REFERENCE

R326.4

Q27b

D0804043

BLACK ABOLITIONISTS

DETROIT
PUBLIC
LIBRARY

C-4   DEC _ 1992

BLACK ABOLITIONISTS

BLACK
ABOLITIONISTS

Benjamin Quarles

A DA CAPO PAPERBACK

Library of Congress Cataloging in Publication Data

Quarles, Benjamin.
    Black abolitionists / Benjamin Quarles.
        p.   cm. — (A Da Capo paperback)
    Reprint. Originally published: New York: Oxford University Press, 1969.
    ISBN 0-306-80425-5
    1. Abolitionists. 2. Afro-Americans. 3. Slavery—United State—Antislavery
movements. I. Title.
E449.Q17 1991   90-27218
973.7'114—dc20   CIP

This Da Capo Press paperback edition of *Black Abolitionists* is an unabridged
republication of the edition published in New York in 1969. It is here
reprinted by arrangement with Oxford University Press.

Copyright © 1969 by Oxford University Press

Published by Da Capo Press, Inc.
A Subsidiary of Plenum Publishing Corporation
233 Spring Street, New York, N.Y. 10013

All Rights Reserved

Manufactured in the United States of America

To my daughter, Pamela

Preface

FREEDOM is and has always been America's root concern, a concern that found dramatic expression in the abolitionist movement. The most important and revolutionary reform in our country's past, it forced the American people to come to grips with an anomaly that would not down—the existence of slavery in a land of the free.

One of the distinctive themes of the American experience, slavery had been firmly established a century before the Declaration of Independence. Its supporters had come to believe that slavery was the normal relationship between black and white. Increasingly concentrated in the South after the Revolutionary War, they rallied to its defense, coming to resent bitterly the mounting Yankee attack. Hence, as nothing else, the abolitionist agitation intensified the cleavage between the North and the South, leading in turn to a resort to arms and the nineteenth century's biggest and most significant war. The seeds planted by the abolitionists carried a germinating force, furnishing the classic American example of the power of ideals in a social upheaval.

Who were these men and women who would not hold their peace about slavery? They did not fit into any particular mold, religious or secular. Embracing a contingent of transplanted Southerners, they comprised a cross-section of America, geographically and otherwise. It is hardly surprising, therefore, that the movement would have its Negro component. Indeed, the Negro could be numbered among the pioneers. The New England Anti-Slavery Society was organized at the African Baptist Church in the Negro quarter of Boston on a snowy January night in 1832. The home of James C. McCrummell, a Negro dentist in Philadelphia, furnished another historic site; it was here in December of the following year that a committee of the American Anti-Slavery Society, headed by William Lloyd Garrison, drew up the Declaration of Sentiments that quickly became the Magna Charta of the movement.

But the black abolitionist phalanx was not just another group of camp followers. The Negro was, in essence, abolition's "different drummer." To begin with, his was a special concern; he felt that the fight against slavery was the black man's fight. Not all Negroes were abolitionists; far from it. But their general attitude was not incorrectly sensed by the British reformer, John Scoble, after a first-hand observation: "The free people of color, with few exceptions, are true to their brethren in bonds," he wrote in 1853, "and are determined to remain by them whatever the cost." Although, as Scoble pointed out, the free Negroes felt a special kinship to the slave, their sense of concern was often rooted in a broad humanity: "I am opposed to slavery, not because it enslaves the black man, but because it enslaves *man*," wrote Daniel A. Payne in 1839. And to John Mercer Langston the abolitionist movement was designed not only for the liberation of the slave but for "the preservation of the American Government, the preservation of American liberty itself."   .

Aside from his varied role as a participant, the black abolitionist constituted a symbol of the struggle. Many of the Negro leaders in the crusade were former slaves, men and women who brought to the platform an experience that in its way was as eloquent, however broken the English, as the oratory of Wendell Phillips. Moreover, it was the Negro membership in the newer abolitionist movement of the Garrison years that marked one of its greatest differences with earlier abolitionist effort, one in which the Negro was regarded as a recipient of good works rather than as an expounder of the faith. And finally an account of the rich role of the Negro participant in the abolitionist crusade would add an element that heretofore has been incomplete or absent in the telling.

The chief reason for the neglect of the Negro abolitionist was the contemporary white media, which took its cue from the Southern press. In Southern thinking the abolitionists loomed large, almost to the point of obsession. But the abolitionists whom the Southerners paraded in such constant if disorderly array were, like so much else in the land of cotton, overwhelmingly of white hue. The white Southerner had to ignore the Negro as abolitionist wherever possible, for to do otherwise would have been to unhinge a cardinal tenet of the Southern faith—the concept of the contented slave and the impassive black. To picture the Negro as civic-minded, as a reformer, might arouse interest in him as a human being and sympathy for him as a figure battling against the odds. Outside the South this neglect of the Negro reformer was less studied but scarcely less prevalent. Indeed, white abolitionists, even those who would never have consciously borrowed anything from the South, would have been more than human had they not inclined to take at face value the ego-soothing role of exclusivity thrust upon them by the supporters of slavery.

To reduce any credibility gap, I have in this work mentioned a number of specific names and places. I hope that at a few points this does not give the impression of mere cataloguing. The nature of the subject would seem to minimize this danger, the role of the black abolitionist being so varied as to dictate that its chronicler keep moving. Hence it is my hope that the reader will not find the narrative impeded by an abundance of name references on the one hand and an undue sketchiness on the other.

I am pleased to make a number of acknowledgments. I owe thanks to Morgan State College for a sabbatical stipend and to the American Council of Learned Societies for a grant-in-aid. I am indebted to many library staffs, especially those in Baltimore. Howard H. Bell, a faculty colleague, placed at my disposal his microfilm collection of colored conventions and newspapers, a boon indeed. Sheldon Meyer, Trade Editor at Oxford, gave the manuscript two careful readings, his suggestions having led to measurable improvement. My wife, Ruth Brett Quarles, read and re-read every line, an invaluable service.

Contents

I

❧ ❧ ❧

Abolition's New Breed

The whole continent seems to be agitated
concerning Colonising the People of Colour.
James Forten to Paul Cuffe,
January 25, 1817

FORTUNATELY the weather was not warm, for Bethel
Church, Philadelphia, was crowded almost to suffocation on
an evening in late January 1817. Never before had such a
large number of Negro Americans assembled, not fewer than
three thousand persons sitting and standing in the main floor
and the U-shaped balcony. On the platform stood James
Forten, a wealthy sail-maker who owned a country residence
and kept a carriage. At a table behind him sat the secretary
for the occasion, Russell Parrott, a public speaker who was
prominent in Negro circles as the assistant to Absalom Jones,
pastor of St. Thomas Episcopal Church. Jones himself was
likewise a platform participant, along with his friend and
early associate Richard Allen, Bethel's pastor and bishop in
the African Methodist Episcopal Church. Conspicuously present was another pioneer Negro clergyman, John Gloucester of
the African Presbyterian Church.

There was only one issue that could bring together a Negro
gathering so numerous, of such diverse sponsorship, and of a
mixture of the well-to-do and literate with the poor and un-

schooled. This binding issue was that of colonization, of sending Negroes to the west coast of Africa. Such a program had been proclaimed a month earlier by the newly formed American Colonization Society from its headquarters at the nation's capital. Any ambiguity in its official title, "American Society for Colonizing the Free People of Color in the United States," was removed by its avowed intent of sending the Negroes across the Atlantic.

Standing before the single-minded audience, Forten called for the "ayes" of those favoring colonization. A complete hush was the only response, as if his listeners were taking a deep breath for a full-throated response in the negative. Forten then called for those who opposed colonization. One long, loud, tremendous "No" went up which, wrote Forten, "seemed as it would bring down the walls of the building." [1]

In more formal fashion the assembly condemned the colonization scheme as an unmerited stigma upon the free Negro, and they vowed that they never would voluntarily separate themselves from their brethren in slavery. They also empowered a committee of twelve, including Forten, Jones, Allen, and Gloucester, to call another general meeting if the need developed.

Within a few days this committee found itself pressed into a most unexpected service—to meet the key figure in the founding of the American Colonization Society, Robert Finley. A clergyman, Finley viewed colonization as a means of uplifting the free Negro and of extending Christian missions to far-off lands. One of those whose advice Finley had sought was Paul Cuffe, a Negro merchant and shipbuilder. In 1814 Cuffe, a Quaker, had petitioned Congress to permit him to transport cargoes to and from Sierra Leone, and to carry a number of families thereto. The bill passed the Senate but was defeated in the House by a close vote after a long debate. But as soon as the War of 1812 was over, Cuffe had transplanted thirty-eight Negroes to Sierra Leone, bearing most of the

$4000 cost of the voyage. In response to Finley's request, Cuffe reported his impressions of west-coast Africa.[2]

Finley had sought other advice and support in the founding of the colonization society. His success had been marred only by the disturbing news of the meeting at Bethel Church. Hence as he left Washington to return to his New Jersey home he arranged to stop over at Philadelphia. Calling upon a fellow Presbyterian minister, John Gloucester, Finley learned of the existence of the committee of twelve and requested an interview.

Finley spent the first hour trying to convince the Negro delegation that the colonization society was benevolently motivated and bent on working for the best interest of the colored people. Convinced of Finley's own goodwill, the Negro committeemen made no embarrassing comments on the motives of some of his fellow workers. Instead they went into a discussion of the most suitable place for colonization. Africa had something to recommend it, said Gloucester, it being so far away as not to invite settlement by restless whites. Richard Allen said that Sierra Leone had attractions of its own, and he praised the work of Paul Cuffe.[3]

Although Finley came out of the meeting with a feeling of optimism, he had not changed any minds. This became evident a few months later when the colonization society selected Philadelphia as one of the five spots to establish its first auxiliaries. The city's black population responded as before. Gathering at the Green Court schoolhouse on August 10, they listened to a succession of speakers, reserving their most thoughtful attention for the statement entitled, "An Address to the Humane and Benevolent Inhabitants of the City and County of Philadelphia." Written by Forten, the statement, which explained their hostility toward colonization, was adopted by unanimous vote.[4]

As initially voiced by the Philadelphia Negroes, and adopted quickly by those elsewhere, the opposition to African colonization resulted from the evil effects it would have on all Negroes, slave and free. Colonization would cause a rise in the price of slaves, thus making it less likely that they would be freed. Colonization would make slavery more secure by removing the free Negro, a source of discontent to the slave and his possible ally in a rebellion. Moreover, free Negroes who went to Africa would be turning their backs on the slave, "our brethren by the ties of consanguinity, suffering, and wrong," as a resolution of the January 1817 meeting phrased it, adding that "we feel there is more virtue in suffering privations with them, than fancied advantages for a season."

Negroes charged that the colonization society threatened them with exile. One of the strongest arguments of the colonization group was that of Negro inferiority, his innate inability to make good in America as a free man. Left to his own devices, ran this line of reasoning, he tended to be corrupt and depraved, a predestined failure. Such baleful predictions provoked Negroes, who knew only too well how much more difficult it is to succeed when no one believes you can. Moreover, as typical Americans, Negroes were suspicious of schemes proposed for them by other people. This attitude on the part of Negroes was intensified in the case of the American Colonization Society, since its officers had never bothered to solicit their viewpoint, with the exception of Finley, who died within a year after its founding.

The Negro protest against African expatriation was recorded by Philadelphia Negroes in 1818 for the third time and once again in 1819. In subsequent years other voices took up the refrain. "Abide in the ship, or you cannot be saved," advised the New York weekly, *Freedom's Journal*. To Lewis Woodson of Chilicothe, Ohio, it was pointless to speak of Africa since "we never asked for it—we never wanted it; neither will we ever go to it." Samuel Cornish, editor of *Rights of All*, the successor to *Freedom's Journal*, said that the best way of repaying Africa the debt we owe her was not to return her sons to her coasts but to do them justice wherever we found them.[5]

Peter Williams, pastor of St. Philips Episcopal Church in New York, in a Fourth of July philippic against the colonization society, forcefully stated the case as the Negro saw it: "We are *natives* of this country; we only ask that we be treated as well as *foreigners*. Not a few of our fathers suffered and bled to purchase its independence; we ask only to be treated as well as those who fought against it." [6]

In a speech at the African Masonic Hall in Boston, the deeply religious Maria W. Stewart, the first native-born American woman to speak in public and leave extant texts of her addresses, strongly rebuked the colonization society, vowing that before she would be driven to a strange land, "the bayonet shall pierce me through." Another young woman, a Washington, D. C., domestic with a "yellowish tint," had a more subdued reaction—to her it "was not fair to send the Negro back after they had disfigured the colour." [7]

Those few Negroes who favored colonization risked obloquy and burning in effigy. In December 1826 when a group of Baltimore Negroes expressed a somewhat mild approval of the colonization society, a mass meeting of Philadelphia protesters, headed this time by John Bowers and Jeremiah Gloucester, drafted a formal "Remonstrance" charging that the Baltimoreans were grossly misleading the public. John B. Russwurm, Bowdoin graduate and the only influential Negro to come out for colonization during the first two decades of the society's existence, was forced as a consequence to resign from the editorship of the newspaper he had established. In letters marked "private" to R. R. Gurley, secretary of the American Colonization Society, Russwurm spoke of the "violent persecution" to which he had been subject by "the most influential of our people." [8]

The colonization scheme had a unifying effect on Negroes in the North, bringing them together in a common bond of opposition. Within a two-year span in the early 1830's Negroes in twenty-two cities held formal meetings of protest.[9] Their resolutions might vary in form—one group might declare themselves the legitimate sons of America, with no desire to leave their native land, and another group might report that they regarded the colonization society in the same light that lambs regarded wolves. But there was no mistaking their common attitude. Indeed, this hostility to the American Colonization Society led the delegates to a national Negro convention meeting in Philadelphia in 1835, to adopt unanimously a resolution "to remove the title of African from their institutions." [10]

The free Negro opposition to African colonization was not chronicled by contemporary observers and as a consequence the credit went elsewhere—to the new abolitionists.

In her work, *The Martyr Age of the United States of America*, the English writer and social critic, Harriet Martineau, credited the American Colonization Society with having "originated abolitionism" by arousing the free blacks and the opponents of slavery.[11] Miss Martineau sensed the interrelatedness of colonization and abolition, but it might be more clarifying to characterize the colonization issue as one of the salient points of difference between two schools of abolitionism— the pioneers who began their work in Revolutionary War times and those who succeeded them half a century later.

Abolitionists of whatever time or place believed slavery to be a wrong and were prepared to act upon their convictions. But a common dislike for slavery and a willingness to work for its downfall did not ensure a common pulling together. Abolitionists differed in their approach; nowhere could this be better illustrated than in the contrast between the old-school, pre-1830 reformers and their more strident successors. A descriptive glance at the earlier school will provide a sharpening of focus.

American antislavery sentiment can be traced back to such colonial figures as Judge Samuel Sewall in Calvinist Massachusetts and the tailor-scrivener John Woolman among the Quakers. The first formally organized society against slavery was founded in Philadelphia in 1775, and it was incorporated fourteen years later under the kind of long title that became characteristic of the early groups, The Pennsylvania Society for Promoting the Abolition of Slavery, the Relief of Free Negroes Unlawfully Held in Bondage, and for Improving the Condition of the African Race. An antislavery society was organized in New York in 1785, and soon after in New Jersey, Delaware, Maryland, Connecticut, Rhode Island, and Virginia. Early in 1794 delegates from five of these groups met in Philadelphia to form a national organization, The American Convention for Promoting the Abolition of Slavery and Improving the Condition of the African Race, a loose federation of state societies.

These earlier abolitionists had a religious orientation, a moderate and conciliatory tone, and, as previously noted, a colonizationist outlook. With branches in the slaveholding South, these reformers counted in their ranks an imposing roster of men of means and high public position. No Negroes or women held membership in their societies, and no attempt was made to form children's auxiliary chapters.

The religious impulse that guided these early reformers was the belief that slavery was a sin for which God would eventually exact retribution. The Friends were prominent in the movement.[12] In Pennsylvania they were its backbone; indeed, only Quakers were admitted to the first two conventions of the Pennsylvania abolitionists. Quakers had good precedents for the work; out of their number had come John Woolman and his close friend and successor, Anthony Benezet, the leading antislavery propagandist in late-eighteenth-century America. Quaker reformers were active in Maryland and Virginia before the 1700's drew to a close. Other religious groups adopted official resolutions condemning slavery, Virginia Baptists taking such a step in 1789, the Presbyterian General Assembly in 1795, and the Methodists during a series of four conferences from 1780 to 1796.

Early abolitionism had a certain Southern flavor. In 1827 the free states had 24 societies with a membership of 1500, but this hardly compared with the 130 societies in the slave states with a membership of 6625.[13] One of the more zealous of the Southern organizers was a Quaker, Charles Osborne, who in 1814 organized the Tennessee Society for Promoting the Manumission of Slaves, thus advancing a reformist outlook in East Tennessee.

With rare exceptions, like that of Osborne, these early abolitionists were gradualists, trusting to what they conceived as the slow but inevitable operation of religious and equalitarian principles. They felt that slavery was not to be abolished overnight but that it would certainly disappear in the fulness of time. They believed "that an abhorrence of slavery would gradually work its way, and that it was the duty of the society patiently to wait the event," wrote William Rawle, onetime president of the Pennsylvania Society. James G. Birney, a slaveholder turned abolitionist, attributed the "declension" of the early societies to their failure to press for immediate emancipation.[14]

Because they expected slavery to die out by slow degrees at some distant, unspecified date, the early abolitionists counseled Negroes to bear and forbear. They advised free Negroes to live within their income so that they would have something to give to the unfortunate, and "to cultivate feelings of piety and gratitude to your Heavenly Father for the many blessings you enjoy." Free Negroes who somehow might be in communication with slaves were advised "to impress them with the necessity of contentment with their situations" to the end that their masters would respond with humanity and gentleness.[15]

In their addresses to the slaveholders, the earlier abolitionists used calm and temperate language, in line with their belief that a harsher tone would seem provocative. They avoided passionate denunciations or the reciting of atrocity stories. They avowed that their plans were of a pacific nature and that any opposition to slaveholders was opposition to a brother rather than to an enemy.

Conciliatory to the core, the earlier generation of abolitionists seemed to go out of their way to win the love and esteem of the South. William Ellery Channing, whose fame as a scholar and a Unitarian clergyman extended far beyond his Boston parishioners, typified this olive-branch approach. In a letter to Daniel Webster in May 1828, Channing suggested that Northerners should allay the fears of Southerners by saying to them, "We consider slavery as your calamity, not your crime, and we will share with you the burden of putting an end to it." [16]

The early abolitionists gave constant and positive assurance to Southerners that they had no intention of interfering with the rights of property. Hence slave emancipation was not to be achieved without compensation to the owners. In part this attitude stemmed from the elite composition of the membership. The founders of the New York Manumission Society, for example, included such distinguished names as Philip Schuyler, James Duane, and Chancellor Livingston, and its first president was John Jay, who was succeeded in that office by Alexander Hamilton. Such men of wealth or high station were highly sensitive to the sanctity of capital investments, however deplorable its form. Not through the purse strings would they strike.

As a national organization the earlier abolitionists were hesitant at first in supporting colonization. Before giving an official opinion, the American Convention for Promoting the Abolition of Slavery invited James Forten to appear at its meeting in December 1818. After receiving his views the convention issued a report opposing colonization on the grounds that Negroes were averse to it and that they were determined not to be transported to Africa unless by force. Again in 1821 the parent organization expressed official disapproval of colonization. But such action had little influence on the subsidiary societies, the Manumission Society of North Carolina having pledged its support to the American Colonization Society before the latter had celebrated its first anniversary.[17]

After 1821 the American Convention quietly abandoned its opposition to colonization, breaking its silence in 1829 to come out in flat endorsement of the voluntary emigration of free Negroes and of Congressional assistance in effecting it. The school conducted by the New York Manumission Society, the African Free School, worked out an agreement with the colonization society in 1828 and 1829 to educate two young Negroes, Washington Davis and Cecil Ashman, for teaching in Liberia. When one of the students of the school, Isaac H. Moore, expressed an interest in Liberia, he was encouraged by principal Charles C. Andrews to write to the colonization society, and when John B. Russwurm was preparing to go to Liberia as a principal in the summer of 1829, Andrews offered to brief him on school administration.[18]

The early abolitionist movement was by no means barren of accomplishment. It had rescued hundreds of Negroes illegally held in bondage, the Delaware Society alone having liberated twelve in the span of a year. True, the organizations did not admit Negroes to membership; the constitution of a Southern auxiliary was likely to be restricted to free, white males, and the Pennsylvania Society for Promoting the Abolition of Slavery admitted only one Negro from 1775 to 1859, the light-skinned Robert Purvis.[19]

But the societies showed an interest in the free Negro, particularly in his education. Its principal work was to maintain schools, reported the New York Society in 1825. Its pride was the African Free School, which in 1834 came under the city-supported system, after an independent existence of forty-seven years. Perhaps the school's more celebrated product was Ira Aldridge, who played Othello at the Royal Theatre in London before he reached thirty and was the rage of Europe for a quarter of a century. In Pennsylvania, too, it was the abolitionists who gave Negroes their first exposure to book learning. In 1802 the legislature authorized public schools, but none existed for Negroes until 1820 when the abolitionists donated a building to the state authorities upon hearing their excuse that they could not build a colored school because no funds were available.[20]

When realistically assessed, however, the abolitionist movement of the federalist era must be accounted a failure. The Northern states had all but abandoned slavery, it is true, but the chief reason had been the availability of a free labor supply which made bonded labor unprofitable.[21] The early abolitionists created no general sentiment against slavery. "Those actively engaged in the cause of the oppressed Africans are very small," lamented the Pennsylvania Society in an address to the national body in 1817.[22]

The operations of the old-school reformers were low keyed; they tended to confine their work to the limits of their own state or community, and even in these bailiwicks they sent out no agents, full or part time, to spread the word. Their national gatherings were little more than periodic exchanges of views. That they did not arouse more opposition was a measure of their ineffectualness. Indeed, they are not thought of as abolitionists in the historical sense that we have come to know the term. It is somewhat ironic that these moderate reformers made use of the strong word "abolitionist" in entitling their societies, thus forcing their more radical successors to adopt the milder designation "antislavery" in their organizational names.

Given the times they lived in, the early abolitionists could hardly have succeeded, whatever their technique. Their original belief that slavery would die a natural death had been shattered by the increase in cotton production in the expanding Southwest. The growing coolness between the North and South was immeasurably increased by the debates leading to the Missouri Compromise in 1820—Thomas Jefferson's famed "fire-bell in the night." For the first time the South began to defend its slave-interest representation in the House of Representatives, and from this it was but a step to a defense of slavery itself.

Obviously the abolitionist approach of brotherly reconciliation found itself progressively weakened in a period in which sectional hostilities were sharpening. The parent organization held no regular meetings after 1832 and formally dissolved in 1838, after forty-four years of existence. These early abolitionists were men of good intention, and their work had not been without its good fruit. But new occasions teach new duties and time makes ancient good uncouth, in the words of one of the new breed, James Russell Lowell.

"We shall spare no exertions nor means to bring the whole nation to speedy repentance," ran one of the resolutions marking the first meeting of the American Anti-Slavery Society in December 1833 at Philadelphia.[23] Thus did abolitionism take on a new character, a direct confrontation—not a flank attack —on slavery. Impelled by a sense of urgency hitherto missing, these new spokesmen insisted that the nation face up to the question. Believing that they best served their countrymen by rebuking them for their faults, they were determined to rivet public attention on an issue most people would have preferred to ignore.

The new school stood for uncompensated emancipation, holding that if anybody deserved payment it was the slave.

When a bondman became free by purchase, even by self-purchase, these abolitionists deplored it as a violation of principle, however much they may have shared the elation of the ransomed. Men of limited patience, they called for immediate and unconditional emancipation. To them gradualism was wrong in theory, weak in practice, and fatally quieting to the conscience of the slaveholder. The doctrine of immediatism had not originated with the new abolitionists,[24] but it had little influence before their arrival. At first the immediatist doctrine was interpreted by some of the new abolitionists to mean gradual emancipation beginning at once, but by 1840 this modification had all but disappeared.

To their radical approach the new breed brought a vocabulary that was equally unsettling. They held that social revolutionaries may have to overstate their case to make their point. "The pleas of crying soft and sparing never answered the purpose of a reform, and never will," wrote the Negro reformer David Ruggles. Thomas Wentworth Higginson held that loud language was needed for those whose ears were stopped with Southern cotton. Hence many of these reformers abandoned the restraints of polite discourse and went in for shock-effect statements. With a fondness for epithet, they might label a slaveholder as a man-thief, a child-seller, and a woman-whipper. At one of their meetings a typical resolution, such as the following by former slave William Wells Brown, might brand the United States as a wilful liar, a shameless hypocrite, and the deadliest enemy of the human race. Wendell Phillips could characterize the South as "one great brothel, where half a million of women are flogged to prostitution, or worse still, are degraded to believe it honorable." Death brought no surcease from their attack; they hailed the "removal" of Webster, Clay, and Calhoun, "those great obstacles of freedom." [25]

However uncharitable their language, most of these reformers were religious men, many of whom felt a personal guilt for the sin of slavery. Abolitionism was to some an outlet for religious anxiety, a seeking for self-purification. The abolition crusade, however, was not church-centered; it was by and large an extra-church movement, in part because the far-reaching whip of the reformers did not spare the clergy.

A broad employment base characterized the post-1830 reformers. Their leaders tended to be college-trained, and they ran the gamut of the professions, including law, medicine, religion, and education. A handful of businessmen joined the cause, among them Arthur and Lewis Tappan, former members of the New York Society for Promoting the Manumission of Slaves. But if the leaders came from an elite class, the movement was essentially grass-roots, its monies coming from thousands of small donors, women as well as men.

By 1833 when the new national society was organized, the abolition movement had become largely concentrated in one section of the country. The numerous societies in the South had all but disappeared in less than a decade. In part this was due to a document which issued from Boston followed by an act which took place at Southampton County, Virginia, both of which alarmed and angered the Southerners,[26] causing them to close ranks.

The disquieting document bore a lengthy title, generally shortened to *David Walker's Appeal*.[27] Its self-taught author was a tall, slender, dark-skinned dealer in clothes, new and secondhand, who had left Wilmington, North Carolina, to settle in Boston. Here he had become a rising figure in the Negro community; he was the local agent for the *Rights of All;* he had been second marshal at a public dinner, held at the African Masonic Hall, for Prince Abdul Rahaman of Footah Jallo; and he had subscribed to the fund to purchase the freedom of George Horton of North Carolina,[28] the most celebrated slave poet since Phillis Wheatley. Walker was a member of the Massachusetts General Colored Association, founded in 1826 for racial betterment and slave abolition.

Walker's Appeal, a seventy-six-page pamphlet that ran into three editions in 1829 and 1830, was a call to militant action. It bore the marks of careful reflection, and its phrasing was often eloquent, although not free of faulty sentence structure and punctuation. Above all, Walker minced no words: "Remember Americans, that we must and shall be free and enlightened as you are, will you wait until we shall, under God, obtain our liberty by the crushing arm of power? Will it not be dreadful for you? I speak Americans for your own good." [29]

Walker's pamphlet "alarmed society not a little," wrote Harriet Martineau. The greatest of the turn-of-the-century antislavery workers, the Quaker, Benjamin Lundy, called it the most inflammatory publication in history, disavowing it as an injury to the cause. *Walker's Appeal* led Georgia and North Carolina to enact laws against incendiary publications and prompted the mayor of Savannah, William T. Williams, and the governor of Georgia, George R. Gilmer, to send letters of protest to the mayor of Boston, Harrison Gray Otis. In February 1830 four Negroes were arrested in New Orleans on the charge of circulating it. Walker's death in 1830 did not diminish the influence of his *Appeal*, Negroes regarding it as "an inspired work" and Southern whites viewing it as "the diabolical Boston Pamphlet." Both would have agreed with their contemporary, Samuel J. May, that "the excitement which had become so general and so furious against the Abolitionists throughout the slaveholding States was owing in no small measure to . . . David Walker." [30]

A much profounder traumatic experience was in store for the South in the Nat Turner insurrection in tidewater Virginia, in the late summer of 1831. The revolt was conceived and planned by a slave preacher, Nat Turner, a dedicated revolutionary but also something of a mystic torn between a New Testament affirmation of love and an even more consuming Old Testament passion for massive warfare against the Sa-

tanic hosts, in this instance, slavery. After receiving what he
considered a sign from heaven, Turner and his followers set
about their grim business, killing some sixty whites.

Turner's rebellion, Walker's pamphlet, and the appearance
of the new abolitionists did not completely crush antislavery
sentiment in the South.[31] But they combined to give it a blow
from which it could never recover, and they were all but fatal
to the organized expressions of antislavery sentiment, the
hitherto numerous manumission societies. Southern abolitionists could not cope with the massive assault by slavery's supporters, who could now put them in a class with Walker,
Turner, and the new militants—the South's new symbols of
outrage, detestation, and fear.

The loss of the South as a recruiting ground for abolitionists
coincided with the acquisition of a new element, greater in
ardor than the lost component if somewhat below it in formal
education and social rank. This new element was the Negro.
"The grand abolition movement of the day, which is now agi-
tating the Northern states, is of a mixed complexion, with a
slice of black and a slice of white, in somewhat unequal proportions," observed the New York *Herald* with a typical touch
of derision.[32] This new black element made its debut at the
same time as and in close conjunction with that of the Boston
reformer destined to become the movement's best known name
—William Lloyd Garrison.

Looking back in 1855 from a vantage of twenty-five years,
J. McCune Smith, the Negro physician and abolitionist, observed that it was hard to tell which loved the other most—
Mr. Garrison the colored people, or the colored people Mr.
Garrison.[33] This reciprocal sentiment first emerged in Baltimore where Garrison spent some eight months during 1829–
30 assisting Benjamin Lundy in editing *The Genius of Universal Emancipation*. The Garrison-Negro bond of affection

was sealed upon Garrison's return to Boston to launch *The Liberator*. Its first issue, dated January 1, 1831, struck the militant note so typical of the new school. He was in earnest and he would be heard, wrote Garrison; moreover, he would be "as harsh as truth, and as uncompromising as justice." The twenty-five-year-old editor had a special message "to our free colored brethren," seeking their support and promising them his, inasmuch as "we know that you are now struggling against wind and tide." [34]

During the early months of 1831 Garrison traveled to half a dozen cities, New York and Philadelphia among them, giving to Negroes a standard speech written with them in mind. In it he promised to devote his life to their service in order to make atonement for the wrongs done them by persons of his own color. "Small wonder," wrote his children, "that there were some who took Mr. Garrison for a black man." [35]

Partly as a result of his growing familiarity with the Negroes' opinions, Garrison reversed his stand on colonization to make it conform to theirs. "It was their united and strenuous opposition to the expatriation scheme that first induced Garrison and others to oppose it," wrote abolitionist Lewis Tappan. *Garrison's Thoughts on African Colonization*, published in 1832, was the sharpest and most sustained attack on the American Colonization Society up to that time. Significantly, the entire second half of the small book is devoted to portraying the negative attitude of Negroes toward emigration to Liberia. Garrison's blast changed many minds, doing much to dislodge colonization from the abolitionist movement.

The Negro's response to this "Daniel come to judgment" was immediate and full. As his black townsmen later pointed out, "We had good doctrine enough before Garrison, but we wanted a good example." Concrete evidence of this regard for Garrison was the support given to *The Liberator*. On the day before the first issue was scheduled to appear, James Forten sent the money for twenty-seven subscriptions, a $54 windfall that enabled Garrison and his publishing associate, Isaac Knapp, to buy the necessary ream of paper. "I seriously question whether there would ever have been a *Liberator* printed," wrote Garrison later, "had it not been for that timely remittance." Five weeks later Forten sent $20 for additional subscriptions. For the first three crucial years the majority of the paper's subscribers were Negroes; in April 1834 whites comprised only one-quarter of the 2300 subscribers.[36]

The early *Liberator* had a corps of Negro agents, including as of February 1832 Richard Johnson in nearby New Bedford, Jehiel C. Beman in Middletown, Connecticut, Abraham D. Shadd in Wilmington, Philip A. Bell in New York City, Josiah Green in upstate Rochester, John Peck in Carlisle, Pennsylvania, and John B. Vashon in Pittsburgh. A veteran of the War of 1812 and a barber with his own shop, Vashon was Garrison's chief benefactor during *The Liberator*'s first years. In December 1832 Vashon sent Garrison $50, which the latter preferred to consider a loan. Eleven months later when Vashon sent $60, the grateful Garrison expressed the wish that it be considered only "an extension of the loan." Garrison was less inclined to demur when a Negro group in Boston sent $30 for life membership in the recently organized New England Anti-Slavery Society for him and his publishing associate, Isaac Knapp.[37]

Money furnished by Negroes enabled Garrison to take his first trip abroad. In the spring of 1833 Garrison decided to go to England for the threefold purpose of spreading the new gospel of freedom, raising money for a Negro manual labor school, and upsetting the fund-raising efforts of Elliot Cresson of the American Colonization Society. Garrison had no money for the trip, but his Negro admirers took up collections, raising nearly $400. Individual gifts ranged from 50¢ to $5, and group gifts from $4 to $124. Some groups, such as the Colored Female Religious and Moral Society of Salem, sent bon voyage presents. On the eve of embarkation he was presented a silver medal by the Juvenile Garrison Independent Society, a group of "colored youth pursuing virtue and knowledge" in Boston.[38]

When Garrison, after four months in England, prepared to return to America, he was again without funds. This time he turned to Nathaniel Paul, a Negro Baptist clergyman then traveling in the British Isles to raise money for the Wilberforce settlement in Canada. Paul advanced Garrison $200, "so that I could return home without begging," as he phrased it in a letter to Lewis Tappan.[39] Upon his return to Boston his Negro admirers held a public reception at Marlboro Chapel, presided over by John T. Hilton, fraternal leader and reformer.

Negroes sought to protect Garrison from bodily harm. Fearing that he might be waylaid by enemies, they followed him late at night wherever he walked the three miles from his office to his Roxbury home, "Freedom's Cottage." These unsolicited protectors were armed with cudgels; therefore it was just as well that Garrison, a nonresistant, was unaware of their services. Negroes were powerless, however, to prevent the daytime mobbing of Garrison on October 21, 1835, when he was led through the streets of downtown Boston with a rope around his middle. Put in jail for safekeeping, Garrison was visited by John B. Vashon, who brought him a new hat, "at a venture as to the precise size required." The pair of pants which had been torn off Garrison became the prize possession of William H. Logan, who solicited them from the sheriff.[40]

At noon on the day of the riot Vashon had dined at Garrison's home. In turn Garrison often dined at the homes of Negroes. While on a visit to Portland, Maine, in September 1832, he was driven around on a sight-seeing tour by Reuben Ruby and entertained at Ruby's home in company with twenty Negroes invited to meet him. While in Philadelphia, Garrison might dine with James Forten or James McCrummell, and in Albany with the tailor, William Topp. While in New York for the historic meeting of the American Anti-

Slavery Society in May 1840 Garrison stayed with Thomas Van Rensselaer, "without money and without price." [41]

James G. Barbadoes, a fellow townsman and clothing-store owner, named a son after Garrison; David Walker's boy was christened Edward Garrison Walker. Negro societies in Boston and New York bore the name Garrison in their titles. The Negro painter, Robert Douglass, Jr., completed a lithographic portrait of Garrison, copies of which sold for 50¢ to further the cause.[42]

Meeting in mid-July 1831 in the African School Room of the two-story brick meetinghouse in Belknap Street, a group of Boston Negroes took note of Garrison's unstinted exertions on their behalf, viewing him as greatly commanding their thanks and gratitude. The man they so honored hardly seemed of hall-of-fame calibre. Certainly in appearance he was not impressive. Prematurely bald and wearing steel-rimmed glasses, he looked mild and benign, with a touch of the funereal in his dress, customarily a black suit and a black cravat. As a speaker he tended to become monotonous. He had a penchant for strong epithets, which his associate, Lydia Maria Child, attributed to "his being very thoroughly imbued with the phraseology of the Bible," [43] and he was overly quick to charge an opponent with moral blindness or a lack of integrity. He was untidy in his ideas and his grasp of history, law, and politics was slight.

But whatever the catalogue of his shortcomings, his unswerving championship of human rights marked him as a providential figure in an age when the forces of slavery and antislavery met head-on in America. This confrontation was welcomed by the latter-day abolitionists, with young leadership, some of it Garrison's, and with new blood, some of it the Negro's.

II

❦ ❦ ❦

Black Sowers of the Word

Now, under the elevated and cherishing
influence of the American Anti-Slavery
Society, the colored race, like the
white, furnishes Corinthian capitals for
the noblest temples.

Maria Weston Chapman, 1843

THE NEW SPIRIT of abolitionism received its widest expression in the formation of the American Anti-Slavery Society at Philadelphia on December 4, 1833. The sixty-three delegates from eleven states proclaimed as their twin objects "the entire abolition of slavery in the United States," and the elevation of "the character and condition of the people of color." Three Negroes took part in the proceedings: James McCrummell, Robert Purvis, and James G. Barbadoes. The Negroes of Carlisle, Pennsylvania, had sent as their representative a white man whom they had swung over to the abolition cause, J. Miller McKim,[1] destined to be a stalwart in the movement for more than a quarter of a century.

No public gathering of abolitionists was more memorable than this three-day organizational meeting at Adelphi Hall. The sessions had to be confined to the shortening daytime hours at the insistence of the city fathers. The police authorities feared an outbreak of violence, and indeed the delegates were taunted as they made their way along Walnut Street to the entrance of the hall. Disorder inside the building was also a distinct possibility inasmuch as no one was refused admission, although the doors were locked once the meeting was called to order. But more than threats would have been required to deter the earnest and able group, a plainly dressed if youngish-looking band of reformers.

At one of the sessions, on the morning of Thursday, December 5, the presiding officer was James McCrummell of Philadelphia. But his fellow townsman, Robert Purvis, was the most observed of the Negro trio at the convention. Soon to marry the daughter of James Forten, but independently wealthy of inheritance from his white merchant father, Purvis could be depended upon to make his presence felt in a public gathering. Forty years later John Greenleaf Whittier could still remember his initial impression of Purvis at Philadelphia: "I think I have never seen a finer face and figure, and his manner, words, and bearing were in keeping. Who is he, I asked." [2]

Purvis himself did not feel that he was at his best, confessing that his heart was too full for his tongue. But he did add: "it is indeed a good thing to be here." The other Negro delegates could have echoed that sentiment, even James G. Barbadoes who en route on the boat trip from Boston had to walk the deck during a stormy night, his color a bar to a cabin berth.[3]

On the final day of the sessions the delegates ratified the Declaration of Sentiments, a forthright call to action couched in revolutionary language. It had been written the evening before at the home of delegate James McCrummell, where its chief author, William Lloyd Garrison, was a house guest. Of the sixty-three signers of the declaration, the twenty-three-year-old Purvis was destined to live the longest. On the board of managers named by the convention, six Negroes were given seats—the three delegates plus John B. Vashon, Peter Williams of New York, and Abraham D. Shadd of Chester County, Pennsylvania.

The founding of an abolitionist society northwide in scope gave a new thrust to the crusade and a fresh hope to Negroes. Within three days after the delegates left Philadelphia, a young colored woman, writing under the pen name "Ada," sang their praises in verse, concluding with the stanza:

> Their works shall live when other deeds
>   Which ask a nation's fame,
> Have sunk beneath Time's whelming wave
>   Unhonored and unnamed.[4]

Negroes took part in the organization of affiliates of the new parent society. The Massachusetts Anti-Slavery Society, successor in 1834 to the New England Anti-Slavery Society, elected James G. Barbadoes and Joshua Easton of North Bridgewater to its board of counsellors. The twelve men who had founded the New England Anti-Slavery Society in January 1832 included no Negroes, but the latter made up one-quarter of the signers of the society's constitution, and Samuel Snowden was named on its first panel of counsellors. At the initial meeting of the Middletown Anti-Slavery Society in February 1834 Jehiel C. Beman was a participant, being elected one of its five managers. In October 1835 David Ruggles was among the four hundred delegates in attendance at the organizational meeting of the New York Anti-Slavery Society, which had to be moved to Peterboro when a mob occupied its first meeting place, the supreme court chambers at Utica.[5]

Seven Negroes took part in the first meeting of the Pennsylvania Anti-Slavery Society, held at Harrisburg in January 1837. As might be expected, this roster included Forten, Purvis, and McCrummell; their associates were John C. Bowers and Presbyterian pastor Charles W. Gardner, both of Philadelphia, John Peck, a barber-shop owner in Carlisle, and Stephen Smith of East Fallowfield. Smith's partner in a lucrative lumber business, William Whipper, sent word from Columbia expressing regret for his absence. As usual, Negroes were moved by the experience: "I never spent a more agreeable time in my life," wrote Bowers. The high spirits of these pioneers must have been matched by those of clergyman Jehiel C. Beman when, a year later, he organized a white antislavery society at Glastonburg, Connecticut. In the summer of 1838 two branches were organized in Maine immediately following a visit by Charles Lenox Remond, then a traveling agent for the parent body.[6]

The new abolitionism was characterized by the organization of women's auxiliaries, and in this effort too Negroes took part. Women had attended the organizational meeting of the American Anti-Slavery Society in Philadelphia, where they had been urged to form their own auxiliaries. They had not been invited to sign the Declaration of Sentiments or to join the society. But even to invite them to become abolitionists was somewhat in advance of the times. Public opinion held that reformist activity was defeminizing and that a woman reformer had somehow unsexed herself. The shout, "Go home and spin," often greeted a woman on the public platform. But the spinning wheel was being replaced, giving women time for something other than household work.

With the coming of the abolition movement many budding women's righters found an outlet for their energies. Hence the invitation from the new national organization was quickly seized upon. On December 14, 1833, the Female Anti-Slavery Society of Philadelphia had its birth, with Lucretia Mott its guiding spirit. Mrs. Mott later recalled that at the opening meeting the women, lacking experience in parliamentary procedures, had called upon James McCrummell for assistance. The best known of the four Negro signers of the society's charter was Sarah M. Douglass, the Quaker principal of the preparatory department of the Institute for Colored Youth, where she doubled as teacher of reading. The other three Negroes were sisters—Harriet Purvis, wife of Robert Purvis, Sarah Forten, and Margaretta Forten, the last chosen by the society as recording secretary. Seven days earlier the sisters had received a moving tribute in poetry, "To the Daughters of James Forten," [7] from John Greenleaf Whittier, as color blind in looking at a person as in peering at a painting.

Founded also in 1833, indeed antedating the Philadelphia society by two months, was the Boston Female Anti-Slavery Society. One of its five counsellors was young Susan Paul, whose brother Thomas was an apprentice in the *Liberator* office, and later a graduate of Dartmouth. At the annual fairs, a money-raising scheme originated by the Boston women, Miss Paul invariably superintended one of the tables.

Early in 1837 the Boston society initiated an exchange of letters with kindred organizations, a step which led to the First Anti-Slavery Convention of American Women. Gathering in New York in May from ten states were more than one hundred delegates, among them Sarah M. Douglass and Sarah Forten. Two particular friends of Miss Douglass were present, Sarah M. Grimké and Angelina E. Grimké. Carolina-born aristocrats turned Quakers, Sarah and Angelina left Charleston in the late 1820's to come north and bear witness against slavery and for woman's rights. At the convention each of the sisters delivered a strong address, both published by vote of the delegates—Sarah's *Address to Free Colored Americans*, and Angelina's *Appeal to the Women of the Nominally Free States*. The convention also issued a circular bearing a poem by Sarah Forten calling upon women to abandon race prejudice.[8]

At the second antislavery convention of the American women, held in Philadelphia in May 1838, Susan Paul was chosen as one of the vice presidents and Sarah M. Douglass as treasurer. Grace Douglass and Harriet Purvis attended the convention, which had to hold its final session in a schoolroom, a mob having burned down its Pennsylvania Hall meeting site. Undaunted by intimidation, Sarah Grimké sponsored a resolution calling upon American women to treat Negroes on the basis of social equality, to appear with them in public places and to exchange home visits.[9]

The third of the women's national antislavery conventions, held also in Philadelphia and in May, met at the Pennsylvania Riding School, no better place being available for so unpopular a gathering. Again two Negroes were given office, Sarah M. Douglass being continued as treasurer, and Grace Douglass, her mother, receiving a vice presidency. The mayor of the city urged the women to hold no meetings in the evening, to avoid unnecessary walking in public with colored people, and to close their convention as soon as possible. The delegates countered by drafting *An Appeal to American Women on Prejudice Against Color*, a plea to roll back the tide of racial bias. "It is worth coming all the way from Massachusetts to see what I see here," said Clarissa C. Lawrence, president of the Colored Female Religious and Moral Society of Salem.[10] The Convention of 1839 was the last held by the women, the time having come for their admission to the hitherto all-male societies.

The participation of colored men and women in the formation of the new national societies was a natural development. Negroes were abolition-minded, having already formed organizations to that end. The Massachusetts General Colored Association dated back to 1826; the colored convention movement, bringing together Negro leaders from several Northern states, began in 1830, and the Female Anti-Slavery Society of Salem, made up of "females of color," was organized on February 22, 1832.[11]

From the beginning the American Anti-Slavery Society vigorously pushed the formation of auxiliary branches, thus giving momentum to the movement among Negroes. In 1834,

Negro antislavery societies were formed in Rochester, Newark, Nantucket, and Lexington, Massachusetts, the last taking the name, Lexington Abolition Society of Colored Persons and Whites Who Feel Desirous to Join. In the same year the Colored Female Anti-Slavery Society of Middletown, headed by Clarissa Beman, was organized.[12]

Six colored auxiliaries to the national society were founded in 1836, including one at Troy, Michigan, plus a woman's antislavery group in Rochester. During the following year Negroes in New York organized the Roger Williams Baptist Anti-Slavery Society as an auxiliary to the national body, and the Negroes in Geneva formed an affiliate of the New York Anti-Slavery Society. In May 1838 black Philadelphians organized the Leavitt Anti-Slavery Society, named after the white abolitionist editor, Joshua Leavitt.[13]

Negroes of a tender age shared in the abolitionist crusade from the beginning. To enlist the sympathies and support of the children was an important phase of most of the reform movements in pre-Civil War America. "Our enterprise is a school for the young," wrote the editor of an abolitionist book for children.[14] *The Slave's Friend*, a monthly designed for juveniles and carrying pictures, hymns, and anecdotes, was distributed without charge.

The formation of juvenile antislavery societies began in 1834, one of them a girl's group at Providence. The six founders quickly added to their number, bringing in several colored misses, making it "a sugar-plum society," said one observer. At their weekly meetings one member would read aloud from antislavery publications while the others sewed. From the sale of their needlework the young women raised $90 the first year, sending it to the national society.

Negro young people felt a similar urge to unite for a worthwhile cause. In Boston in 1833 they formed the Juvenile Garrison Independent Society, youngsters of both sexes and between the ages of ten and twenty who paid an entrance fee of

4¢. Almost at the same time Susan Paul recruited a Garrison Junior Choir, which sang at abolitionist gatherings and gave concerts for the benefit of the Mashpee Indians and similar charities. At a Negro school in Albany in 1834 an antislavery club was formed, each member pledging himself to give 6¢ a month to the national body.[15]

Perhaps the first true Negro juvenile abolitionist societies were formed in 1838 when four of them emerged, at Pittsburgh, Troy, Carlisle, and Providence. The first of these in point of time was the Pittsburgh Juvenile Anti-Slavery Society, formed on July 7, 1838. With David Peck as president and George Vashon, son of Garrison's friend, as secretary, the Pittsburgh group comprised the first "cent a week" society west of the Alleghenies. The forty members also raised money for *The Colored American*, a reformist weekly, and listened to declamations from their fellows. The juvenile society at Carlisle also supported *The Colored American*, and the Providence young people gave their assessments of a penny a week to the national organization. In 1839 the Salem Juvenile Colored Sewing Society, another of the early clubs of its kind, paid $15 to the Massachusetts Anti-Slavery Society for a life membership for an admired adult.[16]

The founding of all-Negro societies did not lead to any substantial withdrawal of Negroes from integrated societies. Indeed, many Negroes were opposed to all-black auxiliaries, holding that they tended to perpetuate the very evils—prejudice and discrimination—they avowedly sought to combat. In truth, however, the Negro abolition societies did not reflect a go-it-alone philosophy on the part of the founders. Doubtless some of them had felt that they would be more at ease and under less of a strain in a racially separate group. Others may have preferred for the time a Negro society in order to spare their white abolitionist colleagues any embarrassment or hostility that their presence might incur. But whatever their reason, the founders of Negro societies did not envision their efforts as distinctive or self-contained; rather they viewed their role as that of a true auxiliary—supportive, supplemental, and subsidiary. Negro abolitionists spoke with the same accents as their white counterparts, although perhaps in a voice of differing pitch.

Negro participants, fittingly enough perhaps, formed a more integral component of the abolition crusade than of any other major reform in America. The larger and far more influential body of Negro abolitionists who never joined a colored antislavery society would, as a natural consequence, work closely with whites. But much the same was true for members of the Negro societies, which in their outlook and operations were closely tied in to the larger movement. This reciprocal, interlocking relationship between black and white reformers may be demonstrated by the support, financial and otherwise, each gave to the other in pursuit of the common goal.

"We do not wish to be burdensome to any, but we are poor," wrote Congregational clergyman Amos G. Berry, in hardly an original vein. Despite their circumstances, some Negroes managed to give for the slave. In the three spring months of 1833 Negroes contributed to the New England Anti-Slavery Society $41 of the total receipts of $324. In August the society received $4.27 from a Negro church in New Bedford and $22.70 from one in Philadelphia.[17] Two months later the society received $15 apiece from Philip A. Bell, Susan Paul, and John Remond for life memberships. In the month of November 1834 Negro groups from twelve cities or towns sent $128.28 to the national society, about one-seventh of its receipts ($858.79) for the period. In 1836 Negro groups in Boston and New York gave $80.52 and $245.60, respectively, to the society.[18]

Group giving by Negro societies, churches, and Sunday schools was supplemented by individual contributions. Ne-

groes like John B. Vashon and Peter Williams, an Episcopalian clergyman, could send $10, and a less affluent giver like
Coffin Pitts of Boston might part with $6. John Jones, who
died in Philadelphia in September 1834 bequeathed $340 to
the Pennsylvania Society, and four years later William Williams left $286.57 to the Massachusetts Anti-Slavery Society.
Over a thirteen-year period the lumberyard owner, William
Whipper, gave $1000 annually to the cause. But an offering
from a Negro was more likely to be of the genus, widow's
mite. Small givers predominated, like the girl from Glaston-
bury, Connecticut, who sent one dollar to the parent society in
1836.[19]

Negro donations were not large, but they came during the
crucial beginning years, when fewer white men of means had
been converted to the cause and hence when money was scarc-
est. Moreover, giving by Negroes had a salutary effect on the
white abolitionists, spurring them on. James G. Birney, writing from the national antislavery office in New York in May
1838, to a Southern congressman, boasted that among the
contributors to their treasury that year was "a colored woman
who makes her subsistence by selling apples in the streets in
this city." [20]

Similarly the support Negroes gave to the antislavery journals in the early years of the crusade had a morale-building
effect on their white co-workers. Negroes felt a continuing interest in the welfare of Garrison's weekly; in January 1835
they organized the Colored Liberator Aiding Association,
which drafted an appeal addressed to the free colored citizens
of the United States. Negroes supported *The Liberator*'s predecessor, *The Genius of Universal Emancipation*. Its editor,
Benjamin Lundy, was not a new-school abolitionist strictly
speaking, but he was second to none in unflagging, continuous
labor in the cause. In October 1829 *The Rights of All*, the
only Negro weekly of its day, urged its readers to subscribe to
the *Genius* on the grounds that its principles were "rare,

sacred and dear." In 1832 John B. Vashon acted as an agent for the paper. In June of the following year a national convention of Negroes, meeting at Bethel Church in Philadelphia, voted to extend the patronage of five reformist sheets—those of Garrison and Lundy plus *The Emancipator*, *The Abolitionist*, and *The Genius of Temperance*. Organ of the American Anti-Slavery Society until 1840, *The Emancipator* had five Negro agents in 1834—David Ruggles, John Peck, Abraham D. Shadd, Stephen Smith, and Vashon—their job to obtain subscriptions and collect "arrearages." Of these the most zealous by far was Ruggles, general agent for New York City, who published a series of six articles explaining to Negroes their stake in the success of the paper. When *The Herald of Freedom* was launched, James Forten sent $5 to its editor, N. P. Rogers, accompanied by a note: "I should like to have some instructions as to future remittances." Stephen Myers of Albany, in a letter addressed to the general public in December 1842, listed the papers that should be supported—*The Liberator*, *The Anti-Slavery Standard*, *The Emancipator and Free American*, *The Western Citizen*, and *The Charter Oak*.[21]

The efforts of Negro abolitionists brought a reciprocal response from their white colleagues, a response that took many forms. Not to be outdone, white abolitionists supported Negro journals, dating back to 1827 when the National Convention and the Pennsylvania Society recommended *Freedom's Journal*. In 1837 the executive committee of the American Anti-Slavery Society recommended *The Colored American* to its members, and at the annual meeting of the society the following year slips of paper were circulated to obtain the names of those who wished to become subscribers. Local organizations took up collections for the weekly, among them the New York State Anti-Slavery Society and the Massachusetts Female Emancipation Society. "I must occasionally send you a few dollars toward sustaining your excellent paper," wrote Gerrit Smith on August 22, 1837, to Samuel Cornish, editor of *The*

Colored American, enclosing $10, and adding, "The Lord bless you." *The Northern Star and Freeman's Advocate*, a small, short-lived sheet published in Albany, had 213 white subscribers in January 1843, making up at least half of the total.[22]

Abolitionist newspapers carried addresses made by Negroes, a long speech often appearing in installments. *The Liberator* carried an address by Robert Bridges Forten, son of James, to the Female Anti-Slavery Society of Philadelphia in November 1834. *The Herald of Freedom* gave three-quarters of a front page to an address by J. McCune Smith at the annual meeting of the national society in 1838. Then twenty-four, Smith held three degrees from the University of Glasgow, bachelor and master of arts and doctor of medicine. At the annual meeting the next year the speech given by Andrew Harris, an 1838 graduate of the University of Vermont, was carried in *The Herald of Freedom*. Similarly a year later *The Anti-Slavery Standard* printed in full the address given by Henry Highland Garnet, which "drew tears from almost every eye," [23] although Garnet was still a student at Oneida Institute at Whiteboro, New York.

The speeches by Negroes at the conventions illustrate another service provided by the white abolitionists—that of providing a sounding board. Negro speakers could air the grievances of their black fellows; they could advise well-wishers who were seeking ways of helping them, and they could, like one speaker, call attention to "the numerous falsifications of history for the purpose of concealing the merits of his people." [24] In similar vein the mulatto schoolteacher, C. V. Caples, gave his fellow reformers a terse reading of the ancient past: "What built up Athens? What extended Rome? The learning and the arts which came from colored men. Who built the Pyramids? Colored men. Who humbled Rome itself? Hannibal, a colored man." [25]

Spurred by the convention speeches of black participants,

the editors of the abolitionist press began to look afresh at the Negro, offering a counterpoise to the daily papers which seldom included him except in the crime columns. Abolitionist weeklies carried original poems by Negroes, some of them signed anonymously, "by a colored lady," or "by a colored girl ten years of age." Two abolitionist weeklies carried the fine piece, "Orators and Orations," an address by William G. Allen at Central College, McGrawville, New York, where he was professor of rhetoric and belles lettres.[26]

At some time or other an abolitionist weekly would reprint stanzas from Phillis Wheatley, along with the bittersweet story of her life, and less often something from the works of George M. Horton, most likely the lines:

> Alas! and am I born for this
> To wear this slavish chain,
> Deprived of all created bliss
> Through hardship, toil, and pain?[27]

The military role of the Negro was not neglected in the abolitionist press. John Greenleaf Whittier, Quaker and pacifist though he was, contributed two such articles to the abolitionist journals, "The Black Soldiers of the Revolution" and "The Black Men of the Revolution and the War of 1812." [28]

Abolitionist publications took due note of Negroes who were successful in business or professional life. They extolled J. B. Smith of Boston as "the prince of caterers." Readers of the antislavery press might learn of attorney Macon B. Allen of the Portland Bar, or of John V. Degrasse, graduate in medicine from Bowdoin College, who had spent two years in London and Paris hospitals, and had made several trips across the Atlantic as a ship surgeon before settling in Boston. In September 1834 *The Liberator* requested Negro inventors to write to the paper so that it could assist them in obtaining patents and also furnish them with proof of colored talent and ability.[29]

Abolitionist newspapers carried advertisements of Negroes who ran clothing or grocery shops, invariably adding an editorial note that the proprietor of the establishment was richly deserving of the patronage extended to him. Some advertisements came from owners of lodging houses, invariably Negroes themselves, who had rooms for the accommodation of "Genteel Persons of Color." Abolitionist newspapers carried letters to the editor praising this or that Negro in business or the professionals—Thomas Jennings, a surgeon dentist of Boston, for example, received such unbilled advertising.[30]

The abolitionist press had a marked effect in making Negroes more active in social and civic affairs. Negro organizations felt no hesitancy in asking these newspapers to carry notices of their coming meetings and lists of their officers. At many Negro meetings the final order of business was a motion instructing the secretary to send a copy of the proceedings to a specified list of journals. Brief notices of Negro weddings dotted the back pages of abolitionist weeklies. How warming to the self-esteem to see one's name in print! But more important was the sense of civic participation it engendered.

As they prepared to organize a state society in the fall of 1838, the abolitionists who assembled at Milton in Wayne County, Indiana, read a sobering letter from Gamaliel Bailey. Bailey was editor of the Cincinnati *Philanthropist*, the first antislavery journal in the West, whose office had been the target of mobs on three occasions. "Your troubles are yet to come, and they may indeed be fiery," wrote Bailey. The prejudice against the Negro would be directed against his friends, ran Bailey's words of warning: their motives would be impeached, their doctrines misrepresented, their good name slandered, and, like as not, their persons assailed. Maria Weston Warren, pillar of the Boston Female Anti-Slavery Society, bore a similar reckoning of the price one paid to join the movement:

"It has occasioned our brothers to be dismissed from the pastoral charge—our sons to be expelled from colleges and theological seminaries—our friends from professorships—ourselves from literary and social privileges." By most of their countrymen, the abolitionists were looked upon as sappers of the social order who incited the slaves to rebel and the free Negro to seek intermarriage. And almost as bad, they endangered property rights, enfeebled the church, and subverted the Constitution.[31]

Ostracism from polite society was one of the crosses an abolitionist might be called upon to bear. The public health pioneer, Dr. Henry I. Bowditch, found himself debarred from many fashionable parties despite his international reputation in medicine. "Ticknor's pleasant literary coteries were no longer accessible," he noted wryly in his journal. For opposing slavery, wrote the clergyman-author Theodore Parker, he had "got nothing but a bad name." While in Philadelphia in May 1833, the clergyman Samuel J. May escorted one of the Forten sisters to an abolitionist meeting. When he returned to Boston he found that the news had preceded him. " 'Is it true, Mr. May,' said a lady to me, 'that you walked in the streets of Philadelphia with a colored girl?' " [32]

To be an abolitionist was to invite economic reprisals, a freezing of one's credit, a loss of employment, or a blacklisting of one's name. A clergyman like Adin Ballou might have a wealthy parishioner suddenly demand payment on a note. An abolitionist professor might lose his chair, as did Charles Follen at Harvard, or an abolitionist judge might lose his seat on the bench, as in the case of William Jay, son of the first chief justice of the United States. Joshua Coffin lost his mailman's job for assisting a kidnaped Negro. James Russell Lowell was loath to take money for antislavery work but he accepted $500 a year to do a weekly article for *The Anti-Slavery Standard*, ruefully noting that his abolitionism had cut him off "from the most profitable sources of my literary emolument." [33] For his antislavery views, John G. Fee was disowned by his father.

Social intermingling between whites and blacks in the abolitionist movement had its special perils. A few white abolitionists, troubled because their colored fellow workers faced discrimination in public places, made it a point to appear with them, courting their lot. Still fewer, like Theodore D. Weld, ate at Negro homes and attended their parties, weddings, and funerals. At the marriage of Weld and Angelina Grimké on May 14, 1838, Grace Douglass and Sarah M. Douglass were among the nearly fifty guests and Theodore S. Wright was one of the two clergymen offering prayers. But such conduct was as unpopular as it was uncommon. When the just-completed Pennsylvania Hall in Philadelphia was sacked and burned two days after the Weld-Grimké wedding, the newspapers charged the abolitionists with bringing it about by having Negroes seated side by side with whites at meetings and by condoning if not fostering interracial arm-in-arm walking in the streets adjacent to the building.

The charge of social intermingling was emotion-laden and hence likely to lead to trouble. In the early days of the movement, abolitionism was synonymous with amalgamationism in the popular mind. Indeed, a white who worked for the repeal of an intermarriage law had as his real object a Negro wife, ran a familiar bit of popular lore. It was unfounded. On one occasion an unnamed white correspondent to an abolitionist newspaper announced that he was prepared to bear testimony against prejudice by marrying a colored woman who was young, respectable, and intelligent. From Baltimore the publisher Hezekiah Niles acidly remarked that he would like to have the honor of announcing the betrothal: "Persons so chivalric should not be thwarted in their desires." [34]

But white abolitionists, almost entirely without exception, were not given to marrying across the color line, even in Massachusetts after the law repealing the prohibition against it was abrogated in 1843. Denying that they were amalgama-tionists, the abolitionists charged that racial intermixing was peculiarly a Southern custom, the natural offspring of slavery. "We do not encourage intermarriage between the white and blacks," said the New Hampshire Anti-Slavery Society in a notice to the public. "We would discountenance it expressly and distinctly." [35]

Such denials by the reformers had little influence on their detractors, particularly the kind who were prone to taking things in their own hands. Amalgamation was a fuse that could be quickly ignited, all the more because the atmosphere was highly charged. Nonviolence was scarcely an American trait, even in the haunts of Thoreau. As Henry Adams ob-served in reflecting upon his salad years, "If violence were a part of a complete education, Boston was not incomplete. Whenever he heard Garrison or Phillips speak, he looked for trouble." [36]

An abolitionist gathering was hardly a smoothly run affair. At the opening of one of the national meetings at Broadway Tabernacle in New York a mob took charge for three hours, "howling till they were hoarse." When the police authorities confessed that they could do nothing, the landlord ordered the abolitionists to leave the building. If property might be endan-gered, so might persons. Reformers ran the risk of rough han-dling, although one of them, a professor at Oberlin, wore a specially constructed "storm suit" while attending abolitionist soirees. Samuel J. May, of quiet manner and fragile build, never forgot an October he spent in Vermont as agent of the New England Anti-Slavery Society: "I was mobbed five times. In Rutland and Montpelier my meetings were dispersed with violence." Henry B. Stanton was manhandled one hundred and fifty times in six years, writes the authoritative Dwight L. Du-mond, and Theodore D. Weld "could be traced from one end of the country to another by such outbursts." [37]

Slavery's critics led charmed lives and were seemingly none

the worst for their ordeals. In his famous encounter with the Boston mob in the fall of 1835, Garrison "sustained certain damages to his clothing, but none in his person." [38] To this seeming immunity from harm there was one tragic exception, Elijah P. Lovejoy. A clergyman who had become editor of a religious journal, *Observer*, Lovejoy moved to Alton, Illinois, in 1836. Here, as in St. Louis, his antislavery views met with determined opposition, his presses being thrown into the river on three separate occasions. On a night in November 1837 Lovejoy was shot and killed as he emerged from a building which the mob, bent on destroying his press, had set on fire. Lovejoy's tragedy was given coverage in the public newspapers and his name became a symbol to reformers.

Negroes were especially moved by the Alton affair. *The Colored American* carried a front page editorial, bordered in black. Boston Negroes held a memorial service at the Smith Street school, and their example was duplicated at Troy, New York, where a saddened company assembled at the Presbyterian church of Daniel A. Payne. A mass meeting of New York Negroes at the First Colored Presbyterian Church mourned Lovejoy "as the first martyr in the holy cause of abolition in the nation." They held no rights dearer than freedom of speech and of the press, ran one resolution, rights especially vital in supplementing "the dumb eloquence of the down trodden slave." A collection of $60 was raised for Lovejoy's widow, to be sent along with a letter of condolence. A few weeks later Joseph C. Lovejoy, one of the martyr's brothers, spoke at the same church.[39]

Although Lovejoy had not considered himself an abolitionist, the colored people did. His sacrifice strengthened their high regard for crusaders against slavery. In truth, the movement had done much for the Negro. In 1830 a great majority of the 320,000 free Negroes were in the habit of regarding all whites as their enemies. The abolitionists changed this stereotype. Now Negroes could witness the labors and the sacrifices of white men and women in a cause inseparably linked with their own. "The devotion and sacrifices of our white brethren should urge us onward," said *The Colored American*. A figure like Simeon S. Jocelyn, zealous abolitionist and white Congregational pastor of a Negro church in New Haven from 1830 to 1834, could not fail to impress Negroes. Congratulated by R. R. Gurley of the Colonization Society, Jocelyn replied that he felt privileged to be laboring among the colored people.[40]

The abolitionist crusade gave to Negroes a heightened sense of self-respect. William Whipper credited it with having a more powerful effect on Negro life than all other influences combined "in checking their evil dispositions and inculcating moral principles." Abolitionism acted as a stimulus to Negroes, "like proclaiming life to a valley of dry bones," and calling forth energies and powers never before exercised. "I confess that I am wholly indebted to the Abolition cause for arousing me from apathy and indifference," wrote Sarah Forten in April 1837, "shedding light into a mind which had been too long wrapped in selfish darkness." [41]

Negroes showed their gratitude by naming their organizations after outstanding figures in the movement. Three of the benevolent societies in Albany in 1837 were named after Benjamin Lundy, Arthur Tappan, and Garrison, respectively. In the same year Philadelphia Negroes formed the Leavitt Anti-Slavery Society, named after journalist and lecturer Joshua Leavitt.

In 1840 the national society split in two, a development that caused the Negro abolitionists to make a fuller use of the resources of the Negro community itself. Their efforts were spurred by a corps of new workers, many of them former slaves, who gave a new dimension to the whole movement.

III

New Tissue for a Broken Body

It is to be regretted that effectual efforts
were not made at an early date to furnish a
history of the services of men of color.

William Yates, 1838

IN THE SPRING of 1840 the abolitionist movement split itself
into two camps. One, headed by Garrison, had its nominal
headquarters in New York but was centered in Massachusetts
with pockets in Pennsylvania and a lonely outpost or two in
Ohio. Drawing its strength from points west of New England,
the opposing faction included a score of outstanding figures,
among them the Tappans, James G. Birney, Gerrit Smith,
Judge William Jay, Henry B. Stanton, and Joshua Leavitt.
Negro abolitionists split also, generally in accordance with the
sectional pattern.

The schism had its dress rehearsal in Massachusetts, the
key issue being the viewpoints of Garrison. By 1839 Garrison
had become an unsparing critic of clergymen, charging them
with upholding slavery. Negroes supported Garrison in his
strictures on the church, but with some misgivings. On one
occasion they stated that Garrison's religious opinions were
not necessarily related to the abolitionist movement, and on
another they pointed out that they were Garrison's followers
as far as abolition was concerned, "but on religious points we
follow Jesus." [1]

Garrison's critics justly charged him with espousing reforms that were far afield from abolitionism, such as the non-resistance movement. Considering the existing peace societies unsatisfactory, Garrison was a founder in 1838 of the New England Non-Resistant Society. Garrison scorned the belief that the Bible was of divine inspiration; moreover, he was an anti-Sabbatarian, holding that no day of the week was holier than any other and hence regarding as superstition the setting aside of Sunday for religious worship.

Garrison was a nonvoter; he vowed that he would never hold office or exercise the franchise in a government that included slaveholders. In a public letter to the Negroes of Boston in December 1834, urging them not to support the Whig ticket, Garrison wrote that he saw little intelligence, and scarcely any conscience, honesty, or fear of God, at the polls.[2] Garrison reasoned that a political party in a country in which slavery existed had to be a proslavery party. Moreover, the Constitution, as Garrison saw it, was a proslavery instrument and hence not to be supported by a true abolitionist.

By 1839 Garrison's critics within the abolitionist ranks felt that a change of leadership was mandatory. At Boston during the annual meeting of the Massachusetts Anti-Slavery Society in May, they raised an objection to women voting at the sessions. Many abolitionists believed that the battle for woman's rights, however praiseworthy, should not be tied to the cause of the slave, and it was on this key issue that they chose to make their stand at the Massachusetts Society. But to no avail. The ruling of the chair that women should vote was approved by a large majority. The defeated faction withdrew, forming without delay a rival state organization, the Massachusetts Abolition Society.

Within a week the Negro abolitionists held a mass meeting in Boston to consider the schism. Predictably they did two things—expressed regret at the division in the ranks and pledged their unanimous support to the Garrison group. For its leader they had nothing but fulsome praise. They de-nounced any colored person, "if any there be," who was hostile to Garrison, likening such an ingrate to a man who fell off a ship and when rescued by a Negro went dripping to the captain to ask "if there was no one on board to save him but a nigger." A week later a mass meeting of Negroes at New Bed-ford took similar action, affirming that Garrison was right and condemning the Massachusetts Abolition Society. "Utter ab-horrence" of the new organization was the sentiment of a Negro gathering in Salem. From Philadelphia, Grace and Sarah Douglass sent Garrison a supporting letter that was couched in religious and moralistic tones.[3]

Negroes in Massachusetts were of a mood to stand by Gar-rison "shoulder to shoulder and foot to foot," as David Rug-gles put it. Hence they were greatly vexed when the Reverend Jehiel C. Beman took a job with the Massachusetts Abolition Society. With headquarters in Boston, Beman was to travel to various towns seeking job opportunities for Negroes, and he was to advertise his services in *The Colored American* and elsewhere.[4] But he got a colder reception in New England than he had anticipated. Garrison and the Boston Negroes, acting in unison, condemned him as a dupe designed to "en-trap" colored people into the new organization.

The script for schism was enacted on a wider scale at the annual meeting of the parent society in mid-May 1840. Garri-son was well prepared for the showdown with the New York abolitionists, even though the site was New York itself. Garri-son had made travel arrangements for over four hundred fol-lowers, hiring boats and extra trains, a step which enabled him to transport his Negro supporters with a minimum of jimcrow, thus ensuring their attendance.

At the meeting, held at the Fourth Free Church, the issue quickly came to a head. Abby Kelley, a staunch Garrisonian, was appointed on the business committee, and the crucial vote was taken as to whether she should be confirmed. The vote of

557 to 451 was in her favor. Thereupon three members of the
business committee withdrew their names on the grounds that
to place a woman on the committee was "throwing a firebrand
into the antislavery ranks." Three days later the seceding delegates held a meeting at the Fourth Presbyterian Church and
brought into existence a new wing, the American and Foreign
Anti-Slavery Society. Its roster of founders numbered 294, of
which 110 came from New York State, including 62 from the
New York City itself.[5] Now, after seven years, no one organization could purport to speak for all abolitiondom. "The pro-
fessed abolitionists were busy abolishing antislavery," wrote
Abby Kelley, herself the symbol of the split.[6]

The results of the rift were immediately reflected in Negro
circles, bringing about a similar parting of the ways. The
opening scene, fittingly enough, was furnished by Garrison.
On May 18, with the meetings just over, the Negroes of New
York held a bon voyage meeting for Garrison, due to embark
for London to attend an international antislavery conference.
The Negroes and some whites packed Theodore S. Wright's
First Presbyterian Church. Following Garrison's speech,
which was largely his version of the breach in the abolitionist
ranks, one of his supporters, Thomas Van Rensselaer, proposed that Garrison and the other delegates chosen by the
American Anti-Slavery Society be approved. But there was
quick opposition to this resolution, substantially on the ground
that it omitted the delegates appointed by the newly organized
national society, one of whom was Samuel E. Cornish.

The issue had come to a head. It was, as S. H. Gloucester
phrased it, "a solemn crisis for the people of color." It was the
Negro phase of the battle between old organization versus new
organization. The surcharged meeting adjourned by passing
no resolution at all, Garrison having made it clear that he
would not have his name linked with those from the new organization. Charles B. Ray, a key figure at the meeting, wrote
to Birney explaining the somewhat changed attitude of the

New York Negro toward the highly revered Bostonian: "If the colored people of this City, or any section of this country, do manifest less warmth of feeling, than formerly toward Mr. Garrison it is in part owing to our friends having multiplied . . . and as a necessary consequence our good feeling is scattered upon all, instead of being concentrated upon one, as when Mr. Garrison stood alone." [7]

Many Negro abolitionists had indeed turned their faces toward the new sun. Eight of them attended the meetings which launched the American and Foreign Anti-Slavery Society, three of whom were named to the twelve-man executive committee. Amos G. Beman served as assistant secretary at the convention and the closing prayer at the final session was given by Theodore S. Wright.

The great majority of black abolitionists in New England would not be drawn into the new society, regarding it as "schismatic." Boston Negroes held a meeting to pledge anew their fealty to the old organization, and Negroes at a gathering in New Bedford saw fit to give a tortured explanation to the word "foreign" in the title of the new society, charging that its tenets were foreign to the principles of freedom and equality. [8]

The old organization did not look kindly upon defectors, white or black. Neutrals fared little better, as John W. Lewis soon learned. Having assumed his duties on February 1, 1839, Lewis was an agent for the New Hampshire Anti-Slavery Society. In his first ten months Lewis had raised $565.37, and the society was pleased with his work. "Nobody thinks of colored inferiority when they hear brother Lewis," said *The Herald of Freedom*, organ of the society. When the parent organization split, Lewis declared his neutrality. Thereupon he quickly lost favor with the New Hampshire society, an old-organization affiliate. Its executive board charged that Lewis drew large crowds solely because he was a Negro and not because of his public speaking, which was long and loud to the point of exhaustion. The board members expressed the hope that "brother Lewis" would take himself to places where he could get more attention and better pay. Lewis fired back with a lengthy reply, in essence expressing the hope that the New Hampshire society would reserve its heavy guns for slavery instead of "disgusting" its members by exhibiting a harsh spirit of contention.[9]

The Lewis episode and the whole split in the abolitionist ranks tended to make Negroes more outspoken toward their fellow crusaders. The Negro's considerable indebtedness to the white reformers had never blinded him to their shortcomings. Now with so much linen being washed in public, the Negro had his bundle to bring, a mixed bundle and of no mean proportions.

To begin with, many white co-workers were charged with harboring race bias. Abolitionists have overlooked the giant sin of prejudice, said Theodore S. Wright in an address at Utica before the New York society, and thus must rid their own bosoms of "this foul monster, which is at once the parent and offspring of slavery." Speaking before the Albany Anti-Slavery Society in February 1838, Nathaniel Paul described the kind of abolitionist who hated slavery, "especially that which is 1,000 or 1,500 miles off," but who hated even more "a man who wears a colored skin." Six weeks after the split, Samuel Ringgold Ward wrote a letter to *The Anti-Slavery Standard* describing abolitionists who "best love the colored man at a distance." In social circles, or in company with other whites, this ilk found it difficult to see Negroes, even "though they had spectacles on their noses." In July 1849 when James Russell Lowell proposed the name of Frederick Douglass for membership in the short-lived, intellectually oriented Town and Country Club, he was astonished at encountering opposition, with the finger of suspicion pointing strongly at the high-principled Ralph Waldo Emerson.[10]

One of the reasons so many whites joined the abolitionist

movement, wrote a Negro editor, was their belief that it stood for abstract principles to be applied to the South, without requiring them to battle the prejudices in their own hearts. James McCune Smith found it strange that in the constitution of the American Anti-Slavery Society, no mention was made of social equality as one of its aims. The editor of the *Northern Star and Freeman's Advocate* had a terse bit of advice: "Until abolitionists eradicate prejudice from their own hearts, they can never receive the unwavering confidence of the people of color." [11]

There were instances in which white abolitionists attended concerts or recitals at which Negroes were barred or segregated. Moreover, some abolitionists, particularly during the formative 1830's, held that Negroes should not be admitted to antislavery meetings or hold membership in the societies, a topic which Charles Follen aired fully at the meeting of the Massachusetts society in January 1836. A year earlier, a few colored young women began to attend the monthly gatherings of the Fall River Female Anti-Slavery Society, a circumstance that almost brought about its dissolution. At its meeting on September 15, 1837, the Junior Anti-Slavery Society of the City and County of Philadelphia debated the question, "is it expedient for colored persons to join our anti-slavery societies?" The vote of 31 in favor to 21 against was hardly reassuring to Negroes in light of the youthful, and presumably more liberal, makeup of the society.[12]

Negroes in Albany were disenchanted with a local abolitionist who refused to rent them a frame tenement, giving as his reason the attitude of his neighbors. This consideration for the feelings of the community was the chief argument advanced by the conservative abolitionists. Undoubtedly, however, it often cloaked a color prejudice of which the practitioner was not aware. In reformist circles, as elsewhere, there was a strong undercurrent of anti-Negro sentiment, mirrored in the common preference for light-skinned Negroes over

those of richer pigmentation. "She was not very dark," wrote
Sarah H. Southwick of Susan Paul, a fellow member of the
Boston Female Anti-Slavery Society. Joshua Easton might
urge his white co-workers to strike not at slavery alone, but
against the spirit which made color the mark of degradation.[13]
However, there were limits to what exhortation would do.
Conquering an aversion to social contacts with Negroes was
not easy; abolitionizing one's own heart was a formidable as-
signment.

Even when they worked side by side, white and Negro
abolitionists scarcely sustained a peer relationship. Whites
tended to be paternalistic, reflecting a "father knows best" attitude. They tended to praise an above-average Negro almost to
the point of eulogy, as if in surprise that he revealed any ability at all. And like the earlier abolitionists they were fond of
giving advice to Negroes, their remarks interlarded with beat-
itudes.[14] The advice might have been good—certainly it was
much like that given by Negro leaders themselves. But if one
Negro criticized another for patronizing a Dan Rice minstrel
show while ignoring a magic lantern exhibition on slavery being held in the same block, the whole thing somehow seemed
freer of racial connotations.

The chief criticism against the white abolitionists by their
black counterparts was their halfheartedness in carrying out
the second of their twin goals—the elevation of the free
Negro. Equal rights for Negroes was an essential corollary of
abolitionism—improving the lot of the Northerners of color
was a clearly stated goal. The Maine Union in Behalf of the
Colored Race, formed in Portland in 1835, was a reflection of
this outlook.[15] Aware of this dual commitment, nearly every
abolitionist society had a special committee on the welfare of
the free Negro. But in most instances this is about as far as it
went—such committees, as a rule, simply did not function.

Hence, in this quarter the abolitionists were vulnerable. In
their strong campaign against slavery in the South, "they half

overlooked slavery in the North," wrote a Negro editor in
1839. The Negro people needed jobs, as their spokesmen constantly stressed. In 1831 Maria W. Stewart asked "several
women" to hire colored girls. Abolitionists were asked to give
Negro apprentices and mechanics an equal chance at least,
and a preference if possible—their "being a neglected people."
In an editorial that brought a flood of approving letters, an
Albany weekly informed the white abolitionists that Negroes
did not expect to ride in their carriages or sup at their parties,
but they did hope that avenues of employment would be
opened up by their alleged friends.[16]

Such thrusts, sharp as they were, brought few changes.
Most white abolitionists simply did not think in terms of the
workingman, white or colored. Men of great understanding in
some things, they never seemed to fully sense that economic
freedom was coequal with, if not basic too, all other freedoms.

To be sure, there were a few gestures by individuals and
organizations. In isolated instances an abolitionist might employ a skilled Negro. Lewis Tappan, for example, paid Patrick H. Reason $70 to do a steel engraving of his brother,
Benjamin. The Tappans were pleased with the product, and
Lewis thought that the antislavery cause would be advanced if
it were known that a Negro was capable of such craftsman-
ship. But, he added in his letter to Reason, "perhaps it will be
best to wait until you have engraved two or three more before
the secret is let out." [17]

Abolitionist organizations made some token efforts to help
the black workingman. Following an address by Charles
Lenox Remond in November 1837, the Rhode Island Anti-
Slavery Society voted to aid Negroes to get jobs as clerks. *The
Philanthropist*, organ of the Ohio society, made its office into a
referral agency at which employers willing to take colored apprentices might leave their names and colored parents with
sons to be apprenticed might follow suit.[18]

Perhaps the most futile attempt at helping the Negro by an

organization was furnished by the American Union for the Relief and Improvement of the Colored Race. Founded in Boston in 1835 and backed by one hundred men in ten states, it proposed to give elementary schooling to the Negro and to teach him trades.[19] The American Union's membership was of the old-school, pillars-of-society type, men who were given more to reflection than to action. Hoping to resurrect the harmony and forbearance of the old days, they shied away from the word "immediate," favored colonization, and preferred to characterize slavery as a wrong rather than as a sin, a vital distinction then.

As could be expected, the union aroused the scorn and hostility of Garrison. Labeling it "An Anti-Garrison Society," he issued an address to Negroes informing them that the object of the union was to put them down, with him thrown in for good measure.[20] This ended the possibility that the union would obtain the necessary co-operation of the colored people in the 1830's. The union expired within two years.

Even under happier auspices an organized effort to assist the free Negro might not have met with success. In 1836 the American Anti-Slavery Society appointed four agents to work among Negroes devising ways to improve their lot. The suggestion had come from Theodore Weld, whose courage, devotion, and success in winning others to the cause had already marked him in reform circles. In February 1836 Weld wrote to Lewis Tappan listing ten reasons why the parent society should turn its attention to the elevation of the free Negro. Tappan agreed fully with Weld's memorandum, rewording it in a handwritten report to his fellow members on the executive committee.[21]

The committee decided to appoint four agents, selecting Hiram Wilson for the Canadian theatre, John J. Miter and William Yates for work in the East, and Augustus Wattles for Ohio. Wattles, a particular protégé of Weld, was designated as "generalissimo of the colored people." A thorough-going equalitarian, he had lodged with a colored family while in Cincinnati as a student at Lane Seminary.

The agents were dedicated men, but this was not enough. Nor did the project fail for lack of co-operation from Negroes. Eight colored clergymen in New York issued a circular urging full support of the agents and addressed not only to New Yorkers but also "to the free colored citizens of the United States and to all their Christian brethren and friends." [22] But the enthusiasm of the Negroes and the high spirits of the agents could not offset a lack of funds. The parent society, in the panic year of 1837, was unable to finance the agents, withdrawing all support by the summer of 1838.

The effort was not wholly lost. Hiram Wilson was launched on a career among Canadian Negroes that became his life's work. Yates made a careful survey of Delaware ("Slavery, and the Colored People in Delaware"), which he found depressing. The Negroes there were undervalued, he wrote, their virtues being disregarded and their degradation magnified. Yates also produced a 104-page pamphlet on civil rights, interspersing it with snatches of Negro history. "The subject is a rich one," he concluded. Yates also produced a survey of the Negroes on Long Island. John J. Miter, apparently the least active of the agents, brought out a study of the Negroes in Newark.[23]

Wattles was a zealous worker. In the three months of the spring of 1837 he traveled 575 miles in Ohio, visiting fourteen Negro settlements and forty-four schools. Late in 1837 he extended his operations into Indiana. Wattles remained on the field for seven years longer. But his funds came from friends and from his own inheritance, the parent society having withdrawn its support. "We are grieved at the discontinuance of the labors of Messrs. Wattles, Yates and Wilson," wrote *The Colored American* on October 27, 1838.[24]

If elevating the free Negro required money, it also called for common sense. And this too was sometimes missing in the proposals made by the abolitionists. In 1839 the New York City Anti-Slavery Society, in a thirteen-point list of ways to help the colored people, recommended that a book on domestic economy be printed for them and that a joint stock company be organized to trade with the West Indies.[25]

Many white abolitionists, as Negroes had sorrowfully came to learn by 1840, had a tendency to abstraction. Such white co-workers viewed the movement as an ideological warfare, the outcome of which was secondary to the stimulus of the mental jousting. To strike a moral posture was more important than to strike at slavery. Wendell Phillips, although almost without peer in the crusade, voiced something of this sense of disengagement in an informal talk to a gathering of fellow reformers at Cochituate Hall in Boston: "My friends, if we never free a slave, we have at least freed ourselves, in the effort to emancipate our brother man."[26]

Negro abolitionists, with the exception of William Whipper, had no fondness for abstraction. Their interest was more personal. A Negro could scarcely muster enough detachment to live in the realms of pure principle, the world being too much with him. An abolitionist who could say, as did Charles K. Whipple, that the principles of morality and religion remain undisturbed by our private exigency,[27] was likely to be white—that is, a person with a less urgent "private exigency."

In their ranks the abolitionists had some question marks. Like any other reform the crusade had its component of deviant personalities who found in it a release for private devils. The movement also had its universal reformers, men who, like Garrison, embraced several causes concurrently, thus diluting their abolitionism. And finally the movement had its summer soldiers who after a season disappeared in the shadows. Impulses to withdraw from the movement were numerous, ranging from a waning sympathy for the slave to a desire to concentrate on making enough money to put one's sons through college.

All of these sobering factors became more evident to the Negro when the abolitionists split in 1840. Negroes realized that a more realistic appraisal of the movement was in order. The Negro would have to look more to his own strength, to put into fuller antislavery use his own organizations.

Fortunately for the Negroes, they were no strangers to acting in national concert. They had been holding national conventions since mid-September 1830 when forty delegates from eight states met at Bethel Church in Philadelphia, with Richard Allen in the chair. For the following five years the Negro leaders held national conventions, generally in Philadelphia.[28] These meetings addressed themselves to three topics (or perhaps three aspects of the same topic); namely, the repeal of the "black laws" of the various Northern states, the advancement of the free Negro, and the wiping out of slavery. After 1835 the national conventions were held intermittently rather than annually. Their place was filled in some measure by state conventions, such as that held by New York Negroes from 1836 to 1850. Already fervently antislavery, the black convention movement would take on an even stronger abolitionist character with the 1840 split in the parent society.

The division in the American Anti-Slavery Society has generally been held to be a weakening of the movement. So it was, if one counts the decrease in the number of auxiliaries and the decline in membership. But the split actually had beneficial effects, taking abolitionism into new channels of expression, thus broadening its base. The division in the national society spewed a variety of isms, resulting in "moral suasion abolitionism and political abolitionism," wrote William Goodell, a highly respected figure in the crusade. "Then came also Church Reform abolitionism—Missionary abolitionism—Methodist, Baptist, Congregational, Independent, and Presbyterian abolitionism. Politicians were careful to supply a Whig and a Democratic abolitionism." [29] And, Goodell might have added, there was a Negro abolitionism.

Following the national division in 1840, the immediate question facing the Negro leaders was whether to adopt a go-it-alone policy, relying exclusively on all-Negro agencies. The issue came to the fore in May 1840 when a group of Connecticut Negroes, meeting in Hartford, recommended that a national convention of black men be held in New Haven in September. Such a meeting was necessary because "of the division among our friends," as the Reverend J. W. C. Pennington phrased it. Another delegate, James Foster, concurred fully, pointing out that "to talk about waiting till our friends get right is nonsense. We must act for ourselves." [30]

But this call met with a cool response from the influential leaders of the American Moral Reform Society, an organization that had been created by the black convention of 1835. Meeting in August 1840 the moral reformists condemned the proposed convention on the grounds that it drew the color line. A week later William Whipper and Robert Purvis, two of the society's leaders, sent word to David Ruggles, organizer of the scheduled convention, that they could not attend any gathering that was "exclusive in character." [31]

To those who favored the proposed Negro convention, it was a means of self-expression. "If we act with our white friends," wrote Charles B. Ray, "the words we utter will be considered theirs, or their echo." Ray and those who shared his viewpoint were vexed by *The Anti-Slavery Standard*, the organ of the American Anti-Slavery Society after the 1840 division, which condemned any separatist movement by Negroes. Such exclusive action strengthens segregation, said the *Standard*, asserting that there was no need for a colored convention when thousands of whites stood ready to help the Negro. Samuel Ringgold Ward, a former slave, fired a letter to the *Standard*'s editor, taking issue with his point of view: "I know that your intention is correct, but had you worn a colored skin from October 1817 to June 1840, as I have, in this pseudo-Republic, you would have seen through a very different medium." [32]

The argument as to the desirability of all-Negro reform societies did not end in 1840; indeed, it never ended in antebellum America. But as concerns the abolitionist movement, the great majority of Negroes preferred to act in concert with whites. The colored convention of 1848, held in Cleveland, recommended that Negroes join white abolitionist societies wherever possible. If, however, Negroes had no choice other than to organize societies, they should do so "without exclusiveness." Hence after 1840, Negro abolitionists continued to participate in the general societies, in many instances holding high office. In 1847 Frederick Douglass became president of the New England Anti-Slavery Society; Robert Purvis served as president of the Pennsylvania Society from 1845 to 1850, declining a sixth term;[33] and Charles Lenox Remond held similar office in the Essex Anti-Slavery Society for a like length of time.

Fortunately for the abolition crusade, a number of able Negro recruits swelled the ranks around 1840, most of them former slaves. Free-born or slave-born, the Negroes who became active abolitionists were generally the most able men in the group, the cream of the crop. For although the Negroes in general favored the antislavery movement, not all of them took part in it.

Indeed, to speak of a "group mind" among Negroes is misleading. "The mind does not take its complexion from the skin," wrote a Negro editor in 1849. "To be a colored man is not necessarily to be an abolitionist." A white abolitionist editor charged that some Negroes were proslavery in feeling, or indifferent to the slave. Such Negroes were "misguided by priestcraft," or swayed by the fear of public opinion, or apprehensive lest any antislavery activity on their part would hurt their business. Oliver Johnson, editor of the sympathetic

Bugle of Salem, Ohio, held that Negroes were so widely separated by sectarian and party lines as to impair their efficiency in breaking the chains of the enslaved. N. P. Rogers, another journalist, asserted that "dark complexioned people are said to be peculiarly hostile to anti-slavery, and there is a good deal of truth in it." [34]

These white observers furnished little evidence for their charges, which might well have been based on a single observation or incident, like that of Rogers who quoted as his only source "a young colored woman." But Negroes themselves levied similar charges. A meeting of Negroes in New York on July 22, 1834, adopted a resolution condemning all persons of color who were not antislavery, denouncing them as "the greatest enemies of our cause." Charles Lenox Remond, in a letter to Garrison, chided young Negroes, male and female, for being indifferent to the antislavery crusade. Henry Highland Garnet expressed the opinion that there were Negroes in Boston who, if they became plantation masters, "would make the blood fly from their slaves." William C. Nell noted that among Negroes there were, unhappily, "complexional distinctions," although he hastened to blame slavery for such intraracial color prejudice. [35]

Obviously not all Negroes had two of the most essential qualities requisite to a black reformer—the will to activism and a full readiness to risk personal assault. Many Negroes were outwardly apathetic, their indifference a shield against a hostile world. Their bystander behavior was a form of survival insurance in a social order that denied them legal and political equality.

A Negro abolitionist might not be called upon to stop the mouths of lions, but he ran risks exceeding those of his white counterpart. When William Lloyd Garrison and Frederick Douglass appeared at the courthouse in Harrisburg, Pennsylvania, on August 8, 1847, to hold a meeting, no attempt was made to molest Garrison—indeed, he was listened to with marked attention and respect. But when Douglass arose there were loud catcalls, followed by a barrage of rotten eggs and brickbats and an explosion of firecrackers. As Douglass observed later, a hated opinion is not always in sight whereas a hated color is. Lecturing in Buck and Montgomery counties in Pennsylvania in the spring of 1845, Charles Lenox Remond wrote that mobs and rumors of mobs were to be expected.[36] Such disorderly and mischief-bent groups had a penchant for Negro properties; in the outbreak of violence against the abolitionists in New York in July 1834, the more than twenty houses leveled to the ground all belonged to Negroes.

Some light-skinned Negroes, not caring to battle against discrimination, passed for white. Some who were Negroes in the South became white upon crossing the Mason-Dixon line. The "colored white," as James McCune Smith called them, were numerous in New York State; six of Smith's acquaintances at The New York African Free School crossed over in 1826, as did ten of Peter Clark's schoolmates in Cincinnati. Negroes believed that as a rule a swarthy person who was hostile to blacks was likely to be a "passer." [37]

Generally those Negroes who were themselves inactive in the movement held a high regard for those who were. This esteem for black movers and shakers reflected a familiar process of identification re-enforced by one of the universal factors in man's experience—a homage to men of mark. For those who had the wish to be active abolitionists but who lacked the will, one enterprising business firm furnished a substitute of sorts. It produced lithograph portraits of black reformers Delany, Douglass, Garnet, and Remond, advertising the portraits as highly suitable for hanging in the parlor.[38]

The most notable of the hero figures who emerged so providentially in the 1840's were former slaves. In most instances their freedom had been self-won, either by flight or purchase. In fewer cases their freedom came from others, either from relatives or friends who purchased it or from kindly or con-science-stricken masters.

Self-purchase was far more common than might have been expected. The turn-of-the-century pioneer leaders, Richard Allen and Absalom Jones, had bought their freedom. The father of Peter Williams, rector of St. Philip's Church, and the father of William Still, the underground railroad operator, were both self-purchased.

Crucial to such a transaction was the co-operation of the master. Generally he was paid in small installments, the former slave raising the money by working, speaking at aboli-tionist meetings, or making door-to-door appeals. Not all attempts were successful. A slave, Lewis Day, about to be sold to Georgia in July 1838, visited John Quincy Adams at his office in the House of Representatives, soliciting help, but Adams could only commend him to mercy and patience. Even after raising the money, a purchaser could face heartbreak. Moses Grandy paid for himself three times, his first master being unscrupulous and his second master a bankrupt.[39]

For all its hazards, self-purchase proved an open sesame to thousands. In 1837 of the 18,768 Negroes in Philadelphia, 254 had bought themselves, paying an average of $278.[40] Cincinnati, nearer than Philadelphia to the cotton kingdom, had a higher proportion of self-purchasers. A firsthand report, made at the meeting of the Ohio Anti-Slavery convention held at Putnam in April 1835, lists in staccato fashion a series of case studies in the stock market:

> David Young, an emancipated slave, had bought his wife and six children. He paid for them $1265. He yet owes $110 for the last child. This he expects to pay this summer.
>
> Henry Boyd bought himself at the age of eighteen. He is now thirty-one, and is worth $3000. He has also bought a brother and sister, for whom he paid $900.

Samuel Lewis paid $500 for himself before he was eighteen years old.

Rebecca Madison paid $1800 for herself, and is now worth $3000.

Henry Blue paid for himself $1000, is now thirty-nine years of age, and is worth $5000. He attends school every day.[41]

As this report indicates, it was common for one member of a family to buy the freedom of another member. In one week in March 1834 Theodore D. Weld visited more than thirty families and found that over half of them were skimping and saving to purchase close relatives still in slavery. Frank McWorter, who came to Pike County, Illinois, in 1829, purchased himself, his wife, their thirteen children, and two grandchildren, raising $10,000 for the seventeen. Former slave John Gloucester, who became pastor of the First African Presbyterian Church in 1807, purchased his wife and their four children. After raising $1400 for her own freedom, Alethia Tanner bought her sister, Laura Cook, and the latter's four chidren, one of whom, John F. Cook, became a civic leader in Washington, D.C. The Cleveland abolitionist, John Malvin, used some of his earnings as a canal-boat operator to pay for his father-in-law, Caleb Dorsey. Pierre Toussaint, hairdresser for fashionable New York women, purchased his wife and sister. Walter Freeman bought his own liberty and that of his wife and six children, paying a total of $2550 to his master, George E. Badger, Secretary of the Navy under President Harrison. This feat was duplicated by Lunsford Lane in North Carolina, except that he raised $3130 for his family of eight. "His exploits so far exceed those of Eneas," wrote an abolitionist sheet, "that could Virgil hear his story, he would be ashamed of his own hero." [42]

In some instances Negroes purchased the freedom of slaves who were expected to pay the purchase price on the installment plan. Such an agreement was made between twenty Negroes and John Berry Meachum, pastor of the African Baptist

Church of St. Louis, who previously had bought his own freedom, that of his wife and their children, and of his father. Hester Lane of New York City, after buying herself and her husband, paid for the freedom of ten others, in some cases receiving small payments from time to time, and in other cases receiving nothing at all.[43]

Former slaves proved a godsend to the cause. The Western Anti-Slavery Society reported that volunteer agents Harmon Bealer and his brother, Halliday, had received their commissions not from the society but from God by virtue of their skin color and their experience of "the depth and damning wickedness of American slavery." Writing in 1850, William Lloyd Garrison ranked such figures as Henry Bibb, William Wells Brown, and Frederick Douglass with the ablest speakers in the movement, and "the best qualified to address the public on the subject of slavery." [44] While not the only black abolitionists emerging in the 1840's, this trio does provide a suggestive portrait of their colleagues of color, illustrating procedures that were commonly employed.

Henry Bibb, born in Kentucky, escaped to Cincinnati in 1837. Returning to the slave states for his wife, he was captured, only to escape for a second time. He made his way to Detroit, where he felt himself to be a man, he said, and not three-fifths of a man. Bibb became an abolitionist lecturer, traveling from Michigan to Massachusetts during the middle and late 1840's. Lewis Tappan, who presided at his lecture to the Brooklyn Female Academy in May 1847, did not put him in a class with Frederick Douglass, but he spoke of Bibb's touching earnestness. Tappan, who had heard all of the leading orators in the movement, found it impossible to listen to Bibb without feeling his heart swell with the deepest hatred of slavery. [45]

Bibb's other lectures in Brooklyn and New York on that

visit constituted an important service to the cause of liberty, in the opinion of Gamaliel Bailey. A master of pathos, Bibb often sang "The mother's lament," a piece purportedly sung by slaves about to be sold. At the end of a lecture by Bibb at the Baptist Church in Blackiston, Massachusetts, the entire audience stood up, signifying their desire to hear him again. Bibb was light-skinned and had straight hair, which prompted the *Blackstone Chronicle* to observe that slaveholders cared very little for the complexion of their victims.[46] Following the Fugitive Slave Law of 1850, Bibb went to Canada, edited the *Voice of the Fugitive* at Sandwich, and became a promoter of Canadian colonization.

William Wells Brown was, like Bibb, a light-skinned escaped slave from Kentucky. During his flight he was aided by a Quaker, Wells Brown, whose name he added to the single name of his slavery days and to whom he dedicated his first book. In the 1840's William Wells Brown served as a lecturer for antislavery societies in New York and Massachusetts. A fair speaker, he was a better writer. He was, says Vernon Loggins, the first Negro American "to attempt seriously the novel, the drama, and travel literature." [47] In 1848 he compiled what was perhaps the best of the song books to come out of the movement, *The Anti-Slavery Harp*, a collection of forty-six pieces to be sung to such familiar tunes as "Oh, Susannah," "Auld Lang Syne," and "My Faith Looks Up to Thee."

During the first six months of 1849, Brown toured the antislavery circuit exhibiting William and Ellen Craft. Slaves in Macon, Georgia, the Crafts escaped late in 1848; Ellen, a quadroon, disguised herself as a man and assumed the role of a slaveholder, with William as an accompanying slave.[48] This dramatic escape became part of the folklore of the abolitionist crusade, in part because Brown took the couple in his charge and gave them maximum exposure. He arranged meetings for them throughout New England, sometimes charging an admission fee, an almost unprecedented practice in abolitionist circles. But the Crafts were drawing cards. They said little, but Ellen's appearance created an instant sympathy in a white audience. Brown arranged for his protégés to be presented at the two largest meetings on the calendar of the Garrisonians in the East—the Massachussets Anti-Slavery Society's convention in January and the New England Anti-Slavery Society's annual meeting in May, both in Boston. Two months after the latter affair, Brown sailed for Paris to represent the American Peace Society at the International Peace Conference. He stayed abroad for five years.

The most influential of the former slaves who joined the abolitionist forces was Frederick Douglass, who ran away from his Maryland master in 1838, settling in New Bedford, Massachusetts. In August 1841, while attending an abolitionist meeting at Nantucket, he was called upon to speak. His sentences were somewhat halting, but William Lloyd Garrison, who followed him, used them as a text for a stirring speech. After the meeting Douglass was approached by John A. Collins, general agent of the Massachusetts Anti-Slavery Society, asking him to become a lecturer. Believing that the public was "itching" to "hear a colored man speak, particularly a slave," Collins had been on the lookout for someone like Douglass.[49]

From the outset Douglass exceeded the highest hopes of his abolitionist employers. He revealed a flair for dramatic utterance: "I appear before the immense assembly this evening as a thief and a robber," ran his opening remarks at a meeting of the Massachusetts Society in January 1842. "I stole this head, these limbs, this body from my master, and ran off with them." Three months later, when Douglass spoke at the annual meeting of the New England Society, a newspaper editor wrote that he had seldom heard a better speech as to language and manner—"the appropriateness of his elocution and gesticulation, and the grammatical accuracy of his sentences."[50]

Fortunately for Douglass, his companions on the reform

circuit in his formative years were likely to be good speakers with well-stocked minds. He could learn much from a figure like Wendell Phillips, who had deserted the bar and turned his back on a political career to cast his lot with the reformers. Philips's oratorical abilities were unsurpassed in nineteenth-century America, entitling him to be called "abolition's golden trumpet."

Douglass, however, was not one likely to be overlooked on the public platform, no matter what the company. From his first weeks with Collins, he was a drawing card. His voice struck the ear pleasantly, and as he gained experience he capitalized on it to the fullest. Melodious and strong, it varied in speed and pitch according to its use, whether to convey wit, sarcasm, argument, or invective. A first-rate speaking voice was not Douglass's only asset—he caught the eye, a man people would come to see. Six feet tall, broad-shouldered, his hair long (as was the custom) and neatly parted on the side, his eyes deep-set and steady, nose well formed, lips full, and skin bronze-colored, he looked like someone destined for the platform or pulpit.

Not relying solely on nature, Douglass had something to say. In his first weeks as a traveling agent and lecturer, he devoted himself to a simple narration of his experiences before freedom. From a description of slavery he began to go into a more direct denunciation of it. Gradually in his public appearances he broadened his subject matter, attacking the church for its timidity on slavery, demanding its abolition in the District of Columbia, and criticizing the annexation of Texas.

In 1845 Douglass added to his growing prominence by the publication of a book describing his life as a slave, *Narrative of the Life of Frederick Douglass*. Storytelling in tone, it was of absorbing interest in its sensitive descriptions of persons and places, including a sharply etched portrait of a slave-breaker named Edward Covey. Boosted by good press notices and reviews, the *Narrative* became a best-seller on two continents, over thirty thousand copies being sold in five years.

Douglass's biography was but one of the nearly one hundred such slave narratives published in book form. These autobiographies and biographies of former bondmen loomed large in the campaign literature of abolitionism, furnishing propaganda of considerable proportions. Their critics would charge that slave narratives were overdrawn, relying heavily upon the pathological—tales of miscegenation, sadistic masters, separation of families, harsh treatment, and cruel punishment. Moreover, it was charged, slave narratives were written without proper documentation, without benefit of notes, diaries, letters, or a revisit to the old homestead for an on-the-spot rechecking. In the preface to his autobiography, Samuel Ringgold Ward apologized for not having "a solitary book or paper to refer to, for a fact or passage." Any conversation appearing in a slave narrative would have to be reproduced, any dialogue reconstructed. In the biography of Lunsford Lane "conversations have been reproduced with a freedom worthy of the Greek historians," wrote James Spencer Bassett. The story which James Williams recited to John Greenleaf Whittier had so many discrepancies that its sale was discontinued in 1838 by the red-faced executive committee of the American Anti-Slavery Society.[51]

Unquestionably the slave narratives were propagandistic—they were, after all, a weapon in the warfare. But if they were to be believed, they had to be as accurate as possible. Hence, aside from a few hoaxes, most of the slave narratives were soundly buttressed in fact. The abolitionists preferred to have former slaves write their own stories, not only to counter the notion of Negro inferiority but to give them the stamp of authenticity. When the abolitionist societies found it necessary to employ ghost writers, they sought persons with a high sense of integrity, such as Lydia Maria Child, John Greenleaf Whittier, and Edmund Quincy.

Whatever their relative admixture of social reality and sensationalism, slave narratives moved well in the book marts. No Negroes, before or since, have ever experienced less difficulty in getting published. Four editions of the biography of William Wells Brown made their appearance in less than two years. In a similar span, over twenty-seven thousand copies had been sold of the narrative of Solomon Northrup, a free Negro who had spent twelve years in slavery after having been kidnaped and put on the auction block as a runaway.

Slave narratives made a deep impression in the North, most readers finding their testimony quite persuasive. To Giles B. Stebbins the narrative by Douglass was "a voice coming up from the prison-house, speaking like a thousand-voiced psalm." Another reader said that she had wept over *Oliver Twist*, that her tears had moistened whole chapters of Eugene Sue's *Mysteries of Paris*, but that Douglass's narrative had "entered so deep into the chambers of my soul, as to entirely close the safety valve." In December 1855 Lewis Tappan wrote Douglass that his wife had read "your history" over and over again: "Its contents will be laid up in our hearts." [52]

A Boston newspaperman defied anyone to have any patience with slavery after reading Bibb's book. The Unitarian clergyman, William H. Furness, confessed to picking up Solomon Northrup's narrative reluctantly, feeling that it would "show the marks of book-making." But what he found was a work that rivetted the reader from beginning to end, giving him a deeper impression of slavery's savage spirit.[53]

The influence of the slave narratives was widened by the abolitionist weeklies, which reprinted extracts from them or ran them in serial form. Chief among the items likely to be selected for reproduction was a slave's letter to his former master. A long letter to one's erstwhile owner berating him for his sins of omission and commission was found to be an effective device. "I intend to make full use of you," wrote Douglass to his former master, "as a weapon with which to assail the system of slavery." [54] Bibb, Brown, and the clergyman, orator, and underground railroad operator, Jermain Wesley Loguen of Syracuse, were among the other more prominent correspondents whose letters to former masters were displayed over and over in the columns of the antislavery weeklies. And if the master could be goaded into making a reply, as in the case of Bibb and Loguen, his letter was gratefully pounced upon by the abolitionist sheets.

Harriet Beecher Stowe praised slave narratives for the vigor, shrewdness, and originality that their characters exhibited, and for their clear portrayal of the slave's own viewpoint. Well might the author of *Uncle Tom's Cabin* speak such words of commendation. Far more than she could ever sense, the vast audience that responded to her classic tale of Uncle Tom was an audience that had already been conditioned and prepared by the life stories of runaway slaves. For, as the knowledgeable Frederick Law Olmsted pointed out, most Northerners got their impressions of slavery from having read slave narratives.[55] Hence if President Lincoln could greet Mrs. Stowe as "the little lady who made this big war," certainly some of this credit might be shared by those former slaves whose stories had been dinned in the public mind, creating an adverse image of slavery that helped make possible the emergence of a Mrs. Stowe and an Abraham Lincoln.

The avowed intention of the slave narratives was to loosen the bonds of the enchained, and, as has been noted, they succeeded in winning a wide readership. There were, however, other publics to be reached and other ways to reach them. Taking this into account, Negro reformers were prepared to plumb the resources within the black community itself. The creation of a distinctive literature was no mean feat, but it hardly left black Americans spent and unfertile.

IV

※ ※ ※

Pulpit and Press

In our onslaught upon what we term separate
institutions, we too frequently lose sight of
the fact that to our church, association and
school we are at this hour chiefly indebted
for whatever of preparation we have made
for the great battle of today.

William J. Whipper, 1855

THE EIGHT NEGROES who were numbered among the founders of the American and Foreign Anti-Slavery Society in May
1840 had one thing in common. They were all clergymen—
Jehiel C. Beman and his son, Amos G. Beman, then on the
threshold of a useful career as pastor of the Temple Street
African Church in New Haven; Christopher Rush, second
bishop of the Zion Methodists; and five Presbyterians—Samuel E. Cornish, Theodore S. Wright, Stephen H. Gloucester,
young Henry Highland Garnet, and the short-lived Andrew
Harris, a graduate of the University of Vermont in 1838 and
pastor of St. Mary Street Church in Philadelphia.

There were many other black clergymen-abolitionists in
1840, among them Charles B. Ray of New York, the former
blacksmith, James W. C. Pennington of Hartford, the ebul-
lient Samuel Ringgold Ward, all Congregationalists; Nathaniel Paul, a Baptist who was active in the Albany Anti-Slavery
Society; and two budding intellectuals, both on the ascetic side

—Episcopalian Alexander Crummell, who served as secretary of the New York State Anti-Slavery Society before he had reached twenty, and Daniel A. Payne, who in June 1839, just before his ordination, delivered a blistering attack on slavery before the Franckean Synod Lutherans at Fordsboro, New York.[1]

Negro leadership in antebellum America was predominantly ministerial, colored men in the other professions being in short supply. This accounted for the key role of the Negro church. "As among our people generally," wrote Martin R. Delany to Frederick Douglass in 1849, "the Church is the Alpha and Omega of all things."[2] Since the turn of the century Negroes had formed independent churches, controlled and conducted by themselves. A small number of Negro Methodists in the North remained in the white Methodist Episcopal Church, but the great majority joined either the Bethel Methodists (AME) or Zion Methodists (AMEZ). In doctrine and in discipline the all-Negro churches were not distinctive; their uniqueness rested in their autonomy, their self-government.

This desire by the Negro to share more fully in the shaping of his own destiny was one of the two major reasons for the establishment of the separate church. It provided an outlet for self-expression. Writing from the vantage point of an insider, John Mercer Langston praised the Negro church for giving to the colored American the "opportunity to be himself, to think his own thoughts, express his own convictions, make his own utterances, test his own powers and thus, in the exercise of the faculties of his own soul, trust and achieve."[3] Significantly, the denominations that held the most attraction for Negroes were those which were democratically organized, thus giving the rank and file a substantial voice in the religious exercises and business affairs.

Another major reason for the establishment of the all-black church was the differing viewpoints between Negro and white churchgoers on public issues and jimcrow practices. Negroes had become sharply critical of white churches, Frederick Douglass in a speech to Philadelphia Negroes in 1847 listing the churches of the land as the chief oppressor of the colored man. Three years later, at a convention of clergymen, Samuel Ringgold Ward charged that on the slavery issue the churches had departed from God and the Bible.[4] Tending to conform to the prevailing pattern, the churches broke no new ground in race relations.

Negroes criticized the white churches for supporting African colonization. In part the churches acted from a missionary motive—spreading the gospel—but this made little difference to Negro reformers. Moreover, many white clergymen were charged with holding themselves aloof from the effort to strike at slavery and prejudice, all the while delivering vague sermons on brotherhood. Others were said to be interested in the Negro's soul but indifferent to his earthly condition.

Churches with branches in the South were condemned for their timidity on slavery. In 1832 at a general conference in Philadelphia, Charles W. Gardner urged his fellow clergymen in the Methodist Episcopal Church to denounce slaveholding in their ranks, but with no success. At the general conference four years later in Cincinnati, the church disclaimed any right to interfere with the relations existing between the master and the slave. The 1840 conference, held in Baltimore, voted to debar Negro church members from testifying against whites in ecclesiastical trials in those states in which law prohibited Negroes from testifying against whites. This resolution drew a long (and futile) statement of protest from two Negro churches in Baltimore, Sharp Street and Asbury. "No man of color can ever be a man in the M. E. Church," wrote black Bishop Alexander W. Wayman in 1858.[5]

The small number of Negroes who were Episcopalians were subject to embarrassing restrictions. In July 1834 Peter

Williams, pastor of St. Philip's Church, was advised by the bishop of the diocese, Benjamin T. Onderdonk, to resign from the executive committee and board of managers of the American Anti-Slavery Society. A dedicated man, one who "was always in trouble about other people's troubles," Williams nonetheless felt obliged to follow Onderdonk's request, although with a heavy heart. Five years later Onderdonk tried to dissuade young Alexander Crummell from seeking admission to the General Theological Seminary in New York. Crummell refused to withdraw his application, but the board of trustees, influenced by Onderdonk, voted against granting the petition. Crummell's fellow students at Oneida congratulated him upon his stand and expressed deep regret at "the outrage against humanity, religion and the Almighty." Crummell later secured ordination in another diocese. But he, like other Negro ministers, could understand the wry comment made by James W. C. Pennington at the general antislavery convention in London in 1843: "If I meet my white brother minister in the street, he blushes to own me; meet him in our deliberative bodies, he gives me the go-by; meet him at the communion table, and he looks at me sideways." [6]

White churches that admitted Negroes seated them in a jimcrow section or pew. There was no interracial mixing before or after services. In Cincinnati in 1840, John Rankin urged his fellow Presbyterians to assist the Negroes in building a church of their own, inasmuch as they were staying away from white churches because of "the prejudices entertained against color." In Washington, D.C., a year later, the Negro members of several Presbyterian churches withdrew to form a colored congregation. Their reason was simply stated: "We do not enjoy in white churches all the privileges we desire." [7]

This was the crux of the matter. As long as white churches practiced jimcrow they were not likely to attract many Negroes. It was a clear knowledge of this fact that lay behind the

founding of St. Thomas's African Episcopal Church in Philadelphia on August 12, 1794, its organizers motivated, as they
phrased it, "to keep an open door for those of our race who
may be induced to assemble with us, but who would not attend
divine worship in other places." [8] The jimcrow practices of
the First Baptist Church of New York prompted its Negro
members to form the Abyssinia Baptist Church in 1808.

Negro criticism of the churches for their lack of reformist
zeal and Christian example left no denomination untouched,
not even the Quakers. In truth the Quakers were vulnerable.
After 1830 their protest against slavery had weakened, in part
because they disliked the harsh language of the new abolitionists. The doctrine of immediate emancipation troubled many
Quakers, who felt that a practice so deeply rooted as slavery
called for time and patience. By 1840 many Yearly Meetings
were advising their members to abandon any lingering abolitionist leanings they might have. Ten years later the Pennsylvania Anti-Slavery Society reported that Quaker hostility to
human bondage was a thing of the past: "They stand entirely
aloof from the antislavery movement." [9] This had the quality
of overstatement common to abolitionists, but it was not easily
challenged, and apparently never was.

Quakers could not divorce themselves from the general feeling of condescension toward black people. "They will give us
good advice," wrote Samuel Ringgold Ward. "They will aid
in giving us a partial education—but never in a Quaker
school, beside their own children. Whatever they do for us
savors of pity, and is done at arm's length." Jimcrow, as Ward
indicated, was no stranger among Quakers. True, the quiet-
ness of their religious exercises caused them to lose some
colored prospects, such as J. W. C. Pennington: "My nature
was sensitive, and I wanted to hear singing. Sometimes I went
and wanted to hear preaching, but I was disappointed." [10]

But there were Negroes of a different temperament from
Pennington's and if they wished to join the Society of Friends

they had a formidable obstacle course to run. And admission to membership did not end their travail. At many meeting halls there were benches in back for Negroes, as one of their nonattending colored communicants, Sarah M. Douglass of Philadelphia, ruefully took note. "This bench is for black people," she had heard whenever anyone sought to sit next to her at Arch Street Meeting.[11] For this reason she had stopped attending, but her mother continued to do so, even though she often had a whole long bench to herself.

In fairness to her fellow Quakers, Sarah Douglass was quick to acknowledge that among them were a "noble few who have cleansed their garments from the foul stain of prejudice." As examples she singled out the Grimké sisters. Negroes had found a number of other Friends worthy of their esteem. As an evidence of their high regard for Elias Hicks, a group of New York Negroes in 1830 named a burial society after him, "The New York African Hicks Association." The death of Thomas Shipley of Philadelphia, whose appearances before judicial tribunals had saved hundreds of Negroes from slavery, led to a memorial meeting by Negroes at the First Presbyterian Church, followed two months later by a more elaborate observance at St. Thomas Church, with Robert Purvis delivering the formal eulogy. "The heart of every colored man that knew him lies prostrate, bruised and bleeding," Purvis had written in a letter to Garrison.[12]

When Benjamin Lundy prepared to move to the West in July 1838 the Negroes held a farewell for him at the Philadelphia Reading Room. They brought tears to his eyes, characterizing him as the father of the cause and one to whom lasting gratitude was due. Thirteen months later when Lundy died, the Negroes in Boston and Philadelphia held memorial services, both groups lauding him for his long and uncompromising efforts on behalf of human freedom. The passing of Quaker Isaac T. Hopper was likewise memorialized by Philadelphia Negroes. Meeting at Bethel Church, they needed no speaker to remind them that Hopper had always been at the beck and call of the fugitive slave and that he had never hesitated to get off a streetcar, even at eighty, if Negroes were not taken aboard.[13]

The Quakers were leading spirits in a movement that Negroes would be likely to support, the free produce movement. This was an effort to strike at slavery by not using anything produced by slave labor. To take the profit out of slavery would hasten its demise. Starting in the late eighteenth century the free produce scheme reached the organizational stage in the 1820's. In 1830, three years after its founding, the Pennsylvania Free Produce Association, based in Philadelphia, extended its work to Negroes.

In October a delegation from the association met with a group of twenty Negroes and exhibited samples of foodstuffs produced by free labor. The Negroes showed much interest. Two months later at Bethel Church five hundred Negroes gathered, with James Cornish as secretary, and formed the Colored Free Produce Society of Pennsylvania. Within three months the officers of the society could report that the demand for free labor articles by its members had exceeded all expectations, some members buying 25- and 50-pound bags of free sugar at one time.[14]

Negro women in Philadelphia, not to be outdone, held a meeting in December to organize a free produce association. On January 24, 1831, at Bethel Church the Colored Female Free Produce Society of Pennsylvania was organized, with Judith James as president and Laetitia Rowley as secretary. By the summer their efforts had won the praises of Benjamin Lundy who expressed the hope that their example would not be lost upon "their sisters of fairer hue" or those of their own color in other localities.[15]

At each of the first five colored conventions, held in the early 1830's, resolutions were passed in support of free labor products, the first convention urging "colored capitalists" to invest their funds in free produce stores and the fifth convention enjoining "every lover of freedom" to abstain from the use of slave labor products as far as practicable. Negro newspapers took up the refrain, *Freedom's Journal* running several articles on free produce. One piece pointed out that every twenty-five persons who used slave sugar provided employment for one slave, with the result that New York City Negroes were subject to requiring the labor of fifty of "our brethren." Hence, to abstain from using such produce was necessary in order to convince the public that Negroes were sincere in their protest against slavery.[16]

Outside of Philadelphia there were a few efforts by Negro groups to foster free produce. In New York in 1838, a group of colored women promoted a display of free labor products at the Broadway Tabernacle, charging 6½¢ for admission, plus additional outlay if one ate, with the proceeds going for antislavery purposes. At the annual meeting of the Geneva Colored Anti-Slavery Society in 1839 the members were invited prayerfully "to ponder the question whether they can innocently or consistently use the products of slave labor." At its organizational meeting in August 1841 at Hartford, the Union Missionary Society besought its members to refuse to receive the known fruits of unrequited labor.[17]

A few Negroes attempted to run businesses on free produce principles. In March 1834 William Whipper opened a free labor and temperance grocery store next door to Bethel Church in Philadelphia. As an added attraction, he reported that the store kept a constant supply of abolitionist books and pamphlets on hand. A Negro confectioner in Philadelphia used nothing but free sugar; he got Angelina Grimké's order for her wedding cake.[18]

The young and serious Frances Ellen Watkins invariably spoke of free produce while on the abolitionist circuit, expressing thanks that she was able to pay a little more for a "Free Labor dress, if it is coarser." In an article on free produce, written for *Frederick Douglass' Paper*, Miss Watkins viewed the movement as "the harbinger of hope, the ensign of progress, and a means of proving the consistency of our principles and the earnestness of our zeal." In December 1852, Jacob C. White delivered a lecture to the Banneker Institute in Philadelphia entitled "The Inconsistency of Colored People Using Slave Produce." White criticized his fellow blacks, saying that if there were only two stores in the city, one of them free produce and the other slave produce, not one colored person in fifty would go out of his way to patronize the former.[19]

But to most abolitionists, white or black, the free produce movement was not a vital issue. For every one who abstained entirely from slave-labor goods or commodities, there were dozens who abstained only in part and then when not too inconvenient and hundreds who simply ignored the whole thing. The nonparticipants ran little risk of censure. More than any other phase of the abolitionist program the exclusive use of free labor products remained a matter between the individual and his conscience rather than a dividing line between the faithful and the backsliders.

If Negroes were not without fond memories of some Quakers and some Quaker efforts, they could also nod approvingly at the work of the Congregationalists in helping to found the American Missionary Association. Founded in 1846 because the existing missionary groups were too quiet about slavery, the American Missionary Association was made up of four organizations founded shortly before 1846. By far the most important of these was the Amistad Committee. The *Amistad* was a Spanish schooner which in the summer of 1839 had been seized by its cargo of fifty-four slaves, led by their headman, Cinque. The two whites who had been spared expressly to navigate the ship back to Mendi, the West African homeland of the captors, brought it instead by a ruse to Long

Island waters where it was seized by the United States brig, *Washington*. The Spanish government demanded the return of the mutineers, who were committed to prison pending trial for piracy. Coming to their assistance, a group of abolitionists headed by Lewis Tappan, Joshua Leavitt, and Simeon S. Jocelyn, formed the Amistad Committee.

Dedicated to the defense, support, and education of the Mendians, the committee secured legal aid to fight their case in the federal courts. A portion of the funds raised came from Negro groups. Two of the self-improvement societies in New York, the Philomathian and the Phoenixian, sent $84.08, the proceeds of a jointly sponsored concert. A benefit in Cincinnati at the Colored Baptist Church raised $50, which a local weekly considered remarkable in view of the hard times.[20]

To raise money the Amistad Committee sold pictures of Cinque at a dollar apiece. The picture was a replica of a portrait by Nathaniel Jocelyn of New Haven, gifted brother of S. S. Jocelyn, whose services had been commissioned by Robert Purvis. The original created a problem for the Artist Fund Society of Philadelphia, to whom Purvis had sent it upon the request of a member. The hanging committee, however, decided against exhibiting the portrait on the grounds that to do so would be injurious to the society's weal in light of the excitement of the times.[21]

In March 1841, after eighteen months of effort, the Amistad Committee was elated when the Supreme Court declared the Mendians to be free, dismissing them from the custody of the court. The committee, along with other abolitionists, gave much of the credit to John Quincy Adams, who had been persuaded to become senior counsel in the final stages of the case. The hundreds of letters of thanks that were sent to him included one, dated March 30, 1841, from a Negro group in Columbus, Ohio. A man who had received countless expressions of approbation over a long public career that included a term in the White House, Adams sent a gracious reply to the black correspondents from Columbus: "I never received from any body of men a vote of thanks more grateful to my feelings than yours." [22]

The Amistad Committee had one final task—to raise money to get the Mendians back to their homelands. As in the case of the defense fund, some of the contributors were Negroes. Like other abolitionists, they responded wholeheartedly to the Mendian mission, inasmuch as they regarded it as the one mission that was free of the taint of the American Colonization Society. In New York in May 1841 fund-raising meetings were held at two colored churches. In Philadelphia four predominantly Negro meetings were held in July, from which $400 was realized clear of expenses. Organized by Lewis Tappan, a twelve-day series of meetings was held in New England, mostly in Negro churches, and $1000 was raised.[23] Invariably, the great attraction at these meetings was a contingent of the Mendians themselves, some of whom had learned enough English to sing a hymn or read a passage of Scripture.

In late November 1841 the remaining thirty-five Mendians sailed from New York on the bark, *Gentlemen*, bound for Sierra Leone, not far from their home. They were accompanied by three missionaries and two teachers, both of the latter being Negroes—Henry R. Wilson of Barbados and James Wilson. The work of the Amistad Committee had been brought to a successful close. Its supporters thereupon formed themselves into a new group, the Mendi Committee, pledged to send assistance to the departed Africans.

The new commitee found that its work was paralleled by the Union Missionary Society, an organization founded at Hartford on August 18, 1841, by Negroes. Attending the meeting were forty-three delegates from five states—Massachusetts, Rhode Island, Connecticut, New York, and Pennsylvania—plus five spectators from the *Amistad* crew. While denouncing the colonization scheme, the delegates felt that

Negro Americans should share in the movement to carry the Christian gospel to Africa. Forming the Union Missionary Society, with headquarters to be located in New York, and with white membership to be welcome, they named J. W. Pennington as president, Amos G. Beman as secretary, and Theodore S. Wright as treasurer.[24]

The next step was enlisting the support of the ubiquitous Lewis Tappan. To the delight of the solicitors, Tappan showed a keen interest and, in typical fashion, soon became a dominant figure in the organization. Since he played a similar role in the Mendi Committee, a merger was inevitable. At Albany in 1846, the Mendi Committee, the Union Missionary Society, and two equally short-lived groups, the Western Evangelical Missionary Association and the Committee for West India Missions, transferred their funds to the newly formed American Missionary Association, and disbanded.[25] At this inaugural meeting of the A.M.A., Pennington and Wright were present. Wright and Samuel Ringgold Ward were named as two of the five vice presidents, and on the twelve-man executive committee four Negroes were placed, Wright, Pennington, Ray, and Cornish.

Although a mission society, the A.M.A. was abolition oriented inasmuch as it considered slavery as one of the most heinous of sins. Its membership was open to anyone who "is not a slaveholder or in the practice of other immoralities." [26] It had no denominational or ecclesiastical ties, but its leadership was predominantly Congregationalist and it was generally thought to be the secular arm of that church. It operated foreign and home missions, the latter quite feebly supported until the mid-fifties. It had one Negro in the foreign field, Mrs. Mary Shadd Cary in Canada, assigned to promote better schools. Of the 263 who were home missionaries before the Civil War, 7 were Negroes.

The Negro appointees of the A.M.A., like the whites, were largely settled pastors whose congregations were too small or too poor to pay them adequately, and who were therefore glad to get $200 or $300 a year as a city missionary. Quite exceptional was a man like Samuel E. Cornish who, since he enjoyed a competence, could volunteer his services free of charge. But other appointees, among them Ward, Charles B. Ray, Jermain W. Loguen, Henry Highland Garnet, and Amos G. Beman, were in no position to decline payment for services. Some of the home missionaries had money-raising responsibilities. Among these was the younger Beman, who held public meetings, generally prefacing his financial requests with a lecture on such topics as "The Origin and History of the African Race" and "What the Colored People Can under God do for Themselves." The collections over one period of five months were meager, Beman amassing a total of $70.17. The other Negro appointees of the A.M.A. were city missionaries, who busied themselves in Sunday school work, distributed tracts in the streets, reclaimed the outcasts, visited the sick and shut-ins, and attended funerals.[27]

The domestic program of the A.M.A was not to be measured by its works alone, particularly its heroic but aborted efforts in Kentucky and North Carolina. By its outspoken hostility to slavery, the A.M.A. furnished an example of a church-oriented group that did not evade or palliate a social and moral problem of the first magnitude. Other denominations, too, had their coteries of concerned churchmen. The American Baptist Free Mission Society, established in 1843, was antislavery in outlook and activity. Among the Methodist clergy there were dedicated abolitionists like Orange Scott, who in 1840 called a convention which formed the American Wesleyan Anti-Slavery Society and who three years later led a "Scottite" secession from the Methodist Episcopal Church.[28]

In 1854 the Brooklyn Presbytery elected a Negro, A. N. Freeman of Siloam Church, as moderator. The third Presbytery of New York voted this office to Theodore S. Wright in 1845 and to J. W. C. Pennington eight years later. In spite of this honor Pennington, in his sermon to the presbytery, felt it necessary to express his keen regret as the indifference of "our general body" on the slavery issue. An attempt at establishing an interdenominational society was made at Cincinnati in 1850 with the calling of a Christian Anti-Slavery Convention. With Lewis Woodson and John B. Vashon among the participants of record, the some two thousand delegates adopted seventeen forthright resolutions to the general effect that slavery contravened the laws of God and the gospel of Christ.[29] But there was no follow-up, and the effort came to little.

The antislavery views of individual clergymen and congregations did give an increasing moral tone to the crusade. Moreover, the hostility to slavery among churchmen was a factor in the breakup within three of the major denominations. The divisive question of human bondage was an issue, however soft-pedalled, in the split in the Presbyterians' ranks in 1837 between the old school and the new school.[30] Differing viewpoints on slavery was the key factor in the disruption of and final split in the Methodist Episcopal Church in 1844, and it led in the following year to a similar break between Southern Baptists and Northern Baptists. But even in the North the church on the whole, reflecting the great majority of individual congregations, preferred to deal gently with slavery in order to preserve harmony on an issue that often brought about disruption.

The Negro church had no such squeamishness about bearing witness against slavery. The Negro church had its weaknesses—its services tended to be emotional with an abundance of "rousement," and many of its preachers were men of little formal training and hence given to substituting sound for sense. However, Negro churches generally conveyed a sense of sincerity, a quality which led such abolitionists as William Goodell and Joshua Leavit to attend them frequently.[31] But from the viewpoint of social reform, the distinguishing mark of the Negro church was its independence from the white control. Its money came from Negroes. Hence it could speak out on such an issue as slavery without fear of losing members or offending someone in the South.

Negro churches formally went on record as opposing slavery. The Zion Methodists at their annual meeting in New York in 1852 declared it to be the duty of all Christian clergymen to denounce slavery at all places and under all circumstances. At its annual meeting in 1853 at New Bedford the American Baptist Missionary Society, representing twenty-six congregations, strongly condemned slavery after the introductory sermon by former runaway Leonard A. Grimes.[32] The 1859 meeting of the Evangelical Association of Colored Ministers of Congregational and Presbyterian Churches dwelt upon the "iniquity" of slavery.

From 1816, the year of its founding, the African Methodist Episcopal Church, in its Book of Discipline, denied membership to slaveholders. Writing in 1856, Jabez Campbell, a spokesman for the denomination, claimed its priority over all others in being "the most free from the evils of slavery." It is to be noted, however, that at the General Conference, which was held that year at Cincinnati, the delegates spent two days arguing whether to adopt a strongly worded resolution against slavery, one which called it the greatest of all crimes and the highest violation of God's law. Delegates who labored below the Mason-Dixon favored a more mildly phrased disapproval of slavery, one of them pointing out that those who spoke so loudly in Cincinnati would likely lapse into silence if they were located 200 miles to the south. Impressed by this viewpoint, the large majority voted to adopt softer tone on slavery.[33] Officially, therefore, the African Methodist Episcopal Church might be termed "emancipationist" rather than "abolitionist." But in actuality most Northern congregations and their pastors made no effort to conceal their decidedly antislavery sentiments.

Church buildings owned by Negroes were commonly put to use for abolitionist meetings. When in 1837 the New York Committee of Vigilance had difficulty in getting a public hall for its meetings, the Ashbury Street Church came forward with an offer of its facilities. In early August 1847 the colored Church in Harrisburg, Pennsylvania, turned its Sunday services over to William Lloyd Garrison and Frederick Douglass. Bethel Church in Philadelphia, with Bishop Daniel Payne presiding, was host to Garrison at a reception in December 1852. Frances Ellen Watkins, having trouble in hiring a hall at Carisle, Pennsylvania, in 1857, wrote reassuringly to fellow abolitionist J. Miller McKim, "I can get the colored church." In 1841 Parker Pillsbury could find no place in Salem, Massachusetts, to hold an abolitionist meeting except at the colored Bethel Church. Unpopular for his outspokenness, Parker was cooly received in white Salem but he praised his Bethel hosts, characterizing them as "noble, manly, womanly, brave and heroic to the last degree." [34]

Generally the black churches asked no fees for permission to use their quarters. Hence Frederick Douglass expressed a hurt surprise when the trustees of the Zion Methodist Church in New York asked him for $13 following an antislavery meeting he had conducted in their building. Douglass contrasted their behavior with that of pastors J. N. Gloucester of Brooklyn and E. P. Rogers of Newark, at whose churches he had recently spoken free of charge. And of course there were a handful of colored churches, three of them happening to be in Philadelphia, where antislavery meetings were not held. Of these the oldest and most socially prestigious was St. Thomas's Protestant Episcopal Church, with its fine organ and its carpeted aisles. Its pastor, the unruffled William Douglass, ignored the angry blast from his namesake, Frederick Douglass, characterizing it as "a corrupt old pro-slavery hag." [35]

Many Negro churches held periodic prayer meetings for the slaves, commonly once a month. Sometimes a congregation would raise money to purchase a slave or the family of a former slave. Fredrika Bremer visited a Methodist church in Washington in July 1850 where a slave member faced the bleak prospect of being sold "down South" and thus separated from his wife and child. "A pewter platter," she wrote, "was set upon a stool in the church, and one silver piece after another joyfully rang upon it." [36]

In their greetings of welcome to visitors at Sunday services, many preachers made it a point to include runaway slaves, their presence imparting a joyful earnestness to the proceedings. More than one Negro church was a station on the underground railroad, its alcove a sanctuary for runaways. Fugitives were housed in the basement of Cincinnati's Zion Baptist Church, the number sometimes rising to fourteen. On one occasion an infant who died was buried beneath the floor in order that the escaping party might not have to risk being seen by the hotly pursuing master. The A.M.E.Z. Church in Rochester was a station on the underground railroad. Quinn Chapel in Chicago, A.M.E. mother church of the Northwest, furnished a conspicuous example of providing accommodations for fugitives.[37] And finally it is to be noted that most of the prominent Negro clergymen, with only a few exceptions, preached a social gospel that stressed the church militant in a fellowship of concern.

In deepening the abolitionist sentiment among Negroes the role of their press can hardly be overestimated. Often the key to the success of a reform movement, the power of the press was certainly a vital factor in the antislavery crusade. The Negro press, even more than the Negro church, presented a united and consistent front against slavery and, as might be expected, a more single-minded attack than could be expected from the clerical quarter.

The seventeen Negro newspapers published before the Civil War struck one note in common—that of freedom—and this included the temperance periodical, *Northern Star and Freeman's Advocate.* Its title, like that of the first two Negro weeklies, *Freedom's Journal,* and its successor, *The Rights of All,* clearly indicate an abolitionist outlook. To attack slavery in all its forms and aspects was invariably proclaimed as the chief object of a newly appearing Negro weekly.

In makeup, the Negro journals were much like those put out by white reformers. They consisted of four pages of six columns each, with seldom a photograph or drawing to relieve the eye or spur the attention. The first page was generally devoted to a long lead article, often a speech or sermon, sometimes from a proslavery source. The back page consisted of canned, filler material, often remote from reformist activities —a serialized story, a travelogue, an "at home with" some literary celebrity, or an essay on nature. The two middle pages contained editorials, reports of meetings, notices of activities to come, letters to the editor, and stories relating to the cause. The last named were often copied, abolitionist sheets feeding heavily on one another.

Negro newspapers carried advertisements of antislavery books, particularly slave narratives, including that of Gustavus Vassa, who after becoming free had devoted his career to abolitionist work in England. The attack on slavery by Negro journals took many literary forms, among them the catechistic and poetical. "What is Slavery? It is the wicked act of the stranger, by which he takes the image of God and reduces it to a thing, a chattel," wrote *The Colored American.* "What is Abolition? It is that light which commeth from above, from the Father of Light, with whom there is no variableness nor shadow of turning." [38] The poetry appearing in the Negro journals tended to be simple in theme if stilted in style, such as the opening stanza of "The Things I Love":

> I love to welcome toil and pain,
>   Earth's cruel frowns and bitter bread,
> That not a man may wear a chain,
>   When I am dead.[39]

For all their similarity with white reformist journals, the Negro papers often addressed themselves to matters peculiarly their own. Their correspondents often struck a note of racial pride and distinctiveness. "I thank our Father," wrote Junius C. Morel, "that it has pleased him in his wisdom to order our color just as he has." J. McCune Smith expressed his gratification that the gifted Elizabeth Greenfield had not tried to pass as an Indian or Moor, but had stood proudly forth on the concert stage as a black woman, pure and simple. "There is one thing our people must learn," he lectured: "We must learn to love, respect and glory in our Negro nature." [40]

In the columns of their newspapers, Negroes debated as to what name was best for their group. The editor of *The Colored American* expressed his displeasure at some of the designations then current: "We are written about, preached to, and prayed for, as Negroes, Africans, and blacks, all of which have been stereotyped, as terms of reproach, and on that account, if no other, are unacceptable." Not surprisingly this editor concluded that the name, "colored American," was the only one above reproach. But there were dissenting voices. At a meeting of Negro leaders later that year, the word "colored" was criticized as being vague and inappropriate.[41]

When James G. Birney was asked in 1838 about the financial status of the abolitionist societies he replied, "We are always in debt, and always getting out of debt." [42] Birney's opening words were tersely descriptive of the financial history of Negro newspapers, his closing phrase less so. Negro weeklies, like abolitionist periodicals generally, operated at a loss, without a single exception. As a rule, abolitonist sheets, white or colored, were short-lived.

Negro newspapers did not pass away without putting up a battle. *The Colored American* employed agents, among them W. S. Jennings of Boston who in February 1837 distributed five hundred copies of its prospectus and obtained more than twenty subscriptions. Another early agent walked twenty-six miles through rain and snow to pick up five subscribers. Lewis Woodson proposed giving the new weekly a needed boost by heading a group of one hundred donors who would give $5 apiece, and another group of fifty donors who would give $10 apiece. Later that year Theodore S. Wright of New York sent thirteen subscriptions. Subsequently the paper employed as its agents Alexander Crummell, John Malvin of Cleveland, and the influential clergyman, Charles B. Ray. In the summer of 1839 Ray announced a subscription meeting at Albany which would feature the last public appearance of the popular figure, Nathaniel Paul, pastor of the Union Street Baptist Church.[43]

Other Negro-run newspapers received pledges of support, including David Ruggles's *The Mirror of Liberty*, whose appearance was hailed by groups in New York, Boston, and Hartford. But in receiving financial support, no Negro reformist journal matched those edited by Douglass, *The North Star*, and later *Frederick Douglass' Weekly*. Aside from substantial aid from whites,[44] Douglass tapped a variety of black sources. Negro women's groups, like The Colored Ladies of Philadelphia, held bazaars in support of his paper. At colored conventions the delegates voted that it be supported, and at public meetings from New Haven to San Francisco, collections were taken up for it. Douglass's papers commanded the unpaid services of half a dozen local correspondents, among them such forceful writers as William J. Wilson of Brooklyn and J. McCune Smith. But despite the most heroic efforts and the expending of more than $12,000 of his own money over an eight-year period, Douglass was forced to terminate his journal in July 1860.

The immediate cause of the suspension was delinquent subscribers, a familiar complaint in Negro journalism. "Pay Us What You Owe Us," ran the title of an editorial in a colored weekly. "Will friend Gloucester [J. H.] please to transmit us some money," begged another publisher: "We hope our Philadelphia patrons will be punctual in paying." The editor of the *Impartial Citizen* observed that many Negroes took the paper on credit for two or three years and then stopped it "without paying up arrearages." Doubtless some of these delinquent subscribers were well-intentioned optimists who simply never were able to get enough money. John B. Russwurm, the pioneer editor, attributed the poverty of his subscribers to their failure to pay.[45]

Delinquent subscribers compounded the other problems of the antebellum Negro newspapers. With possible three exceptions—*Freedom's Journal*, *The Colored American*, and *The North Star*—they started with little or no capital, thus leaving themselves vulnerable to sudden death while still aborning. Unscrupulous operators sometimes posed as agents, pocketing the money for subscriptions. In the fall of 1838 *The Colored American* warned its readers in Ohio and Michigan about one Skipworth who was soliciting funds in its name, but without any authorization other than his own. William Still sent a letter of sympathy to Mary Ann Shadd of *The Provincial Freeman* to express his scorn for anyone who would "lend himself to the base task of swindling the publisher of an anti-slavery paper." [46]

Agents, legitimate or otherwise, had problems in getting an audience. Often they had to work through local preachers and church trustee boards in order to get a meeting place and an audience. Hoping to improve things, Charles B. Ray wrote an article that appeared in the August 12, 1837, issue of *The Colored American* and bore the direct if lengthy title, "Needless Difficulties to be Encountered by An Agent." And, of course, once an agent had access to an audience, the results were often disappointing. At one time or another an agent for a Negro periodical was sure to express some bitterness at the want of interest in the abolitionist cause. William Still, Philadelphia-based agent of *The Provincial Freeman*, complained in 1858 that of the city's 30,000 Negroes, only 400 supported abolitionist newspapers.[47]

For the venturesome who published a Negro reformist newspaper there was no escaping the problem of debit and credit. But the work had its satisfactions, its supporters rightly concluding that their role in the abolitionist movement was not to be despised. Aside from furnishing a vehicle for self-expression, these newspapers furnished an outlet for the frustrations of the Negro, and his blueprints for a new relationship between white and black Americans.

Negro newspapers without exception were not designed to circulate among Negroes alone. Their publishers hoped to attract white readers, thus furnishing an evidence of Negro abilities as well as an exposure to his viewpoints. And in truth a white reader could hardly have picked up a copy of a paper like *The North Star* without some initial surprise at its format and content. It was, as the *Oberlin Evangelist* pointed out, "surpassed by only a very few in the large catalogue of our Anti-Slavery exchange." And readers could not fail to note that Negro newspapers, whether well or poorly edited, had one thing in common. Alike they sounded insistently the two notes which gave to the land of their birth its distinctive cry— freedom and equality.

V

The Users of Adversity

*The elevation of the free man is inseparable from
and lies at the very threshold of the great work
of the slave's restoration to freedom.*

A Call for a National Convention
of Colored Americans, 1855

FOUR YOUNG NEGROES, all of them students at Noyes Academy in Canaan, New Hampshire, were listed as the featured speakers to appear at the public meeting of the New Hampshire Anti-Slavery Society on Independence Day 1835 in a city, Plymouth, which itself bore a historic name. Taking place as scheduled at the Congregational church, the meeting began in the early afternoon with nineteen-year-old Henry Highland Garnet. He walked with a limp and he was dark of skin, "of full, unmitigated, unalleviated, and unpardonable blackness," wrote an eyewitness. His twenty-minute speech was characterized by "pathos and beauty." Next came Alexander Crummell, three years younger than Garnet but of like complexion—"as sable as Toussaint." A boy in years only, Crummell was listened to with deep attention, though doubtless his remarks were unembellished by the parade of references to English literary figures that characterized his later style. The third speaker was orphan Thomas S. Sidney, a graceful orator whose remarks were doubless less barbed than those of his predecessors. The fourth scheduled participant, Thomas Paul of Boston, put in an appearance but did not speak "due to a domestic affliction." The audience was disappointed but hardly felt cheated after Garnet, Crummell, and Sidney. Indeed, the writer and editor, N. P. Rogers, relates that his elation almost moved him to propose a resolution that would surely have passed unanimously: "That colored people have *bona fide* talent enough to be free." [1]

The belief that the cause of abolition would be advanced by evidence of the progress of the free Negro was widespread among reformers, white and black. In 1824 in a farewell address to Baltimore Negroes to be read in their churches, Elisha Tyson, a longtime patron and friend, warned them that any misconduct on their part would give credence to the belief that they were unworthy of freedom. George Thompson, the English abolitionist, told a Negro audience assembled at the Abyssinian Church in Portland in October 1834 that if they conducted themselves blamelessly, there would be an effect on slave emancipation. The Anti-Slavery Convention of American Woman, meeting in New York in May 1837, spoke in similar accents: "Nothing will contribute more to break the bondman's fetters than an example of high moral worth, intellectual culture and religious attainments among the free people of color." The organizational meeting of the Pennsylvania Anti-Slavery Society, meeting in Harrisburg earlier in 1837, issued an address to Negroes, informing them that as they gained wealth and respectability their example would help to undermine slavery.[2]

Negro leaders needed no convincing that they and their followers should seize every opportunity to demonstrate the capacity for freedom and its responsibilities. "Can slaves, if liberated, take care of themselves?" What better way to answer this commonly raised question than to point to a free Negro of good habits and steady behavior. Any other kind of Negro was a liability to the abolitionist crusade. "If we are lazy and idle," exhorted Richard Allen, "the enemies of freedom plead it as a cause why we ought not to be free." J. McCune Smith warned against the seductions of the city, such as "policy gambling, porter houses, with their billiards and cards, women hastening through the streets with their bonnets untied, men hanging around the corner or gutter-tumbling." [3]

Negro groups, like Negro individuals, took the viewpoint that the elevation of the free colored American and the liberation of the slave were very much interrelated. The Negro-controlled Ohio State Anti-Slavery Society, at its meeting in Cleveland in January 1853, viewed slave emancipation and free Negro elevation as simply opposite sides of the same coin. At a meeting of the National Council of Colored People in New York in May 1855, the twenty delegates agreed that the improvement of the free Negro in the North was an effective means of promoting emancipation in the South. Five months later at Franklin Hall, Philadelphia, the Colored National Convention passed a resolution which summed up the point: "In our elevation lies the freedom of our enslaved brethren; in that elevation is centered the germ of our own high destiny, and the best well-being of the whole people." [4]

Here and there, as might be expected, dissenting voices might be heard. The Negro's self-improvement would not gain him any privileges, asserted the *National Reformer*. If a Negro could write like Paul, preach like Peter, and pray like Aminadab, the voice of prejudice would still cry out that he was black. Hence, as the *National Reformer* viewed it, the elevation of the Negro depended less upon his abilities than upon "the improvement of the white man's heart." [5]

Since the abolitionists spent the great bulk of their thin resources on the slave, the twin work of uplifting the free Negroes devolved upon themselves. Self-improvement efforts took many forms, among them the promotion of temperance, mutual aid programs, literary and cultural strivings, and better schools. The temperance cause ran head-on into a commonly accepted practice in early-nineteenth-century America —the daily use of liquor. But among Negroes the temperance movement faced the additional difficulty of dealing with a class of people most of whom were poor and therefore likely to turn to drink as an anodyne, an escape.

Sensing this popular appeal of the bottle, Negro leaders invariably linked abstinence with abolition, holding that to keep sober was to strike a blow at slavery. Among Negroes, as among whites, a supporter of abolition was likely to be a supporter of temperance. Again and again Negro reformers declared that the free colored man owed it to his brother in chains to join the cold water army. Jermain W. Loguen did not see much difference in making a man a slave to rum and in making him a slave to a fellow man. William Whipper condemned liquor for its murderous effect on Africa, inducing its peoples to sell their brothers. Jacob C. White, in an address to the Banneker Institute of Philadelphia in 1854, denounced rum as the ruin of the young, "the very class of our peoples to whom we are to look as the warriors who are to fight for our liberty." Negro leaders were in full accord with the abolitionist editor who asserted that drunkenness and proslavery always went together whereas antislavery, without exception, was totally abstinent.[6] Drinking and slavery, in the eyes of Negro reformers, were twin symbols of the moral decay of the times.

The temperance impulse had deep roots among Negroes, going back to 1788 when the Free African Society of Philadelphia denied membership to anyone with the drinking habit. At every one of the national Negro conventions from their beginning in 1830, the delegates arrayed themselves against the use of liquor. At the second annual convention they passed a resolution authorizing the formation of a society "on the principle of entire abstinence from the use of ardent spirits." This adjunct, the Coloured American Conventional Temperance

Society, had a mushroom growth, reporting twenty-three branches in eighteen cities within a year's time. Again in 1834 the national convention earnestly recommended the principles of total abstinence. The American Moral Reform Society, organized at the fifth annual national convention at Philadelphia in 1835, announced that the promotion of temperance was one of their goals. No one who sold ardent spirits could be a member of the society, which urged the young men of the land to abstain from "every fluid that had a tendency in the least degree to intoxicate." A convention of Negroes of Maine and New Hampshire, held at Portland in 1849, condemned the liquor traffic.[7]

Of all the Negroes in the United States, those in Connecticut were unrivaled in their support of the war against strong drink. The Temperance Society of the People of Color of New Haven, founded in 1829, was a pioneer among Negroes. The addresses given at its meetings were sent to the abolitionist weeklies. In 1833 the Negroes of Middletown organized the Home Temperance Society, with Jehiel C. Beman as president and his son, Amos, as secretary. A year later Hartford had two Negro temperance societies, one of them for juveniles. To the senior Beman went the credit for organizing the Connecticut State Temperance Society of Colored People, which took place at Middletown in May 1836. A year later at its meeting held in Norwich, the society reported a membership of 350.[8] J. C. Beman, the president, became in 1838 the general agent also, periodically visiting the major cities.

Connecticut alone in New England had an effective state-wide temperance organization among Negroes. But local societies sprang up in such cities as Providence, Pittsfield, and New Bedford. Boston, like the much smaller Lenox, had both a men's and a women's society, the latter with Jane Putnam as president and Susan Paul as secretary. Membership in Boston spurted in April 1833 when 114 admirers of William Lloyd

Garrison took the cold water pledge as a farewell tribute to him just prior to his sailing for England.[9]

Of the Middle Atlantic States, New York and Pennsylvania led in temperance activity among Negroes. In New York State, as elsewhere, black abolitionists furnished the leadership in the movement. The New York City Temperance Society, founded in 1829, was assured by Samuel E. Cornish that "a glass of water and a biscuit would answer the purpose of politeness." In the fall of 1831 the society's agents held meetings with church congregations, signing up 39 pledgees at the First Colored Presbyterian Church, 40 at the Abyssinian Baptist Church, and 119 at the Zion Methodist Church.[10] In 1834 the four officers were familiar figures in antislavery work: Theodore S. Wright, Philip A. Bell, Charles B. Ray, and David Ruggles.

Negro temperance work in upstate New York followed a similar pattern of leadership. Schenectady Negroes formed a temperance society in May 1836, following an address by the white reformer, Gerrit Smith. At Buffalo in the spring of 1842, William Wells Brown organized the Union Total Abstinence Society, with 215 members, and remained its president for three years. Another Negro abolitionist, Stephen Myers, acted in 1842 and 1843 as agent for the temperance weekly, *The Northern Star and Freeman's Advocate*. One of the places at which he spoke—Lee, Massachusetts—named its temperance society after him. The meeting had been held in the town hall of Lee, with many whites present, and with twenty persons signing the pledge. In one town, if not in others, Myers served two masters, lecturing one night on temperance and another night on antislavery.[11]

Pennsylvania Negroes had two temperance societies by 1834, one in Pittsburgh and the other in Philadelphia, the latter increasing its number of societies to four in 1837. In this state the women were particularly active in the movement,

Pittsburgh's temperance society being made up of both sexes. The Daughters of Temperance had fourteen unions in the state, numbering a total membership of fifteen hundred. In November 1848 two of the five Philadelphia unions held a joint meeting at the Wesley Methodist Church, at which two hundred women were dressed in full regalia, along with a bevy of cold water girls in white. The two speakers were abolitionists J. C. Beman and Henry Highland Garnet. The latter, after whom one of the unions had been named, was introduced as "apostle of liberty and temperance." Taking an hour and a half, Garnet "portrayed the terrible effects of alcohol and labored to allure the drunkard to the path of soberness and peace." [12]

In proportion to their numbers the Negroes in Cincinnati were unique in their temperance zeal. In 1840 over one-quarter of the city's colored population belonged to either the adult society of 450 members or the youth branch numbering 180. Negro opposition made it impossible for a Negro to sell intoxicating drinks openly.[13] Here again, much of the Negro temperance sentiment was abolitionist-inspired. In the mid-thirties Cincinnati's Negroes had been deeply influenced by Theodore D. Weld and other Lane Seminary students with abolitionist leanings who had done welfare work in colored neighborhoods.

In other Ohio communities the tie between abolition and Negro temperance was even more evident. On an April Sunday in 1849 the Negroes of Salem held a mass temperance rally in the morning, followed by an antislavery meeting in the afternoon, shifting from one to the other with no change of personnel or mood. Three months later the Negroes at Hanover held a mass meeting for the twofold purpose of advocating temperance and slave emancipation. At a statewide convention held at Columbus in January 1853 which went on record as favoring a prohibition law like that of Maine, the featured speaker was abolitionist John Mercer Langston.[14]

The temperance movement among Negroes was a com-
pound of failure and success. Its effectiveness was diminished
by a lack of follow-up and by the prevalence of jimcrow practices within the organized movement. Like the colored convention effort, the temperance crusade among Negroes was
stronger on planning than on performance. Following the periodic meetings, whether annually, quarterly, or monthly, a
hibernation stage set in, with very little activity until the next
coming together. There were no agents, outside of J. C.
Beman and Stephen Myers. The state societies in Massachusetts, New York, and New Jersey were little more than rosters
of officers, although on one occasion—at Hudson in August
1845—the Delevan State Temperance Union of New York
drew an audience of nearly three thousand.[15] A regional organization with headquarters in Boston, The New England
Temperance Society of People of Color, founded in 1835, ran
its course in three years. A later effort at regional organization, the States' Delevan Union Temperance Society of Colored People, founded in 1845, proved to be of shorter dura-
tion and lesser importance.

Temperance work among Negroes was hampered by the
attitude of many white prohibitionists who frowned upon
Negro membership in their organizations. Negroes would
have attended a state temperance convention at Harrisburg,
Pennsylvania, in March 1835 had they not assumed that their
presence would be considered objectionable, wrote William
Whipper in a letter to its president.[16] Reform organizations
that were national in their reach always faced the problem of
Southern reaction to Negro membership. More often than not,
this problem was settled to the satisfaction of the South.

There were a few instances of a co-operative relationship
with Negroes. The Sons of Temperance, which had become
nationwide in 1844, established a Negro local in New York in
1846 and one in Cincinnati in 1848. It was in the latter year
that the Sons reached their high point relative to Negroes, ap-

pointing Charles H. Langston as Deputy Most Worthy Patri-
arch for the West, with full powers to establish divisions and
grant charters west of the Alleghenies.[17] The Cadets of Temperance, a national organization, sporadically granted charters
to groups of colored boys.

For some five years, from 1848 to 1853, Frederick Douglass was active in temperance work in upstate New York. In
March 1848 he was guest lecturer at the Rochester Temperance Society, with a generous sprinkling of Negroes in the
audience. Along with William Allen, he attended the organization meeting of the Woman's State Temperance Convention
in 1852 at Rochester. A year later he was present at the first
meeting of the woman's state temperance society, seconding a
resolution that commended the legislature for limiting the
number of liquor licenses.

After 1853 Douglass grew cool to the organized temperance movement, in part because the woman's rightists with
whom he had worked lost control of the statewide organization. But by 1853, as Douglass was only too well aware, the
pattern of segregation had been firmly established in the organized temperance movement. The Sons of Temperance no
longer granted charters to Negroes or admitted them to membership. When the branch at Cortland, New York, admitted
Samuel Ringgold Ward, it was ordered to expel him or have
its charter annulled. The officers of the Cortland division,
members of Ward's all-white congregation, stood by him and
voted their charter back to the New York division.

The action of the national division in barring Negroes did
not sit well with some of the subordinate branches. Rhode Island's division protested the order and the Massachusetes division threatened to defy it, maintaining that the subordinate
divisions had the right to admit members without regard to
color. In 1850 the Grand Division of New England went on
record as condemning the national division's no-Negroes policy. In Ohio the Ashland County division voted to disband in

protest against the color bar, and the members of the Pollard division declared that such a restrictive policy was tantamount to saying to the colored man, "Our doors are closed against you." [18] Some whites withdrew from the Sons of Temperance, but the latter, with one eye fixed on the South, was hardly in a position to refocus its sights.

If Negro temperance advocates were ignored by white fellow prohibitionists, they ran the risk of causing an overreaction in whites who were "wet," particularly the rum-seller and grog-shop owner. At Philadelphia on August 1, 1842, the Moyamensing Temperance Society attempted to hold a festival and procession, some twelve hundred marchers assembling with banners. Before the parade could get under way, a mob collected, spurred on by the enemies of temperance. Dispersing the paraders and tearing their flags, the rioters then put the torch to the Smith Beneficial Hall and the Second Colored Presbyterian Church. The firemen threw no water on the burning building lest, they said, it bring the fury of the horde upon them. The sheriff and his men put in an appearance, but soon they were retreating before the mob, finally breaking into a full run. It was a bad night for the Negroes, some of them fleeing to New Jersey and others taking asylum in the police station.[19] To crown it all, the brick building that had been used by Negroes as a temperance hall was ordered torn down by the legal authorities, who claimed that it might incite the rioters to renewed activity.

Despite its setbacks, the temperance crusade among Negroes was certainly as productive as it was among Americans on the whole. In an address to New York Negroes in 1837, S. S. Jocelyn deplored the plethora of porter houses in the city, many of them kept by Negroes and still more patronized by them. Yet, he added, intemperance among Negroes was not high proportionally. Joshua Leavitt held a similar view about the Negroes in Washington. Temperance had done a good deal for them after seven years, he wrote in 1841, "much more than among the whites in the same grade of employment." At upper-class social affairs among Negroes in Philadelphia, the standard drink was lemonade, "or some pleasant and whole-some syrup commingled with water." Of the 2200 Negro sea-men who sailed out of New York during 1846, 400 stayed at temperance boarding houses run by the American Seamen's Friends Society.[20]

Individual Negroes, invariably of abolitionist bent, lent their influence to the temperance crusade. The effect of such a zealous temperance advocate as Daniel A. Payne would be hard to measure. Churches and churchgoers in towns and bor-oughs within his ecclesiastical jurisdiction were constantly urged to form temperance societies. Unlike most others in the business, David Ruggles refused to handle spirituous liquors in the grocery store he ran in New York in the early 1830's. Robert Forten, who allegedly never drank a glass of liquor in his life, insisted that the twenty-five workers in his shipyard be nondrinkers. Unlike many employers who would settle for on-the-job abstinence, Forten called for nothing less than tee-totalism from his workers.[21]

In a long letter describing the free Negroes in Washington, D. C., in 1842, Charles T. Torrey attributed their progress to the influence of the abolition movement.[22] A dedicated aboli-tionist who would later give his life for the slave, Torrey may have been seeing what he wanted to see. But whether Negro self-help, in Washington or elsewhere, was rooted in abolition-ism, the two impulses inevitably converged. Negro self-help strengthened the argument of the abolitionists while simulta-neously furnishing the movement with more effective workers.

Mutual aid societies were designed to protect their mem-bers from indigency, helping them in sickness or distress. A Negro family, no matter how poor, was determined that no town hearse would ever drive to its door. The Sons of the

African Society, formed in Boston in 1798, gave as their purpose "the mutual benefit of each other, behaving at the same time as true and faithful Citizens of the Commonwealth in which we live." [23] It pledged its members to attend the sick, to bury a member decently if he had not left enough money for his funeral, to help the widow and children, and to watch over one another in spiritual concerns. Ten years later the New York African Society for Mutual Relief was incorporated, with young Henry Sipkins as secretary. To the regular functions of such a society, it added an annual parade.

The advent of the new abolitionists coincided with, and doubtless stimulated, an increase in Negro self-help organizations. In 1827 at Chillicothe, with Lewis Woodson presiding, an African Educational and Benevolent Society was formed. A year later Providence Negroes took a similar step, and in 1831 at New Haven the Peace and Benevolent Society of Afric-Americans came into existence. But it was Philadelphia that outstripped all other cities, nearly one-half of its adult Negro population holding membership in mutual aid societies in the 1840's. In 1838 the city could count 80 such organizations, with an average membership of 93. Ten years later the roster of mutual benefit societies had risen to 106, comparing most favorably with the total of 119 such groups in the entire state of New York in 1844.[24] In Philadelphia, as elsewhere, the participating members paid dues ranging from $3.00 to $5.00 a year, collected weekly or monthly. Persons of affluence often belonged to two or more societies at the same time.

Like other cities, Philadelphia had its Dorcas Society, a woman's organization to help the poor and bearing the name of a Biblical character of good deeds. The Philadelphia group distributed groceries, clothing and small sums of money. Some groups, like the African Dorcas Society of New York, concentrated on clothing for poor children, particularly those going to school. In 1828 the society provided 232 garments, including hats and shoes, for 123 boys and girls. The Harrisburg Dorcas Society stipulated that none of its food, clothing, or fuel was to go to "drunkards, kidnapers, betrayers and base idle persons." The Dorcas Society of Buffalo, holding that it is sometimes more blessed to receive than to give, occasionally gathered to listen to an address by an invited guest.[25]

Self-help among Negroes was closely related to self-improvement, the acquisition of useful knowledge, and the cultivation of the intellect. A young men's organization in Brooklyn bore the name Esmeralda Benevolent and Literary Club, indicating its dual purpose to combine material assistance and mental outreach. To many Negroes life was something more than a pig foot and a bottle of beer. The self-improvement impulse among Negroes stemmed in part from the general upward and onward spirit so characteristic of American society. But self-improvement among Negroes also had antislavery antecedents, for its advocates viewed it as a means of refuting the charge of racial inferiority while at the same time gladdening the hearts of the reformers. An evidence of this close bond between abolitionism and Negro self-improvement was furnished by the American Moral Reform Society which, at its first meeting, pledged itself to make "one common cause" with the American Anti-Slavery Society. The close affinity between abolitionism and Negro improvement was illustrated by an interracial group in Boone County, Indiana, which organized a society for the moral and literary advancement of the Negro, and then proceeded to organize an antislavery society, thus becoming two societies with an identical membership.[26]

The leadership of Negro self-improvement organizations was invariably of abolitionist hue. The first slate of officers of the Phoenix Society of New York, founded in 1833, included Christopher Rush, Thomas L. Jennings, Theodore S. Wright, Peter Vogelsang, and white Arthur Tappan. The board of directors bore names familiar in reform circles—Samuel Hardenburgh, Peter Williams, Henry Sipkins, and Boston Crummell, father of Alexander Crummell.[27] The abolitionist Nathaniel Paul was the first president of the Union Society of Albany for the Improvement of the Colored People in Morals, Education and Mechanic Arts, and Daniel A. Payne held a similar first presidency of the Troy Mental and Moral Improvement Association. Hosea Easton was the presiding officer of the Hartford Literary and Religious Institution upon its founding in 1834.

Most of the self-improvement societies sponsored a series of public lectures, from five to twenty-one a season. Open to the public, these lectures were generally free of charge, as in the case of the Philadelphia Library Company, but sometimes not, as in the case of the Adelphic Union Association of Boston, which charged a modest 50¢ for a single ticket for the entire series and 75¢ for a combination ticket admitting a man and a woman. For its series of weekly lectures the Philomathian Society of New York charged $2.50 for a season ticket, and 12½¢ for a single lecture.

The guest lecturers at Negro self-improvement societies generally included a good sampling of abolitionists. Edmund Quincy opened the season's series for the Adelphic Union in 1838, subsequently mailing a copy to the officers, at their request, to have it published. During the 1840 season the union's roster of speakers included abolitionists Theodore Parker, Samuel J. May, Henry I. Bowditch, John Pierpont, William Lloyd Garrison, James Freeman Clarke, and, for a return appearance, Edmund Quincy.[28] The Adelphic Union opened its 1846 series with the abolitionist politicians, John P. Hale and Charles Sumner. The lecture topics, particularly those in the New York forums, were not confined to political and social issues, but included chemistry, geography, logic, and organs of sense. Such broad topical coverage was especially valuable in those cities in which Negroes were barred from attending lectures other than those sponsored by themselves.

Most of the self-improvement societies provided opportunities for active participation by the members. A lecture would often be followed by a general discussion. Some societies, particularly those made up of young men, inclined toward oratory and declamation, with some of the speakers delivering original pieces. Others made use of the English essayists and poets, on one occasion Ransom F. Wake reading Dryden's "Alexander's Feast." Some societies staged debates; at its meeting in December 1842 the Philomathian Society of Albany, with abolitionist William H. Topp presiding, listened to the pros and cons of the question: "Is the human mind limited?" [29]

Some of the societies had libraries of their own. Upon organizing in January 1833, the Philadelphia Library Company of Colored Persons issued a public notice appealing for books or for money to buy them. The letter of solicitation carried the names of abolitionists Robert Purvis, Frederick A. Hinton, and Junius C. Morel. By 1840 the library had six hundred volumes, acquired in part by the monthly dues of 25¢ a member. The San Francisco Atheneum and Literary Association, whose members were required to be moral and intelligent, had a library of eight hundred volumes in 1854. The sixteen colored library societies in New York State in 1844 had libraries whose holdings ranged from one hundred to fourteen hundred volumes. The Adelphic Union of Boston, a bit better off than the others, sent its duplicate books to newly organized libraries. Many of the libraries stocked newspapers and periodicals, particularly those of abolitionist hue. Some libraries were able to announce a set schedule of opening and closing hours, the Phoenix Society of New York, for example, operating from four o'clock in the afternoon to nine at night, on Monday, Wednesday, and Friday. [30] Circulating libraries asked that the borrowed books be returned in a week's time.

To use a Negro reading room required no fee. The New York Vigilance Committee assessed its members $2.75 a year for the upkeep of its reading room but "strangers" were admitted free of charge. These libraries were open to the public, and this meant that whites were welcome, a policy which bore an implied criticism of libraries that excluded Negroes, which most of them did. There was only one society made up of both sexes, the Gilbert Lyceum of Philadelphia, founded in 1841 with Jacob C. White as president and Grace Douglass as treasurer.[31]

The all-male Negro self-improvement groups, however, did not exclude women from their reading rooms or from attending meetings open to nonmembers. But such partial acceptance was hardly satisfactory to all concerned, and as a consequence a half-dozen women's societies were started. Leading the way in 1831 was the Female Literary Association of Philadelphia, to be joined the following year by the Afric-American Female Intelligence Society of Boston. But the Philadelphia women were not to be outstripped, forming two additional societies in the 1830's, the Minerva Literary Society and the Edgeworth Society. And the last of the antebellum woman's societies, as the first, was founded in Philadelphia, the Sarah M. Douglass Literary Circle, which held its first meeting on September 22, 1859.[32] These literary societies sent reports of their proceedings, along with examples of their creative writings, to the abolitionist press.

Juvenile self-improvement societies among Negroes were few in number, doubtless because they were in competition with the schools, public and private. The strongest of these fewer than a half-dozen groups was the Garrison Literary and Benevolent Society of New York, founded in 1834 and made up of males from four to twenty years of age. The society held its weekly Wednesday afternoon meeting in the classroom of a public school until the school trustees decreed that an organization that bore the controversial name of Garrison could not be permitted to use its facilities. Led by master Henry Highland Garnet and shouting, "Garrison! Garrison! Garrison! forever," the boys voted against changing the name of their society.[33] Fortunately for them, the Philomathian Society, through Philip A. Bell, offered the use of its hall without charge.

Negro self-improvement organizations strengthened the abolitionist effort, although admittedly to an extent not open to scientific measurement. "Many of the self-improvement societies were influenced by the antislavery struggle," writes a present-day authority, "and were in the main anti-slavery societies until around 1857 when they took on a more definite literary aspect." There were at least fifty such organizations. Some were short-lived, like the Saramento Young Men's Musical and Literary Society, reflecting the incurable optimism of Americans, black and white. Some were small—J. McCune Smith described the New York Literary Union as not being large but as having at least a president and a secretary who were not the same person.[34] By contrast the Philadelphia Library Company had a roll call of 150. In some cases the membership count may have been larger if there had been no admission fee, generally of one dollar.

But a number count was not the full measure of the impact of these societies. They raised the aspirations of their own members; they lent support to the abolitionist cause, and to nonjoiners, white or black, friend or disparager, they furnished an evidence of black enterprise in a somewhat unexpected quarter.

Negro self-help was expressed in the movement for more and better schools. This effort, too, bore an abolitionist stamp inasmuch as school training would demonstrate that the Negro was capable of improvement and hence not doomed by innate inferiority to be a slave perpetually. In 1827 there was a total of ten Negro schools, primary and grammar, in five cities—Portland, Boston, New Haven, New York, and Philadelphia. In the early 1830's, with the simultaneous emergence of the colored convention movement and the new-type abolitionists, the Negro school effort received much more attention.[35]

In the summer of 1831, Garrison, S. S. Jocelyn, and Arthur Tappan conceived of forming a Negro manual labor college at New Haven, Connecticut. Manual labor schools combined a curriculum of classical studies with useful physical labor in the shop or on the farm. Traveling to Philadelphia, the three abolitionists broached the idea of the delegates at the colored convention, mentioning New Haven as the proposed site. The delegates, laboring under the impression that the New Havenites were "friendly, pious, generous and humane," [36] voted their approach enthusiastically, adding, however, that the trustee board of the proposed college should have a Negro majority. As a follow-up, the convention appointed a so-called Committee for Superintending the Application for Funds for the College for Colored Youth, composed of Philip A. Bell, Boston Crummell, Peter Vogelsang, Peter Williams, and restauranteur Thomas Downing, already famed for his Oyster House.

The proposed college got no further. The mayor of New Haven, Dennis Kimberly, strongly opposed it, and his stand was supported by a town meeting which voted to "resist the establishment of the proposed college in this place by every lawful means." The school was denounced as a threat to the prosperity of Yale and the other educational institutions in the city. The belief was widespread that the proposed Negro school would be an abolitionist auxiliary or "front." [37]

One of the reasons given for the hostility to the proposed school was its designation as a college, which bore the implications of high achievement by Negroes and their resultant pressing for social equality. But this explanation could hardly hold true for the school which Prudence Crandall proposed to establish for "young ladies and little misses of color" two years later in near-by Canterbury. Miss Crandall had announced this step after she had lost practically all of the students from her boarding school following the admission of a Negro, seventeen-year-old Sarah Harris. Canterbury, like New Haven, called a town meeting, at which its leading citizen, Andrew T. Judson, strongly denounced Miss Crandall and her school. The meeting was adjourned before abolitionists Samuel J. May and Arnold Buffum could get the floor for a rebuttal. Judson and his numerous supporters urged the state legislature, then in session, to enact a law prohibiting any school from instructing Negroes who were not inhabitants of the state. Miss Crandall held out for sixteen months after the passage of the law, but in September 1834 she closed the school and quit the state.[38]

A similar fate was in store for abolitionist-sponsored Noyes Academy in Canaan, New Hampshire, which in 1834 announced itself as open to youth of good character without distinction as to color. Twenty-eight whites and fourteen Negroes studied together for a year, while the townspeople grew increasingly restive. A public meeting was convoked in the summer of 1835, which decreed that the academy should be physically transplanted. On August 10 some three hundred men with ninety to one hundred oxen dragged the building away, leaving it in ruins.[39]

These setbacks were dismaying to the abolitionists, but they could take comfort when they looked elsewhere. However abortive at New Haven, Canterbury, and Canaan, education for Negroes, spurred by their zeal, had been given a fresh impetus. The spirit of self-help took on another form, with Negroes themselves assuming the task of providing additional schools. Again the Negroes who led the way were abolitionist activists.

In January 1832, a group of Pittsburgh Negroes established the African Education Society, with John B. Vashon as president and Lewis Woodson as secretary. The school, its personnel all-Negro, was attended by "many of the respectable colored people" of the city. During the same year John Malvin organized the School Education Society in Cleveland, the costs to be borne by subscriptions and appeals. In 1836, Providence Negroes founded the New England Union Academy, with tuition of $3 a quarter. New York Negroes established the Phoenix High School in 1836, with Theodore S. Wright as president, Dr. John Brown as secretary, and Samuel Cornish and David Ruggles as solicitors. Philadelphia in the mid-thirties had ten self-supporting colored schools. Cincinnati in 1838 had two Negro schools "deriving no aid from their white neighbors." In 1857 Wilmington, Delaware, had two schools supported by Negroes, with considerable assistance from Quaker Thomas Garrett, who purchased the land site and hired the building contractor. For six years, 1854 to 1860, San Francisco Negroes supported a one-teacher school, touching a total of some two hundred and fifty students. Baltimore, which outstripped any other city in free Negro population, had fifteen colored schools in 1859, every one of them self-sustaining.[40]

These efforts by Negroes themselves were supplemented by white individuals or groups. In Boston in 1815, the merchant Abiel Smith left an endowment of $4000 for the Negro school, held in the basement of the African Baptist Church. The Quaker silversmith Richard Humphreys left $10,000 in 1832 for the founding of a school for Negroes, which emerged five years later as the Institute for Colored Youth. In 1855 Homer Treat of Litchfield County in Connecticut left $4000 for the founding of a colored school or for assisting needy Negro students, whichever the trustees of the fund decided. Jermain W. Loguen was one of the school fund executors named in Treat's will. In 1840 the Ohio Ladies' Society for the Education of Free People of Color was founded at Massillon, its purpose to elevate the Negro and thus undercut the opposition to the abolitionist movement. The founders announced a second compelling motive: "Long enough surely have we received the taxes of the colored man to help educate poor white children, and now let us as a band of sisters unite in vigorous efforts to repair their wrongs."[41] In some of the schools conducted by this society the salaries of the teachers were paid by the Ohio Female Anti-Slavery Society.

The clergyman, Charles Avery, gave an initial donation of $25,000 in 1849 to found a college bearing his name at Allegheny, Pennsylvania, to train young Negroes for teaching and the ministry. Serving on the board of trustees was the abolitionist, John Peck. In 1852 the General Conference of the African Methodist Episcopal Church, meeting in New York, had high words of praise for Avery, who was present. Later that year a more concrete expression of Negro esteem came to Avery from Robert S. Duncanson, who gave him a painting, "The Garden of Eden," for which the struggling artist had been offered $800.[42]

Privately supported colored schools, whether financed by Negroes themselves or by their supporters, were obviously not the total answer to the question of educational need in a day when publicly supported schools had become widespread throughout the North. Poor as a group and taxed like everyone else, Negroes saw no reason for their not benefiting like others from the public school system. Gradually the states began to assume a grudging responsibility for the education of their Negro children.

Schools attended by Negroes were all-colored in student body and predominantly so in teaching staff. Such schools were invariably feebly supported in comparison with their white counterparts, the New York Board of Education, for example, spending $1,600,000 for sites and buildings for white pupils over a twenty-year period, while spending only $1000 for such facilities for colored students, a ratio of 1 to 1600, although the school population ratio was 1 to 40. But it was not their feeble support alone that made segregated schools a prime target of Negroes and abolitionists. These challengers proclaimed that racially separate schools were relics of slavery, fostering prejudice and discrimination.

In Massachusetts alone did the protesters crack the segregated school system, with Boston providing the most spectacular victory, although not the first. In the 1840's the Negro school in Boston, named after early benefactor Abiel Smith and supported by the city after 1820, came under increasing attack led by Negroes and abolitionists. In 1846 a petition signed by eighty-six Negroes protested the segregated school, terming it insulting. The Primary School Committee thought otherwise, defending the all-Negro composition of the Smith School. However, two members of the committee, Henry I. Bowditch and Edmund Quincy, submitted a blistering minority report, to which they appended a statement by an even more ardent abolitionist, Wendell Phillips, castigating the city solicitor for upholding the legality of a jimcrow school.[43]

Three years later another petition, this one bearing 202 signatures and characterizing the Smith School as "a great public nuisance," was laid before the Primary School Committee. Again, rejection soon followed. Negroes then turned to the courts, Benjamin Roberts bringing suit in the name of his young daughter Sarah, alleging that she had to pass five other schools before she could reach the one for Negroes. Taking the case for the plaintiff was Charles Sumner, assisted by a young Negro, Robert Morris. Despite Sumner's learned plea, the court upheld the school committee.[44]

But its victory was but a staying action. The airing given to the case had its effect on public opinion. Negroes, led by William C. Nell, kept up a drumfire against the school, holding indignation meetings and presenting numerously signed resolutions at abolitionist gatherings. The state legislature proved more responsive than the courts or the school board. Noting that Boston lagged behind the other chief cities in the state, the legislature in April 1855 prohibited the exclusion of any child from any school because of race, color, or religion. When the new school year began on September 3, 1855, a group of abolitionists, headed by William C. Nell, went from one schoolhouse to another to see the new policy in operation. There was no disturbance of any kind, the school committee having acted in good faith, despite their earlier opposition.

Once the schools were integrated, the Negroes held a meeting of celebration, also integrated. The person honored at the happy occasion was William C. Nell who received a gold watch along with verbal bouquets from Lewis Hayden, physician John V. DeGrasse, attorneys Robert Morris and John S. Rock, as well as Garrison, Phillips, and Charles W. Stack. Because she had sustained an accident, Harriet Beecher Stowe could not be present, but she sent Nell an autographed copy of *Uncle Tom's Cabin*.[45] At this joyous celebration there was little mention of the Smith colored school, which indeed had already closed its doors for lack of pupils.

The admission of Negroes to white colleges—no Negro college was incorporated until 1854—was an abolitionist concern, as might be expected. White reformers were highly indignant that some black co-workers had been denied admission to colleges—Thomas Paul, senior, by Brown, Charles B. Ray and Amos G. Beman by Wesleyan, and J. McCune Smith by both Columbia and Geneva. At the annual meeting of the New England Anti-Slavery Society in 1836 at Boston, a resolution was passed recommending that abolitionists support Oneida Institute because it was the only literary institution east of Ohio which officially welcomed Negroes. Other colleges had no stated policy barring Negroes but, as an abolitionist put it, "they encouraged a prejudice which created an atmosphere in which a colored student could not live."[46] Colleges feared that if they enrolled Negroes they would lose white students, particularly from the South.

Oneida, located at Whitesboro, near Utica, was not the first college to admit Negroes. In August 1826 of the year in which Oneida was founded, Amherst graduated Edward Jones and two weeks later Bowdoin conferred a degree upon John B. Russwurm.[47] But these were one-shot affairs, hardly to be compared with Oneida's enrollment of six Negroes in 1836. Negroes were attracted to Oneida because it was a manual labor school, one which combined physical effort with mental effort. It thus had a practical aspect important to job-conscious Negroes, many of their improvement societies bearing in their titles the words, "mechanic arts." Oneida further attracted Negroes because it was strongly abolitionist. Its president, Beriah Green, was elected president of the American Anti-Slavery Society at its first meeting in December 1833. Six months earlier students at Oneida had organized the first of the new type abolitionist societies in New York. Theodore D. Weld spent three formative years at Oneida, one of its many dedicated abolitionist alumni.

Oneida's influence spread westward, many of its students enrolling at Lane Seminary in Cincinnati and at Oberlin. The latter particularly bore a strong abolitionist stamp, the trustees having voted, although by the narrowest of margins, to encourage Negroes to enroll. This was deemed especially venturesome inasmuch as Oberlin, truly a pioneer, also took the lead in admitting women. Again and again the charge was made that "we intended to encourage marriage between colored and white students, and even compel them to marry," wrote the noted theologian-evangelist, Charles G. Finney.[48]

True to her antecedents, Oberlin remained liberal. Abolitionist lecturers were welcomed to her halls, and runaway slaves found her campus a sanctuary. At a public meeting in August 1842, President Asa Mahan stated that the connection of Negroes with the college had been a source of pleasure to the officers. The A.M.E. clergyman, J. M. Brown, writing on June 8, 1844, observed that there was no place in the United

States where a Negro might get an education "as cheap as he can at Oberlin, and at the same time, be respected as a man." The college expelled a white student for calling a colored man a "black nigger," even though the student was, in the words of Professor Amasa Walker, "a very consequential young man," from a rich and respected family. Of the 245 Negroes who attended Oberlin before the Civil War, 3 per cent of the total, apparently not one lodged a formal complaint of discriminatory treatment by faculty or fellow students.[49]

For all its liberalism, Oberlin was not the first college to appoint a Negro to its faculty. This pioneering step was taken by New York Central College founded in 1849 at McGrawville, New York, by the American Baptist Free Missionary Society. Pledged to "the morality of anti-slavery," the coeducational school welcomed Negroes as students and as teachers. During its dozen years of existence three Negroes served successively as professor of belles lettres—Charles L. Reason, who left for Philadelphia in 1852 to become principal of the Institute for Colored Youth, William G. Allen, product of Oneida College, who left somewhat precipitously after marrying a white student, and George B. Vashon, an Oberlin graduate. At the commencement exercises in June 1858 one of the speakers was black John B. Reeve, a graduating senior.[50]

Abolitionists, white or black, found Central College a haven. Frederick Douglass came to the campus in July 1852 for a series of four lectures. William C. Nell put his stamp of approval on the school, hailing it for "doing a mighty work in uprooting prejudice." But praise from the faithful, however gratifying, did not solve the college's chronic financial troubles. In 1858 the trustees, with bankruptcy imminent, prevailed upon Gerrit Smith to buy the land and buildings. Smith attempted to persuade J. McCune Smith to accept the presidency but the latter demurred, doubtless sensing that the college's day was done.[51]

By then, however, the loss of Central College could be more

easily borne. There had been an increase in the list of colleges and professional schools that would accept a Negro, and the day was passing when the racially restrictive policies in American higher education would force a J. McCune Smith to enroll at Glasgow or an Alexander Crummell to turn to Oxford.

VI

Duet with John Bull

*Slavery in America is not a domestic
question; it is a question for all mankind.*

J. W. C. Pennington, London, 1843

IT WAS a summer afternoon in Harrisburg, Pennsylvania, in
1859, but not just any summer afternoon. It was August 1—
a day of celebration to Negroes in the North. For it was on
August 1, 1834, that an act of the British Parliament decreeing an end to slavery in the British West Indies went into
effect. Hence the Harrisburg celebration in 1859 by Negroes
was in line with the best in abolitionist tradition.

Augmented by visitors from Philadelphia and Baltimore, a
procession formed at the head of Harrisburg's main street to
march through the town to a picnic grove. The grand marshall and his aides, wearing blue sashes decorated by
wreaths, led the way on horseback. Then came a color
bearer, a few paces in front of the Henry Highland Garnet
Guards, who were carrying new muskets and wearing gray
coats and pants, fatigue caps, and white belts. In uniforms
scarcely less resplendent marched the Philadelphia Brass
Band. Sandwiched between the Good Samaritan Lodge of the
Daughters of Temperance and the flag-bearing, music-
making Odd Fellows were the three speakers of the day, pro-
ceeding in a dignified stroll. Bringing up the uniformed rear

were the Carlisle and Toussaint L'Ouverture Clubs, followed by the throng of spectators turned paraders and participants.

At the grove the formal program proceeded, with the band playing and the choir singing, followed by prayers. Now it was the turn of the speakers of the day—Jacob C. White, Jr., Charles W. Gardner, a Harrisburg clergyman, and Henry Highland Garnet. Dinner followed, with a number of whites eating and drinking with everyone else. One could not tarry too long at the table lest he be late for the music concert scheduled from eight to ten o'clock at Brant's Hall back in town. After the concert the celebrators went to the Walnut Street exchange for the day's finale—the Grand Emancipation Ball.[1] Thus did a group of Americans commemorate a day not on their country's calendar of holidays, but an import from across the Atlantic. Thus did a group of Negroes hail Britannia, linking her past to their future.

The agitation against slavery in antebellum America was not solely a domestic phenomenon. In early Victorian England the humanitarian impulse was strong, one of its manifestations being a deep hostility to slavery. Rooted in religion and philanthropy, British abolitionism was tinged with the current romantic spirit in literature. To the poets and the essayists the watchword was freedom, and this sentiment embraced the black people in bonds. If they were savage they would need only to be freed, and, since they were unspoiled and uncorrupt, they would soon become noble. These impulses—religious, philanthropic, and literary—bore substantial fruit. An act of Parliament in 1833 abolished slavery in the colonies. Six years later the British and Foreign Anti-Slavery Society was formed, its purpose to strike at slavery wherever it existed.

The American antislavery movement owed much in inspiration and support from reformers in Great Britain.[2] But if

America received much, she brought something in return. To the antislavery cause in England during the twenty-five years before the Civil War, Negro abolitionists made a distinctive contribution. During this period a procession of black reformers crossed the Atlantic, to be lionized in London, Edinburgh, and Dublin. The full effect of their influence would be felt during the Civil War when the abolitionized sentiment of the British rank and file became a factor in preventing Her Majesty's government from extending diplomatic recognition to the slaveholding Confederate states.

American abolitionists did not share the coolness toward John Bull felt by many of their countrymen. Abolitionists were quick to forget the Revolutionary War and the War of 1812 and to focus their admiring attention on Britain's work in abolishing the African slave trade and finally, in 1833, in decreeing an end to slavery in the British West Indies. The day that this Parliamentary act went into effect was August 1, 1834. As a result the first of August became a revered entry in the abolitionist calendar, a day to commemorate.

Negroes and abolitionists celebrated West India Emancipation Day because they did not have much to choose from. A law abolishing the foreign slave trade went into effect on January 1, 1808, and Negroes in New York took due note of the occasion. On that day they gathered to listen to orator Peter Williams describe the rape of Africa, the horrors of the slave trade, and the noble efforts of John Woolman, Anthony Benezet, and William Wilberforce. The following year New York Negroes held three celebrations of the abolition of the foreign slave trade. At the African Methodist Episcopal Church the speaker was Henry Sipkins, whose address was reminiscent of Peter Williams in tone, if inferior in literary expression. Williams himself attended the exercises sponsored by the New York African Society for Mutual Relief, where he read a brace of original poems and listened to the orator of the day, William Hamilton. The third observance was the work of the Wilberforce Philanthropic Association, with Joseph Sidney as orator.[3]

These 1809 celebrations were the high point. Within three years the January 1 observances would be discontinued. For by then Negroes had unhappily taken note that the law prohibiting the foreign slave trade had become almost a dead letter, being blatantly flouted.

Beginning in 1827 Negroes in New York celebrated July 4 for a few years. In 1799 the state legislature had passed a gradual emancipation act covering the slaves born after that year. A law passed in 1817 extended slave emancipation to cover those born before July 4, 1799, stipulating that they were to become free as of July 4, 1827. With the approach of the day for the almost complete extinction of slavery in the state, Negroes made plans to celebrate. Meeting at the Mutual Relief Hall in New York in mid-April 1827, a group headed by William Hamilton and Thomas L. Jennings recommended that all Negro churches in the city hold services of prayer and thanksgiving on July 4.[4]

The largest July 4 celebration in the city took place at the African Zion Church, its walls adorned with banners of the participating societies and with pictures of Thomas Clarkson, the English abolitionist, along with those of John Jay and Daniel D. Tompkins, former governors who had pushed emancipation measures. A group of original hymns served as a prelude to William Hamilton's oration. "This day we stand redeemed from a bitter thralldom," ran one of the sentences in a stirring address that would soon be printed for sale at 12½¢ per copy.[5]

Since the Fourth of July was a national holiday, most Negroes throughout the state preferred to postpone the emancipation celebration until the following day. This included New York City blacks who on July 5 held a parade through the downtown streets en route to Zion Church. The procession was led by grand marshall Samuel Hardenburgh, his cocked hat vying with his drawn sword for attention. Hardenburgh's mounted aides dashed up and down the line of some four thousand marchers. At the City Hall the grand marshall saluted the mayor to a roar of cheers.[6] Indeed, the meeting at Zion Church, with an oration by John Mitchell, was something of an anticlimax.

Albany Negroes had begun preparing for their celebration nearly four months in advance. Gathering at the African meetinghouse in late March, they had appointed a committee of twelve, headed by Lewis Topp, to make all arrangements. On July 5 the celebrants gathered at the African Baptist Church whose pastor, Nathaniel Paul, was the chief speaker. Paul paid tribute to a host of reformers and political personages, English and American, living and dead. His denunciation of the foreign slave trade took on the note of apostrophe typical of the times: "Tell me, ye mighty waters, why did ye sustain the ponderous load of misery. Or speak, ye winds, and say why it was that ye executed your office to waft them onward." [7]

In Rochester the Negroes ushered July 5 in with a booming cannon. In the forenoon a procession moved through the principal streets to the public square where a stage had been erected and seats set up for the speakers and audience. The guest of honor was the chief architect of the emancipation measure—Governor Tompkins himself. The featured speaker, too, was a symbolic figure—Austin A. Steward, a runaway slave turned grocer. "Let us, my countrymen, henceforth remember that we are men," he exhorted.[8]

At Cooperstown the Negroes held a celebration at the Presbyterian Church. As at Rochester, a number of whites were present. Doubtless many of them had come out of curiosity, but none left until leaving time. A few out-of-state observances were held. At New Haven a meeting was held at the Temple

Street African Church, with white N. S. Jocelyn, the pastor's brother, as speaker. At Baltimore the Friendship Society held a dinner, with a long round of toasts which ended with a lifting of the glasses to "our emancipated brethren in New York." A group of Negroes in Fredericksburg, Virginia, also sat down to a celebration dinner, opening with a song, "Hail Columbia, happy land," and closing with a toast: "May the anchor now cast for freedom by the State of New York sink deeply in the breasts of our Southern States."[9]

Of the slaves who were freed in New York on July 4, 1827, the woman who named herself Sojourner Truth was destined to be the most remarkable. An abolitionist and an advocate of woman's rights, she remained a lifelong illiterate, but she made a deep impression by her rude eloquence and gaunt, commanding figure. With a hopeful heart and an unshakable confidence in ultimate justice and the goodness of God, she bore pity rather than bitterness toward the slaveholders.

The annual observance of emancipation day in New York State lasted only three or four years. Negroes in New York City celebrated the day in 1828 and in 1831, and those in Troy observed it in 1829. Twenty-seven years later the celebration was resurrected for a single time at Auburn's Sandford Hall, with a majority of whites in attendance. A cluster of leading Negroes took part, with J. W. Loguen presiding and the elderly Austin A. Steward on the platform. Speaker Henry Highland Garnet, just returned from six years abroad, was followed by Frederick Douglass, who held forth for two hours. Lucretia Mott, long-time friend of the Negro, and a woman's righter, also spoke, without expecting equal time.[10]

But New York's emancipation day was no longer commemorated. It had never really captured the Negro's imagination inasmuch as it came at an unpropitious time. To Negroes the Fourth of July simply was not a day for poetry and song. They felt no warmth for it—a reaction that extended to anything held on July 5. While other Americans were moved to patriotic demonstrations on the Glorious Fourth, the Negroes were moved to bitter reflection. Unlike most of their white compatriots, Negroes could hardly fail to note the disparity between the rhetoric and the reality, between their country's high professions of liberty and equality and the existence of slavery and the high wall of color.

"What to the slave is the Fourth of July," was the title given by Frederick Douglass to one of his notable orations. A holiday based on the Declaration of Independence and its fine phrases was without savor to Negroes, who wondered why whites with good taste did not react similarly. The Fourth of July moved William J. Watkins to "retire from the exulting multitude, pensive and solitary, to contemplate the past and present as connected with our history in the land of our nativity." The colored convention of 1834 voted against holding any kind of celebration on July 4 and urged Negroes not to join in public rallies. In 1838 a Negro newspaper suggested that on July 4 a large slave whip should be unfurled in place of the stars and stripes. Another Negro weekly proclaimed the fourth day of July as "the bleakest day of the year. We wish we could blot it from the calendar." [11]

Finally, Negroes were cool toward celebrating on July 4 because of the danger of assault by boisterous whites who had drunk too much. This apprehension had its role in making New York Negroes substitute July 5 for July 4 as state emancipation day. Colored people in other localities tended to make a similar substitution in their infrequent Independence Day celebrations. "On account of the misfortune of our colour, our fourth of July comes on the fifth," mourned Peter Osborne at a New Haven church on July 5, 1832. By the mid-fifties this risk of personal attack when holding a July 4 celebration had lessened, but the Negro's other reasons for withdrawal still remained. When in 1859 the Banneker Institute decided to celebrate the Fourth of July the *Anglo-African* remarked that such an observance was something new in Philadelphia and at variance with the general practice among Negroes coast to coast.[12]

Having no Fourth of July the black man did the next best thing—he celebrated August 1. Did not British emancipation augur ill for American slavery? This was the note struck at the initial August 1 celebrations in America, held in 1834 at Philomathian Hall in New York. The three main speakers, Thomas L. Jennings, John Berrian, and Henry Williams, hailed the coming day when Britain's example would be followed by the United States. A meeting held by the New York Committee of Vigilance on August 1, 1837, similarly expressed the conviction that the "disenthrallment" of the West Indies was a sure sign of what was in store for America.[13] Of the August 1 celebrations during the early years, the most important took place in 1838. It was then in the British West Indies that the apprentice system would come to an end and slaves would become unconditionally free. On July 31, 1838, the Negroes of Cincinnati held a watch night service, remaining mute and motionless for the final fifteen minutes before midnight. At twelve o'clock the silence was broken with a loud cheer, followed by song and prayer. The celebrants dispersed at 2 P.M. but were back eight hours later to resume. The festivities, including a "total abstinence" dinner, went on until early evening.[14]

Philadelphia witnessed a more formal observance, with clergyman William Douglass discoursing on the contagious influence of moral justice as it confronted wrong and outrage. Colored churches in Philadelphia remained open throughout the day, inviting all who would to pray. In New York the colored people held a monster meeting at Tabernacle Hall at which Theodore S. Wright presided, joined on the platform by Thomas Van Rensselaer, William P. Johnson, Thomas Downing, Philip A. Bell, and Samuel Johnson. The occasion called for no less a personage than William Lloyd Garrison. Expansive on such a historic day for freedom, Garrison must needs praise his hosts: "The fact that you are now observing this jubilee—that this meeting is under your direction—is another decisive proof that you regard liberty as a jewel above all price, and a state of slavery the worst of all conditions." [15]

On the eve of the 1838 observances by Negroes, the reformist sheet, *The Emancipator*, recommended that henceforth August 1 be celebrated by abolitionists universally. The suggestion did not go unheeded, although until 1842 there were few such observances in Massachusetts. But to no group did an August 1 mean more than to the Negroes. It was "a day that should be remembered, observed and consecrated by every colored man," wrote Samuel E. Cornish. At an August 1 meeting of the New England Freedom Association, held at Boston's Chardon Street Chapel in 1843, J. C. Beman asserted that white people could not quite celebrate the day like Negroes. Another speaker, S. R. Alexander, said that he had advised his nine-year-old Hannibal "to swear this day eternal enmity against slavery," and he exhorted other parents to follow his example. [16]

August 1 became the Negro's Fourth of July and his celebration of the national holiday. Street parades with brass bands and carriages were common to both. On August 1 celebrations the banners borne in the parades often depicted a slave with his fetters broken, his arms outstretched, and his face upward-looking. Often the parades included military companies. A New Bedford celebration in 1852 featured a company of cadets from New York. Three years later the New Bedford observance boasted the presence of the National Guards of Providence, plus their own Union Cadets. On August 1, 1858, the New Bedford Blues, accompanied by a brass band from Bridgewater, marched to the depot to receive the Liberty Guards of Boston, sporting twenty-five muskets and accompanied by the Malden Brass Band. A Boston celebration in 1859 included the local Liberty Guards, the New Bedford Blues, and the National Guards of Providence.[17]

Despite the bands and the marching, an August 1 celebration was much lower in decibel count than a Fourth of July affair with its firecrackers and other noisemakers. Although nighttime programs in town were part of many August 1 agendas, the daytime activities were the most popular, by far. The site of the latter was generally a shady grove, accessible by railroad at excursion rates. In the center of the grove a large stand had been erected for the chaplain, speaker, and musicians. The tables, laden with chicken and ham, were roped off until mealtime. Such a pastoral setting made for a tranquil afternoon. Since all beverages other than "pure and cold water" were contrary to regulations, there were likely to be fewer fist fights than at a Fourth of July affair. An August 1 celebration at Christiana in Pennsylvania in 1858 was described by William Wells Brown as "all peaceable and quiet, not a drunken person on the grounds," even though the attendance ran to two thousand, the largest single gathering of Negroes Brown had ever seen.[18]

An August 1 observance was likely to be well attended, in part because it might draw from several communities. A celebration at Dayton in 1854 brought ten carloads from Cincinnati, plus contingents from Xenia, Hamilton, Troy, and Piqua. For the celebration at Galesburg, Illinois, in 1857, groups of Negroes came from four towns—Quincy, Monmouth, Kewanee, and Burlington, and two counties—Coles and Edgar. An August 1 held at Marshall's Grove on Staten Island in 1856 brought together Negroes from New York, Brooklyn, and Williamsburgh. Of the 7000 attending the celebration at a New Bedford grove in 1855, some 500 came from Providence and 250 from Boston. The group planning the observance at New Bedford in 1858 sent out an invitation, through secretary John Freedom, to Negroes throughout Massachusetts. In Providence, Rhode Island, the seven Negro societies, whether benevolent, cultural, or reformist, all joined forces in celebrating August 1.[19]

The attendance at Negro-run August 1 celebrations was invariably swollen by the presence of whites. Negroes generally sent out blanket invitations. In announcing their observance in 1854, the Negroes of Dayton, Ohio, courted the attendance of the "citizens of every state, county, city, town, village and settlement." In sending out such a general invitation it was sometimes necessary to add a footnote asking that everyone bring his own refreshments. Whites were more receptive to an August 1 affair than any other kind conducted by Negroes. An observance at Harrisburg, Ohio, in 1849 drew an interracial crowd of two thousand, the largest ever seen in the village. One-quarter of the celebrators of an August 1 at Morris Grove, Brooklyn, in 1855 were whites, many of them good-looking young women. Presumably they were the daughters of abolitionists, mused a reporter from *The New York Times*, inasmuch as the latter had homely wives but pretty daughters.[20]

At the Brooklyn affair Sydney H. Gay presided and J. Miller McKim and Garrison were among the speakers. Whites like these were occasionally scheduled as speakers at Negro-planned August Firsts. At a morning service at a church in Newark in 1839 Charles G. Finney shared the speaker's platform with his colored fellow clergymen, James W. C. Pennington and Samuel Ringgold Ward. At Cleveland in 1853 the featured speaker was James A. Thome who in 1837 had spent six months in the British West Indies assessing the results of emancipation. At New Bedford in 1858 one of the guest speakers was the Reverend Henry Bleby of Barbados, who had been in Jamaica when slavery came to an end ("I saw the monster die," he related). When New Bedford Negroes held their annual parade on August 1 they usually halted at the home of Mayor Rodney French, a trusted friend.[21]

In accounting for the popularity of an August 1 picnic, the

role of relaxation must not be overlooked. The advance publicity for a celebration at Dayton, for example, came right to the point, "Every provision will be made to make the day one of pleasure as well as productive of good." Often the speeches were followed by dancing under the spreading trees. At the San Francisco observance in 1855 dancing was not on the program but seemed to be the high point for many: "With a majority of colored people in San Francisco dancing is the acme of human happiness," wrote the local correspondent of a reformist weekly.[22] An August 1 was a family affair, and hence there were aerial cars and other amusements for those children who were not encircling the vendors of watermelon and ice cream.

But to most adults the pleasurable features were a concomitant to their seriousness of purpose rather than a substitute for it. Many observances had a distinctly religious tone. In-town affairs were generally held in churches, with ministers prominent in the proceedings. At Troy in 1839, Daniel A. Payne spoke at the Bethel Free Church in the morning and the Liberty Street Presbyterian Church in the evening. At each service Payne read original odes in commemoration of the day, a typical stanza running thus:

> Ransomed islands! lift your voices
> Louder than the roaring sea!
> While your bounding heart rejoices,
> Praise the God of Liberty.[23]

In New York City on the same August 1 a morning service of prayer was held at Theodore S. Wright's Presbyterian Church, followed in the evening by a concert of sacred music. In 1854 the Indiana District Conference of the A. M. E. Church ordered each minister to deliver a West Indian Emancipation sermon or lecture during the first week of August in 1855.[24]

But whether in city churches led by clergymen or in coun-

try groves led by laymen, an August 1 celebration was characterized by an insistence that slavery must go. The speakers
might be of tender age, such as those of the Yates Juvenile
Anti-Slavery Society, meeting on August 1, 1839, at the Liberty Street Presbyterian Church in Troy. Or the speakers
might be college students, such as sophomore George B.
Vashon and freshman and former slave William P. Newman
appearing at the observance at Oberlin in 1842, one arranged
by Negroes. The speaker might be a semiliterate recent runaway or a polished performer like the tall, well-proportioned
J. B. Sanderson, who could hold forth for an hour without a
grammatical error.[25] At an August First a poet like James M.
Whitfield might deliver an original ode, or a toast might
come from a figure in the professions, such as David J. Peck,
the first Negro to win an American medical degree. Whatever
their background or calling, these participants struck a common note. And its refrain was echoed by the inscriptions on
the banners that decorated the platform: "Liberty the birth-
right of all." "Let the oppressed go free." "Give us our rights,
we ask for nothing more."

Not all Negroes thought that August 1 was a day worthy of
being celebrated. West Indian emancipation had been com-
pensated emancipation, with the masters having received payment. Hence, to some critics such emancipation was an admission that man could hold property in man. Moreover, ran the
charges, West Indian emancipation was a "given" freedom—
it was a boon conferred rather than a right seized. "Let us seek
some day in which some enslaved black man in our own land
swelled beyond the measure of his chains and won liberty or
death," exhorted J. McCune Smith. He would prefer the day
when Denmark Vesey suffered gloriously in Charleston as
head of an abortive rebellion or "when Nat Turner turned all
Virginia pale with fright." Robert Hamilton, editor of the
Anglo-African Weekly, shared Smith's point of view. The
West Indies slaves had not liberated themselves, he wrote, and

hence he would prefer to commemorate the kind of day which marked the downfall of slavery in Haiti or the birthday of Nat Turner. A white editor of a Columbus, Ohio, paper expressed the hope that Negroes would soon have a better day to celebrate than August 1 in this land of "Life, Liberty and the 'Pursuit of Niggers.'"[26]

Negroes who celebrated August 1 could not refute these charges, nor did they try. But at their observances they invariably invoked the future, certain that it would furnish a more glorious day to commemorate than was then on the calendar. At their August Firsts they paid their respects to the past by reading aloud the Declaration of Independence and the West India Emancipation Act. But the speakers, even those who glorified pre-colonial Africa, placed great emphasis on the new day a-coming. Dissatisfied with the status quo, constant in their seeking for a change, Negroes did not believe that August 1 was destined to be their only freedom day for limitless years to come.

"These black brethren constitute an argument against American slavery which nothing can overthrow," wrote a British weekly in 1854. "If these are not men, where shall they be found?" For nearly fifty years Negro reformers had been journeying to England in search of support. Paul Cuffe had gone to London in 1811 seeking a grant of land for colonization in Africa. The well-known essayist Leigh Hunt was impressed by his "good countenance and manly presence," considering him "an excellent specimen of what freedom and instruction can do for the outcasts of colour." During his stay of four months Cuffe became personally acquainted with the great English abolitionist trio—Thomas Clarkson, William Wilberforce, and Zachary Macaulay, dining with the last named. In their annual report the directors of the African Institution extolled Cuffe and his crew for having attracted respect throughout Great Britain by the propriety of their deportment and the proficiency of their navigational skills.[27]

Three years after Cuffe's unsuccessful quest, another New Englander, Prince Saunders, came to London and was soon moving in good society. Self-assured and of polished manners, he was presented to the King. John Quincy Adams, who attended a dinner to which Saunders had also been invited, believed that some people feted him because they mistook his Christian name for a title.[28] But this was hardly likely in the case of Wilberforce, who helped him to obtain an appointment in Haiti.

After 1830, with the advent of the new school abolitionists, the number of Negro American reformers journeying to the British Isles took a sharp increase. The first in point of time was Nathaniel Paul, who after ten years as pastor of the Hamilton Street Baptist Church in Albany had gone to the Wilberforce settlement in Canada. This community, badly in need of funds, commissioned Paul to go to England. Armed with a letter of introduction from Sir John Colborne, Lieutenant-Governor of Upper Canada,[29] Paul sailed from New York on December 31, 1831.

Paul's four year sojourn across the Atlantic did not realize any money for the Wilberforce settlement, his expenses matching his collections. But he did much to advance the cause of abolition. He spoke before a select House of Commons committee that was considering the West India Emancipation bill; he breakfasted twice with William Wilberforce, and his audiences averaged between 2000 and 3000.[30] In his speeches Paul stressed the importance of promoting religion and education among Negroes, but he never failed to attack the American Colonization Society, or to give Uncle Sam "due credit for his 2,000,000 slaves."

Paul was joined by Garrison in the summer of 1833, and together on July 13 they journeyed to Playford Hall, Ipswich, for a visit with the aged and sightless Thomas Clarkson. Dur-

ing the four-hour interview, Paul described the attitude of Negroes to the American Colonization Society, a disclosure that
"seemed powerfully to agonize the mind of the venerable
man," as Garrison reported it. Upon Garrison's return to
America, Paul toured northern England and Scotland in company with John Scoble, later the Secretary of the British and
Foreign Anti-Slavery Society.[31]

In the summer of 1834 Robert Purvis came to England,
after facing the usual difficulties of a Negro trying to get a
United States passport. In August, at the House of Commons,
Purvis was presented to the great Irish patriot, Daniel O'Connell. Mistaking Purvis for a white American, O'Connell hesitated to shake hands with him. Apprized by John Scoble of the
identity of Purvis, O'Connell greeted him warmly, explaining
that he never took the hand of an American without first
knowing his stand on slavery and its ally, the American Colonization Society. A month later, armed with a letter of introduction from Garrison, Purvis paid a visit to Sir Thomas
Fowell Buxton, parliamentary leader of the antislavery forces
after 1824.[32]

Making a greater impression abroad than Paul or Purvis
was their Negro successor in the British Isles, Charles Lenox
Remond. Although not imposing in physique, Remond had
proved to be one of abolition's most effective speakers. He did
something for the colored man, wrote Cyrus M. Burleigh, removing any doubt as to his mental capacity.[33] Chosen by the
American Anti-Slavery Society in 1840 as one of its four official delegates to the first World Anti-Slavery Convention at
London, Remond's trip was financed by the Bangor Female
Anti-Slavery Society, the Portland Sewing Circle and the
Newport Young Ladies' Juvenile Anti-Slavery Society. Remond did not take his seat, however. The London convention
voted against the seating of women delegates. As a result,
Garrison, Remond, and Nathaniel P. Rogers, in a dramatic
gesture of protest, left for the gallery to join their fourth col-

league, Lucretia Mott, and the other unseated women delegates from the United States.

Remond became a spectator rather than a participant, but
during the sessions he and his colleagues were surrounded by
admirers, almost to the point of holding court in the gallery.
Lady Bryon, the Duchess of Sutherland, joined the self-exiled
party and conversed freely with Remond. After the convention
held its final session the American abolitionists remained for a
day at Freemason's Hall to hold a meeting of their own. At
this rump gathering Remond's speech won the loudest applause and the greatly impressed Charlotte Upscher, daughter
of Zachary Macauley, asked Mrs. Mott to brief her on the
Negro orator.[34]

Remond remained in the British Isles for nineteen months,
holding forth on slavery, colonization, temperance, and race
prejudice. His schedule was crowded; during one stretch he
spoke twenty-three evenings out of thirty. But a true reformer
never complained of being overbooked, even though, as in the
case of Remond, his standard speech ran to two hours. Audiences of that day were inured to long addresses, but Remond
seems to have held their attention throughout. Buxton paid
tribute to his platform effectiveness by seeking to enlist him as
a lecturer against the slave trade.[35]

Remond, like Purvis before him, formed the acquaintance
of Daniel O'Connell, a name highly revered in Negro circles.
A meeting of Negroes in New York in December 1832 at the
Abyssinian Baptist Church had been devoted to honoring
O'Connell, reading a portion of an address he had made at a
meeting of the London Anti-Slavery Society earlier that year,
and then adopted six laudatory resolutions to this "uncompromising advocate of universal emancipation, and the friend of
the oppressed Africans and their descendants."[36] It was
O'Connell who, after the overthrow of slavery in the British
West Indies, demanded that British abolitionists turn their
attention to the United States.

Remond met O'Connell in July 1840 while both were in London attending the annual meeting of the British and Foreign Anti-Slavery Society. At one of the sessions Remond followed O'Connell on the program, and opened his speech with a tribute to him. A month later the two reformers dined together.[37] In his remaining months abroad, particularly those spent in Ireland, Remond spoke of O'Connell in unrestrained praise. When he returned to America in December 1841 he brought with him a Great Irish Address, signed by Daniel O'Connell and 60,000 other Irishmen, urging their countrymen in America to treat the Negroes as friends and to make common cause with the abolitionists.

In his speaking tours back home, Remond exhibited the address, which in most halls extended from the rostrum to the front door. Hundreds would examine the document, including some Irish. But the American sons of Erin were not abolition-minded; indeed, as much as they admired O'Connell they bitterly resented his proddings as to the Negro. Irish abolitionists —O'Connell, Richard D. Webb, and James Haughton, among others—were totally unable to transfer their attitudes to their transplanted countrymen. The fear of labor competition from Negroes was the dominant reason for the coolness of the Irish American toward the abolitionist movement. There were other reasons, but none could be so tersely expressed as that of William C. Nell: "The opposition of Irishmen in America to the colored man is not so much a Hibernianism as an Americanism." [38]

For the twenty years following Remond's visit abroad, a veritable host of Negro reformers made their way across the Atlantic. These included former slaves turned clergymen, like James W. C. Pennington, Henry Highland Garnet, Samuel Ringgold Ward, Jermain W. Loguen, and Josiah Henson, the last named soon destined for fame as "the original Uncle

Tom." Former slave laymen who journeyed abroad bore names equally notable in reform circles, such as Frederick Douglass, William Wells Brown, William and Ellen Craft, and Henry "Box" Brown. To these must be added a complement of free-born Negroes, among them J. McCune Smith, Robert Douglass, Jr., William G. Allen, William H. Day, Sarah P. Remond, Martin R. Delany, and clergymen Alexander Crummell and William L. Douglass.

Robert Purvis was one of the few Negro abolitionist leaders who did not come to England during the peak decade of the 1850's. He never repeated his visit of 1834, a circumstance much regretted by Sarah Pugh, onetime president of the Philadelphia Female Anti-Slavery Society and herself a sojourner in the British Isles in 1853. The presence of "the noble and gentlemanly Purvis" would do a great good, wrote Miss Pugh in March 1853, because he was "allied to the oppressed race" and because of his "knowing all things & everybody connected with the cause from the beginning." But Purvis remained in America even though later that year he and his wife seriously considered moving to England for good as a result of the refusal of the Philadelphia Chicken Fanciers to receive into their exhibition any poultry from Purvis. He attributed his denial to their color prejudice, their coolness toward him having been made all the stronger by having won the first prize at the three preceding annual exhibits.[39]

Of the Negro Americans journeying to the British Isles some were bent on pursuing academic training study or professional study, as in the cases of Smith, Crummell, and Robert Douglass. Brother of Sarah Douglass, the last named had come to London with a letter of introduction from the well-known portraitist Thomas Sully. Some made the trip, like Remond, as delegates to a conference. Pennington journeyed to London in 1843 as a representative of the Connecticut Anti-Slavery Society to the World Anti-Slavery Society. William Wells Brown sailed from Boston in July 1849 as an officially accredited delegate to the Paris Peace Congress. Samuel Ringgold Ward came to England in June 1853 as an agent for the Anti-Slavery Society of Canada, his main mission to solicit funds for the assistance of needy fugitives.

As if to spread their thin ranks as widely as possible, these visiting Negroes did not travel in company with one another, as a rule. Occasionally, however, their paths crossed in attending official or specially called meetings. For example, the annual meeting of the British and Foreign Anti-Slavery Society, held in London in 1851, was attended by Crummell, Garnet, Henson, and Pennington, each of whom spoke. Three months later, on August 1, at the Hall of Commerce in the same city the American Negro performers held a public meeting for the dual purpose of celebrating West India emancipation and condemning American slavery. With William Wells Brown in the chair, the large audience included two literary luminaries, Thomas B. Macaulay and the newly appointed poet laureate, Alfred Tennyson.

The length of stay of the visiting blacks varied, ranging from six months to five years, both J. McCune Smith and William Wells Brown remaining for the latter span. A few came with the intention not to return, like William G. Allen and the Crafts. Those who originally planned to stay for a short time found reasons for extending their sojourn. J. McCune Smith spent his entire span in one place, but the others, including the university-based Crummell, did considerable moving around. In this respect none could quite match William Wells Brown whose wide-ranging travels took him, as he reported, to "nearly every town in the kingdom."

If there was one Englishman above all others to whom the visiting blacks were indebted it was George Thompson. No stranger to Negro Americans, Thompson had first come to the United States in 1834 as an agent of the British and Foreign Society for the Universal Abolition of Negro Slavery and the Slave Trade. A close friend of Garrison, Thompson shared his attitude toward Negroes, addressing them as "brethren and sisters." Unpopular with Boston's nonreformist element, Thompson had constantly faced mob violence: "I cannot describe the emotions of my soul in view of the wicked murderous and fiend-like disposition exhibited toward you, in this land of Bibles and Christians," Susan Paul had written in a letter expressing gratitude for his labors.[40] The Negroes who came to England were happy to meet such a long-time champion. Winner of a seat in Parliament in 1847, Thompson did all that he could for the visitors—furnishing them with letters of introduction, arranging their itineraries, traveling with them to meetings, and introducing them to audiences.

Thompson's graciousness was characteristic of the general reaction to the Negroes. Abolitionists as a class were more highly esteemed in England than in America. Certainly the mission-bent blacks who crisscrossed the British Isles were most cordially received. Small in number and transients for the most part, they posed no threat to the laboring man or to the purity of the national blood stream. Hence they received that heartiest of welcomes that comes from a love of virtue combined with an absence of apprehension. A few examples may be in order.

James W. C. Pennington was given a tea at Surrey in June 1843 attended by five hundred guests. A month later he preached twice at the Queen's Street Chapel in Leeds, a local reporter characterizing everything about him as "impressive." Frederick Douglass had a similar experience upon his arrival in the British Isles in 1845. Wherever he goes, wrote visiting William Lloyd Garrison to his wife, he is "the lion of the occasion." For twenty months Douglass was hailed and feted, whether in England, Ireland, or Scotland, whether in large cities or quiet crossroads. Mayors presided over assemblies gathered to hear him. He dined with the great abolitionist, Thomas Clarkson, a month before his death, and he spent an evening with the economist-statesman John Bright and his sister. At a packed public farewell in his honor in London on March 30, 1847, he could truthfully point out that "although I speak of it myself, I have steadily increased the amount of attention bestowed upon this question by the British people." [41]

William Wells Brown arrived in London in late September 1849 after a ten-day stay in France where he "spoke admirably" at the World Peace Conference and attended a reception given by the French foreign minister, Alexis de Tocqueville. In England, Brown was "overwhelmed by public meetings." At a January soiree in Newcastle he was given a purse of 20 sovereigns as a token of regard for his character and admiration of his zeal in advancing the cause of the slave. At Bristol in April 1850 four hundred guests sat down to tea in his honor. [42]

In December, Brown was joined at Liverpool by William and Ellen Craft, and for six months the three former fugitives journeyed through the midland counties, northern England and Scotland. The trio repeated its triumphs of a year earlier in New England. "All who see and talk with them cannot but feel a deep thrill of indignation at a system that would rob such persons of their humanity," wrote the Liverpool *Mercury*. Hundreds were turned away at a meeting arranged for the three visitors by the Glasgow Female Anti-Slavery Society. The Crafts were received with "rapturous applause," and Brown delighted the crowd with his observation that the United States welcomed the refugees from the banks of the Danube and Tiber whereas "here in Glasgow 3,000 persons are assembled to welcome refugees from the banks of the Mississippi." At Bristol the three reformers gave a new impetus to the abolitionist spirit. [43]

Arriving in England within months of Brown was James W. C. Pennington, there for a repeat visit. Hired by the Glasgow Female Anti-Slavery Society, he toured the length and breadth of Scotland, his tearful tales exciting sympathy and sorrow. In 1850 he attended the World Peace Conference at Frankfort, returning to England with Henry Highland Garnet. For three years the latter sounded his voice of vast compass in public places throughout the British Isles. Garnet so impressed the United Presbyterian Church of Scotland that they sent him to Jamaica as pastor of the Stirling Presbyterian Missionary Church.

As Garnet sailed westward to his new charge, two other Negro abolitionists debarked to enliven the British scene. The most conspicuous of these was Samuel Ringgold Ward, whose circle of black chin whiskers could be observed only at close quarters. Huge in stature, witty and vivacious, Ward was an immediate favorite wherever he went. Although called upon to speak on behalf of a variety of reform causes and on the same platform with distinguished public figures, he "never failed to acquit himself with honor." [44] The Earl of Shaftesbury, who presided at his first two meetings, became his patron, and the Chelmsford Quaker, John Candler, offered him fifty acres in Jamaica.

The other abolitionist notable who came to England in 1853 was the youthful, light-skinned William G. Allen. Formerly a teacher at Central College, Allen had married one of his students, Mary King. When their engagement became known, Allen had been visited by a group of townspeople armed with tar and feathers, and his fiancée had been moved to a neighboring county by her protesting parents. But the determined couple married on March 30 and sailed for Liverpool nine days later.

Once in England, Allen quickly published an account of his experiences, *The American Prejudice against Color: An Authentic Narrative, Showing How Easily the Nation Got into an Uproar* (London, 1853). Priced at one shilling and written in Allen's typically forceful style, the book sold well. With his wife, Allen toured the reformist circuit relating their story. Subsequently he added three addresses to his repertoire, one on the history and prospects of the African race, another on the present condition of the American Negro, and a third on his probable destiny. In Dublin for two years, he supplemented his lecture income by giving lessons in elocution. Befriended by such prominent abolitionists as Joseph Sturge and George Thompson, Allen solidified his support by his ability and integrity. In a letter to Garrison he contrasted his reception in the land of John Bull with the patronizing attitude Negroes met with in America, even among abolitionists. As if to bear him out, his British admirers purchased control of the Caledonia Training School at Islington, and installed him as master, "the first instance in this country of an educational establishment being under the direction of a man of colour." [45]

Allen's success in promoting the cause in England was fully matched by that of Sarah P. Remond of Salem, Massachusetts, sister of Charles Lenox Remond. Well and favorably known in Garrisonian circles, Miss Remond had in 1856 been employed as a visiting lecturer by the American Anti-Slavery Society. Her moderate success on the platform in her native country was overshadowed by her triumphs abroad in 1859 and 1860. The somewhat supercilious Maria W. Chapman, who had spent six years in Europe, wrote to Sarah on September 4, 1859, asking whether she would like to have "special letters of introduction from me." [46] Miss Remond had no such need. She bore a beguiling air of refinement, a genteel pattern of manners so esteemed as an ideal of womanhood in Queen Victoria's England. She carried herself with an air of high seriousness; her speech was dulcet-toned and quiet, and her fluent vocabulary was free of unladylike turns of phrase. Unlike many of her colleagues, she avoided the sentimental, the heartrending tales of Tom and Topsy.

But of Miss Remond's effectiveness there could be no doubt. In August 1859 she gave three lectures in Bristol, her first appearance having been advertised by printed handbills. At one of the crowded meetings she was asked to express an opin-

ion on the religious revival in America. She replied that it was
not genuine since it did not include the abolition of slavery.
The Bristol and Clifton Ladies Anti-Slavery Society, sponsors
of her visit, expressed their deepest appreciation for her visit
and their "mournful sympathy" for the slave.[47]

At its December 1859 meeting, the Leeds Young Men's
Anti-Slavery Society hired Miss Remond as an agent and arranged a tight schedule. For three months her life was a whirl
of appearances at town halls, chapels, and school auditoriums
that invariably were crowded to excess. When she appeared at
Warrenton in March, her address was signed by the mayor,
the parish rector, the member of Parliament for the borough,
and by 3522 inhabitants, no previous address in Warrenton
having ever been more numerously autographed.[48]

At Dublin in March, at a meeting arranged by the Dublin
Ladies' Anti-Slavery Society, Miss Remond's audience included university clergymen and professors, who were held as
spellbound as those of lesser learning. At a meeting in Edinburgh in October, Miss Remond attracted an audience of over
two thousand, with hundreds turned away. After speaking an
hour and a half she "resumed her seat amidst enthusiastic
cheering, which was prolonged for several minutes." Sum-
ming up the value of her services, the Leeds Young Men's
Society reported that the thousands who heard her would
never forget the experience.[49]

In point of time, Martin R. Delany was the last of the better
known black abolitionists to pay an antebellum visit to the
British Isles. Timing things so as to attend the International
Statistical Conference at London in mid-July 1860, Delany
arrived fresh from a safari into equatorial Africa. At the opening session of the conference the chairman, Lord Brougham,
called attention to his presence. Amid great applause, Delany
bowed, and for the five days of the conference he was a center
of attraction. His subsequent stay of seven months was capped
by his attendance as a special guest at the Congress of the

National Association for the Promotion of Social Science, held at Glasgow, and his appearance before the Royal Geographic Society in response to an invitation to give a report on his African exploration.[50]

From the time of Nathaniel Paul's visit in 1832 to that of Delany nearly thirty years later, Negro Americans had worked to strengthen the current of antislavery sentiment in Great Britain. Their audiences had been large and sympathetic, and their influence had been correspondingly great. After listening for a quarter of a century to their unsparing condemnation of human bondage, the British public found it hard to conceive of a single good argument in its support. On the eve of his departure from the British Isles William Wells Brown could tell a Manchester audience that he returned to America knowing that he could truthfully assure Negroes and abolitionists "that something is being done here for their cause." [51]

This deepened British hostility to slavery took many forms, such as supporting American abolitionist weeklies, particularly the one published by Frederick Douglass, sending money for the underground railroad, and publishing and circulating books on Negroes of ability, such as Wilson Armistead's, *A Tribute for the Negro* (1848), and H. G. Adams's, *God's Image in Ebony* (1854). But the most significant manifestation of British hostility to slavery came with the outbreak of the Civil War when the English masses and middle class became strongly Northern in their sympathies, regarding the Confederacy as slavery's strongest bastion in the Western world. Thus did British abolitionist sentiment, nurtured by visiting blacks from across the Altantic, influence international diplomacy and the outcome of the Civil War.

Negro abolitionists who could not do their bit by journeying to the British Isles might express their sentiments toward the great English reformers, Wilberforce and Clarkson. Upon the death of the former in late July 1833 Negroes showed their sorrowful esteem. The members of the Phoenix Society wore badges of mourning for a month, and another New York group sent a letter of condolence to the family. In Newark one of the self-improvement groups held a memorial service, and at the Baptist meetinghouse in Boston John T. Hilton delivered a commemorative oration.[52] Negroes in Philadelphia likewise assembled in solemn tribute to Wilberforce. His birthday, August 24, was annually observed by the Young Men's Wilberforce Debating Society, and one of the two antebellum colleges founded for Negroes bore his name.

Wilberforce's coworker, Thomas Clarkson, was likewise honored in colored circles by having literary and self-improvement societies named after him. Upon his death in 1846 Negroes in New York held a commemorative service, with Alexander Crummell delivering a long and carefully prepared eulogy. Charles L. Reason recited an original poem, "Freedom," of comparable industry—42 stanzas—of which the following lines are suggestive:

> Well hast thou fought, great pioneer,
>   The snows of age upon thy head
> Were freedom's wreaths, by far more dear
>   Than finest sculpture o'er the dead.[53]

Perhaps the best way to pay tribute to a fallen abolitionist was to stretch out one's hand to the slave. This could be done most directly through the underground railroad.

VII

The Black Underground

A fugitive slave—"a living gospel of
freedom, bound in black."
Lydia Maria Child, 1846

ON A DAY in early August 1850, William Still of Philadelphia was approached by a man who gave his name as Peter
Freeman and said that he was looking for his long-lost mother
and father, Levin and Sidney, former slaves like himself. William Still was an underground railroad operator and hence familiar with dramatic incidents. But as Peter unfolded his story
Still stood almost transfixed. For it happened that Levin and
Sidney were his own parents and therefore the man talking to
him was an older brother he had never seen before.[1]

Such human interest stories about former slaves who journeyed northward looking for relatives or in pursuit of freedom, or both, made effective propaganda for the abolitionist
cause. Fugitive slaves on the wing tended to arouse sympathy
and to stir the public conscience. Slavery was weakened far
less by the economic loss of the absconding blacks than by the
antislavery feeling they evoked by their flight and the attempts to reclaim them.

Sympathy for the runaway slave was created and sustained
by the Fugitive Slave Act of 1793. Heavily weighted in favor
of the master, this measure offended the popular sense of fair

play. Without first obtaining a warrant, a master had only to seize his slave, bring him before any judge, and prove to the court's satisfaction that the person in custody was guilty as charged. The judge would then issue what was in essence a certificate of repossession. The alleged slave was permitted no trial by jury and given no opportunity to present witnesses to give testimony on his behalf.

The abolitionists attacked the measure on the dual grounds that it was unconstitutional and that it legalized kidnaping. The latter contention was the more readily provable, particularly in the instance in which Richard Allen was claimed as a fugitive, much to the subsequent discomfiture of the claimant.[2] The law was one-sided, but, even had it been more fairly drafted, there would still have remained a great reservoir of sympathy for those who made the dash for freedom. A blend of the desperate and the heroic, their actions could hardly fail to win the admiration even of the great mass of people who did not care for the abolitionists and to whom the free Negro was someone to be tolerated rather than welcomed.

Hence the work of assisting runaways was in popular favor in the North, many whites being drawn into the work. Possibly the best known of these was the Quaker, Levi Coffin, whose thirty-five-year record of slaves assisted ran to well over two thousand. Formerly from North Carolina, Coffin's success as a storekeeper in Newport, Indiana, and then in Cincinnati, afforded him the means for underground railroad activities. Two other abolitionists with long and almost as notable careers in helping fugitives were Thomas Garrett, whose Wilmington home was perhaps the best known station in the East, and Canadian-born Alexander M. Ross, who took time from his career as a physician to recruit escape-minded slaves in Richmond, Nashville, Selma, and New Orleans.[3]

Any balanced analysis of underground railroad operations must include its Negro workers. In Ohio, for example, black people were particularly active. Abolitionist leader James G.

Birney noted in February 1837 that slaves were escaping in great numbers to Canada by way of Ohio. And, he added, "such matters are almost uniformly managed by the colored people. I know nothing of them generally till they are past." The fugitive slaves who made their way through Sandusky were aided almost wholly by the town's one hundred Negroes, led by a barbershop owner, Grant Richie. The state numbered not fewer than one hundred Negro underground railroad workers. In Missouri the loose network included a cluster of all-Negro associations in St. Louis which sped the fugitive to Chicago and points north.[4]

The great authority on the underground railroad, Wilbur H. Siebert, points out that the list of towns and cities in which Negroes were co-workers with whites in the movement was a long one. Moreover, he adds, many Negroes in states that bordered the slave regions found numerous ways to help the fugitives without much risk to themselves. Although Siebert is as objective as one could wish in his assessment of the Negro's role in the movement, he unwittingly does not do it full justice. In his monumental "Directory of the Names of Underground Railroad Operators," embracing some 3200 entries, Siebert designates 143 names as Negroes. But in listing the following he did not identify them as colored: James J. G. Bias, Frederick Douglass, George T. Downing, Robert Morris, Robert Purvis, Charles B. Ray, Stephen Smith, and William Whipper. Similarly, in listing the membership of the Vigilance Committee of Boston, Still omits the Negro identity of William C. Nell and John T. Hilton, and in the roster of the General Vigilance Committee of Philadelphia, he does not indicate that Charles H. Bustill, Robert Purvis, C. L. Reason, William Still, Josiah C. Wears, and Jacob C. White were colored men.[5]

Of the variety of ways to assist fugitives, one in particular was suited to the Negro operator—that which entailed going into the South and making contact with those who were escape-minded. The slave was more likely to place his trust initially in a black face. Moreover, some Negro conductors were former slaves who were familiar with the territory in which they operated. Some of these secret returnees were willing to run this special risk in order to rescue their wives and children.

The most renowned of these black conductors was Harriet Tubman who, like Nat Turner, was given to dreams and to prayers. Herself an escapee from Dorchester County, Maryland, in 1849, she made some fifteen excursions into slave territory and brought back more than two hundred fugitives. Short and spare, she hardly looked like a person with a price on her head. But she was skillful in avoiding detection, her coolness in a tight spot matching her courage. To her abolitionist associates she became something of a legend, Thomas Wentworth Higginson calling her the greatest heroine of the age.[6]

A less noted and less lucky conductor was Leonard A. Grimes, a free Negro. Grimes became a hackman in Washington, D. C., eventually owning a number of horses and carriages, all as available for rescuing slaves as for conveying paying passengers. In one of his ventures in Virginia, his native state, he was seized after spiriting a slave family away in a hack. Grimes spent two years in the state prison at Richmond. He then went to Boston and became the pastor of the Twelfth Baptist Church. But, as in Washington, he neglected no opportunity to assist a runaway.

Most of the conductors whose names are lodged in record were based in the free states and hence were engaged in speeding the slave on his way rather than leading him out of the South. These "middlemen" included George L. Burroughs of Cairo, Illinois, whose job as a sleeping-car porter between Cairo and Chicago gave him an unusual opportunity for smuggling slaves. The most enterprising conductor in Salem, Ohio, was George W. C. Lucas, whose false-bottomed wagon conveyed fugitives to Cleveland, Sandusky, and Toledo.[7] At

Elmira, New York, former slave John W. Jones secreted slaves in baggage cars bound for Canada.

For some black conductors the water was the freedom route. Slaves were carried across the Ohio on skiffs from Kentucky to Indiana. Negro crewmen might bring slaves aboard as stowaways on vessels leaving Southern ports and bound for the North. Elizabeth Barnes, who worked for a ship captain at Portsmouth, Virginia, hid slaves on vessels sailing for Boston and New Bedford. New Yorkers Edward Smith and Isaac Gansey of the schooner *Robert Centre* were charged by the Virginia Governor Thomas W. Gilmer with having abducted slave Isaac, and $3000 was offered for their delivery to the jailer at Norfolk.[8]

Shipping slaves from one Northern port to another was far more common than the intersectional traffic, not to say less hazardous. James Ditcher piloted slaves along the Ohio from Portsmouth to Proctorville. Fugitive slaves were a common sight on the canal boat running from Cleveland to Marietta and owned by Negro abolitionist John Malvin.[9]

It is to be noted that many runaways never left the cotton kingdom, taking refuge either in the towns or the swamp lands. Other slaves preferred Mexico as their destination. A letter from a "free, colored Floridian," in an abolitionist journal in October 1831, urged slaves to turn toward Mexico because of its convenient location, its mild climate, its generous land policy, and its freedom from color prejudice.[10] But to the great majority of footloose slaves, the region above the Ohio River had one irresistible attraction that Mexico lacked—a substantial black population like themselves in language and outlook and one whose feeling of "sympatico" needed no proving.

A prominent feature of the Negro underground was the providing of overnight accommodations for the absconding slave. A white host might well be an object of suspicion to a newly fledged fugitive. Upon reaching Philadelphia, where they revealed their true identities, William and Ellen Craft were placed with Barkley Ivens, a non-Negro, much to Ellen's alarm. "I have no confidence whatever in white people," she told William, "they are only trying to get us back into slavery."

Levi Coffin noted that the fugitives who passed through Newport, Indiana, generally stopped among the colored people, although the latter were not always as skilful in concealing them as they might have been. But carelessness could hardly be charged to Chapman Harris of Jefferson County and his associate, Elijah Anderson, despite the fact that their cabins were well-known stopping places for fugitives.[11]

Coming to Cincinnati in 1847, Levi Coffin found that there, too, most of the fugitives who landed in the city soon vanished into the colored quarter. Some of those who were taken to the Negro section wound up at a place most unlikely to be suspected of harboring fugitives—the well-appointed Dumas House, famous for its ornate saloon where one might find the "biggest colored faro game in the country." At Ross, Ohio, the Reverend William H. Mitchell gave overnight housing to some thirteen hundred fugitives over a span of twelve years. Mitchell's lodging-house activities ceased in 1855 when the American Baptist Free Mission Society engaged his services as a missionary to the former slaves in Toronto. Runaway slaves reaching Detroit could find asylum at the residence of George DeBaptiste, who had worn out his welcome in Madison, Indiana, because of his underground railroad activities. A slave coming to Chicago might be lodged with the well-to-do tailor, John Jones.[12]

At Philadelphia the physician-clergyman James J. G. Bias "gave his bed freely" to slaves directed to his house by the white abolitionist Charles T. Torrey. Not stopping with his bed, Bias also gave to his overnight guests a quick medical checkup. Just outside Philadelphia the Byberry residence of Robert Purvis, a well-known station on the underground, had a special room reached only by a trap door. Another wealthy black abolitionist, William Whipper of Columbia, a port of entry for fugitives from Maryland and Virginia, resided at the end of the bridge leading into the town. He put up as many as seventeen slaves in one night, the next day sending them west by boat to Pittsburgh or by rail to Philadelphia in the false end of a boxcar he owned. In one instance Whipper alerted Jacob C. White at Philadelphia that the fugitive he was dispatching was in a "perilous situation," having seen his master that very day. At West Chester, Abraham D. Shadd, fairly well-off but not in a class with Whipper or Purvis, "entertained and forwarded" black transients.[13]

In New York City, the home of Charles B. Ray was a haven for journeying fugitives, fourteen of them walking up the front steps one summer morning. But Ray was not the only black New Yorker to be so blessed. "One hundred and fifty, in a single year, have lodged under my roof," wrote Henry Highland Garnet, "and I have never asked or received a penny for what I gave them, but divided with them my last crust." [14]

Colored abolitionist leaders in upstate New York knew that runaways would be directed to their doors. Jermain W. Loguen at Syracuse fitted an apartment in his house for these unannounced visitors. Those who came to Rochester made their way to the office of Frederick Douglass on Buffalo Street, early morning arrivals sitting on the steps until opening time. In Albany the home of Stephen Myers was an overnight sanctuary for black drop-ins on the last leg of their northward journey. The Buffalo home of William Wells Brown was a station on the underground railroad, Brown himself conducting sixty-nine to Canada over a period of seven months in 1842.[15]

In the Northeast the best known rendezvous for runaways was the home of Lewis Hayden in downtown Boston. Hayden himself was a fugitive from Kentucky, his rescuer Calvin Fairbank having been arrested and jailed for helping him es-

cape. Hayden had turned down an earlier opportunity to escape because he could not bring his future wife along with
him. As if to prove himself worthy of Fairbank's sacrifice,
Hayden welcomed fugitives to stop under his roof. When the
owner of William and Ellen Craft, Dr. Robert Collins of
Macon, Georgia, sent two deputies to reclaim them, William
took lodging in the Hayden dwelling, temporarily barricaded
for the occasion. One day when Harriet Beecher Stowe visited
the Haydens she was surrounded by thirteen escaped slaves.[16]
Upon settling in Newport, Rhode Island, in 1855, George T.
Downing quickly established himself as the friend of any fugitive alighting in that city.

Individual assistance to runaway slaves was supplemented
by the work of vigilance committees, and here too the black
people in the North played a distinctive role.[17] A vigilance
committee aided the fugitives in a variety of ways—boarding
and lodging them for a few days, purchasing clothing and
medicine for them, providing them with small sums of money,
informing them as to their legal rights and giving them legal
protection from kidnapers. A primary function of the vigilance committee was to help a slave establish himself in a new
location, to furnish him with letters of introduction, to help
him find a job, and to give him guidance and protection while
he was thus engaged in getting started. Hence a vigilance
committee was a combination underground and upperground
railroad, the latter comprising its efforts to help the slave lo-
cate within the United States. "The time has come to stop running," announced Jermain W. Loguen, manager of the Fugitive Aid Society of Syracuse.[18]

Many of the vigilance committees had a totally or predominantly Negro membership. The greatest of these Negro-run
organizations was the New York Committee of Vigilance,

founded in November 1835, with David Ruggles as its secretary and general agent. As its monthly meetings the committee listened to speakers like James Emerson, a seaman who had almost been sold into slavery after accepting work on a ship running to Petersburg, Virginia. Appearing at committee meetings were speakers like the wife of kidnaped Peter John Lee, her fatherless sons at her side.[19]

The committee listened to stories of colored children who had been hired as domestics and then carried into the South and sold. The committee publicized descriptions of missing Negroes, and informed its members as to the arrival and departure dates of ships suspected of harboring slaves. At one of its meetings three destitute Africans were introduced, with a plea for funds to help them return to their native land. On one occasion Isaac Wright told his story of being rescued by an agent of the committee after having been sold into slavery at New Orleans by the captain of the *Newcastle*, J. D. Wilson. It was through the committee that Wilson was arrested and detained for the illegal sale of Wright and two other Negro seamen. To attend a meeting of the Vigilance Committee tended to tear at the heart strings. At the annual meeting in 1837 at the Zion Church, Alvan Steward, founder in 1835 of the New York Anti-Slavery Society, was deeply moved by the strong emotions of gratitude expressed by the fugitives whom the committee had assisted. "I could almost submit to become a slave for the privilege of making such a friendship," he said to the gathering.[20]

Much of the success of the New York Committee of Vigilance could be credited to David Ruggles. "He is a General Marion sort of man," wrote a contemporary editor, "for sleepless activity, sagacity and talent." [21] Ruggles personally gave assistance to hundreds of runaways. The case of Frederick Douglass was a typical one. Ruggles sheltered the young Douglass for nearly two weeks, made his marriage arrangements, and sent the newlyweds to New Bedford, Massachusetts, with a five-dollar bill and a letter of introduction to a locally prominent Negro, Nathan Johnson.

Ruggles boarded incoming ships to see whether slaves were being smuggled in. He went from door to door in fashionable neighborhoods making inquiry as to the status of black domestics, New York law freeing any imported slave after a residence of nine months. In one instance Ruggles went to the Brooklyn home of Daniel K. Dodge and brought away a domestic, Charity Walker, a former slave. Although Ruggles got her a job, the obliging Charity succumbed to a ne'er-do-well and soon became pregnant, opening Ruggles to a volley of criticism, however unjustified, from those hostile to the abolitionists.[22]

Ruggles resigned as secretary and agent in February 1839 because of trouble with his eyes and a clash with the committee. Ruggles kept no books and hence was never able to render an accurate account of monies received and expended. The committee could never tell whether Ruggles overdrew his salary of $400 a year, and Ruggles, secure in his own sense of honesty, resented any probing of it.[23]

With the resignation of Ruggles the New York Committee of Vigilance lost its driving spirit and much of its influence. But its record over a five-year span had been commendable. During its first year it had "protected" 335 Negroes from slavery, and this figure was a sound approximation for each of the succeeding four years. The committee also won public acceptance of its contention that persons claimed as fugitives should have a trial by jury, a measure they had advocated from their opening meeting. In May 1841 Governor William H. Seward signed such a bill, and a month later the Vigilance Committee held a victory celebration at Asbury Church. The presiding officer, Charles B. Ray, hailed the measure for sweeping clean from the statute books the last vestiges of slavery in the state.[24] But the law was not firmly enforced at the outset, and before it could prove itself it was nullified by a Supreme Court decision (*Prigg v. Pennsylvania*, 1842) giving Congress the exclusive right to enforce the Fugitive Slave Law.

Negroes in Boston and Detroit had all-Negro vigilance groups, although neither had as dramatic a figure as Ruggles. Founded in Boston in 1842 and lasting for five years, the New England Freedom Association aimed to "extend a helping hand to all who may bid adieu to whips and chains." It solicited donations of money or clothing for the fugitives and places of residence, temporary or permanent, and advertised in the abolitionist press for persons who would give them jobs. Two of its seven directors were women. Founded in the same year as its Boston counterpart, the Colored Vigilance Committee of Detroit was headed first by William Lambert and then by George DeBaptiste. In the absence of competing white abolitionist organizations, the Detroit group maintained an independent existence until the Civil War, reaching its peak in the mid-fifties. In one two-week period in 1854 the committee gave assistance to fifty-three freedom-bound blacks, a figure which grew to 1043 for the period from May 1, 1855, to January 1, 1856. Cleveland had an all-colored committee of nine, of whom four were women, which sped 275 slaves to Canada from April 1854 to January 1855.[25]

In Boston and New York the all-Negro vigilance groups were succeeded by racially mixed prototypes. In Boston in September 1846 a committee of vigilance was formed by Samuel Gridley Howe following public indignation over the return of a slave who had secreted himself on a vessel bound from New Orleans to Boston. The committee included Robert Morris and William C. Nell along with many prominent white reformers and literary figures; for example, Ralph Waldo Emerson sent word that if the economic well-being of Massachusetts depended upon making Boston a "slave-port," he would willingly forego such prosperity and "turn to the mountains to chop wood." [26] The Boston Committee of Vigilance performed its most conspicuous services in the early 1850's following the passage of the Fugitive State Law. [27]

New York City was the headquarters of another racially mixed group to assist the runaway slave—the New York State Vigilance Committee. Founded in 1847 with the Quaker Isaac T. Hopper as president, but with a membership over 50 per cent Negro, the committee assisted 166 fugitives during its first six months. In 1848 the committee was reorganized with white philanthropist Gerrit Smith as president and Charles B. Ray as corresponding secretary. One of the committee's accomplishments during its first year was the instigation of action in the federal courts in nine cases in which a person was held as a slave in a slave state even though he was entitled to his freedom by the laws of the state. From January 1851 to April 1853 the committee assisted 686 former slaves, many of whom received little more than periodic counseling, but of whom thirty-eight were freed after being brought into New York City by their reputed masters. [28]

Upstate New York had two interracial slave-assisting organizations, although the one in Albany might well have been called the Myers Vigilance Committee. Its guiding spirit, Stephen Myers, held few meetings, although he acted in the name of the committee. That Myers was able and honest muted any criticism. At Syracuse the abolitionists founded the Fugitive Aid Society, with Jermain W. Loguen as its manager. Engaged in helping runaways since 1850, Loguen devoted full time to the work beginning in 1857. He wrote letters to the local newspapers urging their readers to hire fugitives in their shops and on their farms. How many jobs he found for the more than three hundred former slaves that passed through his hand cannot be known, but it earned for Syracuse the title of "the Canada of the United States." [29]

Loguen's good work in Syracuse was overshadowed only by that of William Still in Philadelphia, the secretary of the Gen-

eral Vigilance Committee. This organization had a predecessor, the Philadelphia Vigilance Committee, which was
founded in 1838 and was in existence six years. This parent
group was interracial on paper; eleven of the thirteen members of the first so-called Standing Committee were whites.
But the president was Purvis and the agent (executive secretary) was another Negro, Jacob C. White. After 1839 the
monthly meetings were no longer attended by whites, so that
the committee was all-Negro in its operations and increasingly
Negro in its personnel. This committee assisted some three
hundred fugitives a year—its high for one week, the first
week in September 1842, running to twenty-six.[30] It dispatched the fugitives to Canada or to David Ruggles in New
York.[31] The committee expired in 1844, although many of the
former members, Purvis, White, J. J. G. Bias, Daniel Payne,
and Stephen H. Gloucester among them, continued to assist
slaves in an individual capacity.

The successor of this pioneer organization, the General
Vigilance Committee, was more consistently interracial. Robert Purvis was made chairman of the new organization, seven
of whose nineteen founders were Negroes. But, most impor-
tantly, black William Still was made chairman of the four-
member Acting Committee, thus becoming the executive secretary of the organization and its dominant figure.

A more resourceful and hard-working operator could
hardly have been found. The full scope of Still's activities may
be gleaned from his 780-page work, *The Underground Railroad*, published in 1872. In this fact-crammed, semi-docu-
mentary work, Still reproduced scores of letters from workers
in the field, such as Joseph C. Bustill from Harrisburg describing the beginnings of the local Fugitive Aid Society. Still
exchanged fruitful letters with such white supporters and colleagues as Thomas Garrett in Wilmington, Sidney Howard
Gay in New York, Levi Coffin in Cincinnati, and Hiram Wilson at St. Catherines in Canada. Still received scores of letters

from fugitives he had helped, such as the one John J. Hill sent from Toronto: "I am as Free as your President Pearce [*sic*], only I have not been free so long. It is true that I have to work very hard for comfort but I am Happy, Happy." [32]

The general Vigilance Committee aided hundreds of black bondmen, the number running to 495 from December 1852 to February 1857. But the episode that Still was least likely to forget was the delivery of Henry Brown, shipped in a box from Richmond to Philadelphia by Adams Express. When the shipment reached the antislavery office, Still, one of the four receiving agents, pried off the lid. Whereupon "the marvellous resurrection of Brown ensued," wrote the author of *The Underground Railroad*. "Rising up in his box, he reached out his hand, saying, 'How do you do, gentlemen?' " [33]

It was well that underground railroad work had its rewards. For there was no lack of problems, a need for funds ranking first. As in the case of all other antislavery operations, money was in short supply. The three major sources were Negroes, a sprinkling of whites, and a corps of women's groups on both sides of the Atlantic.

Negro giving was fair to good. The $284.31 raised by the New York Vigilance Committee from January 1, 1839, to May 23 of the same year came almost wholly from Negroes. The racial identity of one of its donors in 1837 could hardly be mistaken—George Jones, who had contributed $12.50, "was dragged to slavery by an order from our City Recorder," according to the committee's first annual report. Many members of the committee pledged themselves to contribute 50¢ a month, and in cases of dire need the members advanced money out of their own pockets. At its annual meetings the committee passed the hat, the average collection running to $75. In Detroit the bulk of the money of the Vigilance Committee seems to have come from collections taken up at meetings, particularly at call meetings growing out of quick-breaking incidents. Some of the funds of the Vigilance Committee of Philadelphia came from small donors, fifty-two of them contributing a total of $95.94½ from September 11, 1839, to January 13, 1840. This committee also solicited from Negro churches and it held soirees, raising $42 at one of these held in June 1841.[34]

At Rochester the Negroes "systematically aided their hunted brethren," wrote William C. Nell to William Lloyd Garrison on February 19, 1852, having just held a "donation festival" on their behalf. At Syracuse in January 1859 the manager of the Fugitive Aid Society, Jermain W. Loguen, received a financial contribution from thirty of the escaped slaves for whom he had gotten jobs, some of them adding a personal gift to him, such as an engraved sugar spoon or butter knife. To put something into its ever-exhausted treasury the New England Freedom Association sponsored juvenile concerts, charging a small fee at the door. On one desperate Sunday in August 1846 the association sent delegates to five of the colored churches in Boston, succeeding in raising a total of $23.19.[35]

Some of the support of the vigilant groups came from white donors. In 1840 the New York Committee received $25 from Arthur Tappan and $10 from John Rankin, both New York merchant-abolitionists. At Albany, Stephen Myers could operate independently of his committee because he had only to call upon three wealthy whites for whatever monies he needed. Upon assuming the presidency of the New York State Vigilance Committee in 1848, Gerrit Smith authorized the committee to draw upon him for $500 for the year's operations. On occasion a collection for underground railroad operations might be taken up at an abolitionist gathering, Harriet Tubman receiving $37 from such a source at Framingham, Massachusetts, in July 1858.[36]

Raising money for fugitive slave assistance had its appeal

for wives and mothers. In New York the Negro women held annual fairs at the Broadway Tabernacle for the benefit of the Vigilance Committee. An admission fee of 12½¢ was charged, thus guarding against a poor sale of the "useful and fancy articles" on display. Many of the women who conducted the fair also worked for the committee by collecting a penny a week from friends. At Syracuse a group of women busied themselves in soliciting food, clothing, and money, channeling their collections to J. W. Loguen.

The women of Philadelphia outstripped all others in the work. Over a four-year span the colored Women's Association made donations for fugitive slave work, giving $50 in 1851. The earlier Vigilance Committee had a short-lived women's auxiliary, from which it received $10 in 1839. The interracial Philadelphia Female Anti-Slavery Society generally dipped into its treasury after receiving a touching appeal from the committee, usually to the effect that it had on hand a group of fugitives ready to move northward but had no funds to get them on the road. The society sent $20 in September 1841, $50 in January 1842, and $10 in January 1843, and an additional $25 later that year. In May 1845 the society gave $10 to one of its members, Hester Reckless, to assist fugitives, following her plea on their behalf.[37]

Women in the British Isles lent a sisterly hand in the work. Beginning in 1852, the year of its founding, the Glasgow Female New Association for the Abolition of Slavery held an annual bazaar for the New York Vigilance Committee, designating it as the principal recipient of its funds. The New York group also received grants of $50 each from the women in Dundee and Edinburgh in both 1857 and 1858. The Rochester friends of the fugitive received $100 in 1857 from the Edinburgh Ladies' New Anti-Slavery Association. The Philadelphia Vigilance Committee received remittances from the women of Dundee and Newcastle-on-Tyne, the latter through Anna D. Richardson who in 1846 had been instrumental in raising $700 to purchase the freedom of Frederick Douglass. In the spring of 1858 the Philadelphia Committee and Thomas Garrett in Wilmington each received $50 from Eliza Wigham, on behalf of the Edinburgh Ladies Emancipation Society.[38]

The work of Loguen at Syracuse drew support from women's antislavery groups throughout Great Britain—Edinburgh, Aberdeen, Berwick-on-Tweed, Halifax, Liverpool, Barnsley, and Huddersfield. The women from the land of Daniel O'Connell were not to be left out, the Irish Ladies Anti-Slavery Society sending Loguen $72.79 in February 1859 "for the benefit of fugitives coming to his house in Syracuse." [39] It is possible that over the five-year span from 1855 to 1860 Loguen received from the women in the British Isles some $400 a year, a sum which perhaps equalled their combined contributions to the other fugitive aid societies in the United States during the period.

Hundreds of women, British and American, white and black, gave sacrificially to help the fugitive slave. But their efforts fell short of the need, this phase of the abolitionist crusade sharing with the others a chronic lack of funds. The modest salaries of the full-time agent were generally in arrears. Collections were slow, and only the zeal of the workers kept the work going as fruitfully as it did. But even the most dedicated worker might have felt a bit dispirited over the plight of the Philadelphia Vigilance Committee, which as of November 11, 1841, reported that its funds were gone, that it was in debt, and that its total collections over the past month had been "a bundle of clothes, two hats and a bonnet." [40]

Resources that were badly needed to help the fugitive from the South went sometimes to unworthy recipients—those who pretended to be runaways or their relatives. Since a fugitive aroused sympathy and received aid, it is not surprising that a small corps of impersonators sprung up. Most impostors claimed themselves to be slaves; others put forth the more modest honor of being a slave's relative—husband, father, son, or brother, whose freedom they were allegedly raising money to effect.

During the first week of December 1839 the Philadelphia Committee of Vigilance turned down the requests of two men claiming to be slaves, although one of them looked so woebegone that the committee relented and gave him $20 and some food. Generally the warnings against detected impostors were to be found in the columns of the antislavery journals. At Hartford in the summer of 1845, James W. C. Pennington advised the public to be on guard against one James Thompson, who was passing himself off as a slave from Lynchburg, Virginia. Early in 1850 the abolitionists of New York City were alerted about one William Johnson, an alleged fugitive in search of his alleged spouse. Johnson was all the more reprehensible for having recently deserted a real wife. Late in 1855 an antislavery weekly gave a personal description of one O. C. Gilbert who was pocketing monies he collected for fugitives. Gilbert was a large, robust man, 5 feet, 9 inches, of dark brown hue, practically bald and quite bowlegged: "Let all the papers pass him around," ran the warning.[41]

In January 1858 the inhabitants of Middlesex County, Massachusetts, were warned against a short, slender, light mulatto of twenty-two, who called himself George Thompson. Namesake of the British abolitionist, this "strolling knave" George Thompson had already collected $15 from sympathizers in Leominster. Abolitionists were advised that George was a reckless liar, varying his story according to circumstances. The breed was not unknown in England, Reuben Nixon spending a jail term for falsely soliciting funds as a fugitive.[42]

Elizabeth Buffum Chace, a Quaker at Valley Falls, Rhode Island, encountered only two known impostors in her long career of helping runaways. But one of these impersonators turned out to have been a hardened criminal. The "gentlemanly, light-colored, handsome man" she had protected for ten weeks from the slave catchers allegedly trailing him turned out to be an escapee from the New York state prison at Auburn. Mrs. Chace might have been forgiven, confessing that she had been impressed by his "great desire to learn our ideas about right and wrong, and for the improvement of himself in all directions." [43]

Abolitionist weeklies often advised their readers to be less credulous when approached by someone claiming to be a runaway. Some fugitive aid societies were hesitant about giving assistance unless the alms-seeker could produce a certificate of identification from friends or acquaintances in the border states. But such a precaution could have had little real effect. The counterfeiting of certificates of freedom ("free papers") was common in underground railroad operations; hence, a person who chose to become an impostor would have found it no real obstacle to borrow this technique and proceed to acquire forged letters of introduction.

To the friends of the fugitive slave there was one class more hated than the impostors and this was the informers—those who could be bribed to reveal the whereabouts of a runaway. Levi Coffin, head of the underground railroad at Cincinnati, found that not all Negroes were to be trusted in fugitive slave operations. [44] But such a group of betrayers of the slave remained very small, in part because of the adverse publicity given them and in part due to more forceful action.

Dating from its origin, the Negro press printed the names of black informants, *Freedom's Journal* listing those of Moses Smith, formerly of Baltimore, and Nathan Gooms of New York, in its issue of November 7, 1828. The mere appearance of these names in the columns of the weekly was a sufficient deterrent to the other informers whose identity the editors threatened to reveal. When Martin R. Delany was editor of the *Pittsburgh Mystery* he was sued on two occasions for charging Negroes with having assisted the slave-catchers.[45]

A Negro who assisted the slave-catchers ran the risk of bodily harm, as two of this ilk found out in Cincinnati. Robert Russell decoyed a fugitive to a wharf where he was seized by his master's agents. But before Russell could enjoy his informant's fee of $10 he was tarred and feathered by a group of young Negro men. In August 1858 two runaways were betrayed by John Brodie, who had promised to assist them in returning to Covington, Kentucky, to effect the liberation of relatives. Brodie's treachery nearly cost him his life. He was seized by a group of Negroes, who proceeded to give him three hundred blows with a paddle, a stroke for each dollar he was supposed to have received from the slave-catchers. Only the presence of the influential Henry Highland Garnet saved Brodie from further punishment. The badly mauled informer delivered himself to the police authorities, to be placed in jail for safe-keeping. In Jefferson County, Indiana, an informer was whipped within an inch of his life. During the court trial it was impossible to get any Negro to testify against his floggers.[46]

Telltale Negroes were dealt with harshly because underground railroad work was hazardous enough as it was. Whether black or white, in the North or South, the benefactor of a fugitive slave ran a variety of risks. Imprisonment was an ever-present threat to those whose theatre of activity included the slave states, as some Negro operators could ruefully attest. For journeying into the South to recruit runaways Samuel D. Burris was placed in jail at Dover, Delaware, for fourteen months. He was then auctioned off as a slave to serve for seven years, but his abolitionist friends arranged to have him purchased by a dummy. Elijah Anderson of Indiana died in 1857 at the state prison in Frankfort, Kentucky, where he was serving a term for conducting fugitive slaves across the state line.

For the same offense and at the same penitentiary Oswald Wright of Corydon, Indiana, served a five-year term. Samuel Green, a local Methodist preacher at Dorchester County, Maryland, who attracted public attention upon receiving a sentence of ten years for possessing a copy of *Uncle Tom's Cabin*, was actually being punished for his suspected aid to fugitives, the original reason that brought the search party to his house.[47]

David Ruggles, executive secretary of the New York Committee of Vigilance, had to stay on the alert lest any attempt be made to assault him. He took the precaution of changing his lodgings periodically, but this did not save him late one night in January 1837 when a small group attempted to force open his door, possibly with kidnaping in mind. In 1838 Ruggles was jailed for two days on the charge that he had harbored Thomas Hughes, a slave charged with felony. At Columbus, Pennsylvania, Negro businessmen William Whipper and Stephen Smith risked no bodily harm or jail sentence for secreting slaves but two attempts were made to set fire to their lumberyard.[48]

Whites who were made to suffer for assisting fugitives received public expressions of sympathy and esteem from Negroes. Amos Dresser, who had received a public whipping in Nashville in 1836, allegedly for distributing abolitionist literature, received a different reception later that year at Theodore S. Wright's Presbyterian Church and at a crowded call meeting of the New York Committee of Vigilance. Daniel Drayton of the schooner *Pearl*, who spent over four years in jail for making arrangements to smuggle seventy-seven slaves from Washington to New York in April 1843, was an honored name among Negroes. The Colored Ladies' Anti-Slavery Sewing Circle of Canandaigua sent him $7 and an effusive letter, the latter described as being "exceedingly gratifying to the feelings of Captain Drayton." In New Haven at the Temple Street Church of Amos G. Beman he spoke to an overflow audience, many of whom purchased copies of his *Personal Memoirs*.[49] Perhaps there was a touch of self-guilt in the attitude of Negroes toward Drayton, a colored informer having been a contributing factor in his capture.

For assisting runaways Calvin Fairbank served two prison terms, totaling nearly seventeen years. His first stay came to an end in August 1849 when Lewis Hayden, the former slave whose escape had led to Fairbank's arrest, raised $650 from 160 donors to pay Hayden's owners, who thereupon joined in the petition for a pardon for Fairbank. Detroit Negroes, led by George DeBaptiste, took up a collection for Fairbank upon his release.[50] In less than three years, however, Fairbank was back in a Kentucky jail, again for aiding a fugitive. This time he remained behind bars until late in the Civil War, in the meantime sending letters to Frederick Douglass and others, addressed from "Louisville Jail."

The fugitive slave movement had its martyr in Charles T. Torrey, who died in a Maryland penitentiary in May 1846. A clergyman-abolitionist who felt compelled to live out his convictions about the brotherhood of man, Torrey worshiped only in Negro churches while in Washington in the winter of 1841. From his base at Baltimore, Torrey helped to speed some four hundred runaways on the road to freedom over a two-year span. But in 1844 he was charged by a Winchester, Virginia, master with helping his slaves escape, and the court sentenced him to six years at hard labor. At Boston "a Torrey meeting of Negroes" took up a collection of $30 for their jailed friend and called upon the abolitionists in general and the Negroes in particular to rally to his aid.[51] Detroit's black reformers gathered at the First Colored Baptist Church to offer prayers for him.

Torrey's death in May 1846 brought from Negroes many expressions of grief, mingled with indignation and purpose. At Oberlin the colored citizens adopted a series of resolutions drafted and read by William H. Day, tendering sympathy to

Torrey's wife and children and condemning the governor of Maryland for not having pardoned him so that he might have "breathed his last among his native hills." Boston Negroes, meeting in Zion Church on June 15, 1846, voted to erect a monument to Torrey and invited the co-operation of colored people throughout New England. On July 31, 1846, the Negroes of the city held a service at Tremont Temple in honor of Torrey, with eulogies by John T. Hilton, William C. Nell, Joshua B. Smith, Henry Weeden, former slaves Samuel Snowden and Lewis Hayden, and a visiting speaker, Methodist minister Lucius C. Matlack, a friend of Torrey's.[52]

Meeting the next day at an August First celebration the colored people of Providence passed a resolution in favor of the Torrey monument proposal made by the Boston Negroes. But the Torrey Monument Association received very few contributions, Garrison having expressed the opinion that abolitionist money might be put to better use. The absence of such a stone did not keep Negroes from visiting Torrey's grave at Mt. Auburn cemetery at Cambridge, Massachusetts, Daniel Payne making a trip there in the summer of 1850.[53]

During the four months he spent in the Moyamemsing Prison in 1855 Passmore Williamson of Philadelphia evoked the sympathy of Negroes throughout the North. Williamson, a member of the General Vigilance Committee, was charged with contempt of court for having refused to reveal the whereabouts of three slaves whom he had persuaded to leave their master, no less a personage than the United States Minister to Nicaragua, John H. Wheeler. In truth Williamson did not know the whereabouts of Jane Johnson and her two boys, Daniel and Isaiah, inasmuch as they had been spirited from the wharf by William Still and five Negro porters. Still and his accomplices were brought to trial, two of them, John Ballard and William Curtis, receiving a week in jail for assault and battery on Colonel Wheeler.[54]

While the trial of the six black rescuers was going on, Wil-

liamson remained behind bars. But he received hundreds of
letters and scores of visitors. Among the latter was a five-man
delegation—George T. Downing, Stephen Myers, Robert
Purvis, Charles Lenox Remond, and John S. Rock—from the
Colored National Convention, which was meeting in Philadelphia in mid-October 1855. The delegates reported that Williamson had assured them that he would not sacrifice a single
principle on the altar of slavery. A month later the high-
minded Quaker was triumphantly acquitted, his case having
been greatly strengthened by Jane's testimony that, in the language of the court record, she had "willingly left the boat,
aided in the departure by several colored persons, who took
her children, with her consent, and led or carried them off the
boat, and conducted your petitioner and her children to a carriage, a short distance from the boat." [55]

The friends of the fugitive included a small corps of lawyers and to these, too, the Negroes found a way to express
their gratitude. At Bethel Church in February 1841, a group
representing the colored citizens of Philadelphia gave a set of
silver plates to David Paul Brown for his services in defending
runaways. At Cincinnati, Salmon P. Chase regularly defended
fugitives, receiving no fees for his services but acquiring a
silver pitcher from the city's grateful blacks. In July 1851,
attorneys E. C. Larned and George Maniere each received a
silver cup from the colored citizens of Chicago as a token of
high regard for their successful services on behalf of Moses
Johnson, an alleged fugitive. For their legal services in the
Shadrach rescue case in 1851, Richard Henry Dana and John
P. Hale received from the Negroes of Boston an eight-volume
set of Henry Hallam's *Constitutional History of England*
which, as the donors pointed out, was "a history marked by
the progress of free institutions and by the virtue of courage
of great lawyers." Both recipients sent gracious replies, Dana
stating that the set gave him a feeling of pride and gratifica-

tion and Hale saying that he would cherish his set while he lived and bequeath it to his family when he was gone.[56]

To a Negro abolitionist few things could be so satisfying as helping a runaway. But the great majority of black leaders felt that there was a complementary work to be done—one that would not only strike at slavery but would simultaneously elevate the free Negro. This was the use of political power—getting the ballot and putting it to the proper use.

VIII

The Politics of Freedom

Political power is a mighty Anti-Slavery engine.
We hold that all true abolitionists should
go to the polls and vote.

Colored American, August 17, 1839

THE RIGHT to vote never loomed so large to Negroes as in the two decades before the Civil War. Through political action slavery might be rooted out and equal justice brought into play. A Negro electorate could give needed support to anti-slavery men and measures in Congress. Fairer treatment of the Negro could be gotten locally if white legislators had to reckon with a colored constituency.

But the Negro who wished to vote faced a sea of troubles. The great friend of the colored man, William Lloyd Garrison, decried politics, holding that the Constitution was proslavery and that all who took an oath of office to support it were ridden with the virus. But Garrison's theories of nonvoting and disunion were maintained by only a handful of Negro leaders. Robert Purvis held fast to the Garrisonian viewpoints, crying in May 1857 that the United States government was "one of the badest, meanest, most atrocious despotisms that ever saw the face of the sun." During the same month, Charles Lenox Remond, in a debate with Frederick Douglass at Shiloh Church in New York, argued that the Constitution was pro-slavery. But in 1848 Remond had temporarily abandoned his nonvoting stance when he cast a ballot for Stephen C. Phillips, Free Soil candidate for governor, justifying his action on the grounds that Phillips had favored larger appropriations for Negro schools.[1]

If the great majority of Negroes could not support Garrison's views on politics, they could sympathize with his single-minded devotion to the principle of nonvoting. But what left them unsympathetic and stirred up was the lukewarm reaction toward Negro suffrage that characterized the majority of the voting abolitionists. Ahead of their times in some important respects, the abolitionists nonetheless were in the main much like other Americans of their day when it came to political equality for the Negro. The freedom of the slave, yes. But to stand at the polls on a par with the black man, this was another matter. The friends of the colored people took part in antislavery work as a matter of duty, wrote the San Francisco correspondent of *Frederick Douglass' Weekly*, but they were no more likely to believe that Negroes were naturally equal to whites than they were to believe that chalk was cheese.[2] Many white abolitionists shared the common belief that political equality would lead inevitably to social equality, something for which they were not ready.

Another discouragement for the vote-minded Negro was the legal barrier. By 1860 equal suffrage existed only in New England, excluding Connecticut. In the remaining states the Negro was barred outright from the polls or, as in New York, faced with a property requirement.[3] Colored men found their exclusion particularly galling since it came during a period in which voting rights were being expanded. In many states the political disfranchisement of the black man took place almost simultaneously with the removal of all barriers for white men.

This conferring of the ballot upon the white workingman brought a special problem to the Negro, for it added to the electorate a class which opposed his advancement. The white mechanics and workers in the North feared the Negro as a labor competitor, and this fear was well known to politicians. Increasingly, therefore, the voteless black man became a whipping-boy for office-seekers pandering to race prejudice. In 1855 a Negro San Franciscan likened the colored people of California to a beast of burden by which political demagogues rode into power.[4]

Participation in political life would not be easy for Negroes —this they knew. But the outlook was not wholly bleak. The colored people would have to bear the brunt of the battle themselves, but they knew there were some whites, men of influence if small in number, upon whom they could count. And, best of all, politics and political parties were in a state of flux after 1840, and out of the new equilibrium might come a new niche for the Negro. "Amid the confusion of parties and the death struggle of old political dynasties," wrote J. W. Loguen to Frederick Douglass in the spring of 1855, "we cannot fail to accomplish much with proper exertion." [5]

The Negro seeking to strike at slavery through political action operated on both state and national levels. He had to win the ballot in his own commonwealth and then to support the political party best serving his interests in the Congress and, if possible, at the White House. It was the first of these steps that was crucial and difficult—to wipe out the states' legal requirement that the ballot be conferred upon whites only, or that Negroes meet special qualifications.

Negroes in New York had faced this "strings attached" problem since 1821, when a state constitutional convention decreed that before a Negro could vote he had to own $250 worth of landed property. The convention, and subsequently the voters, ignored a petition of protest from fifty Negroes, twenty of whom could write their own names. In 1826 the state legislature added to the vexation of the Negroes by voting to retain the property proviso.

With the rise of the militant abolitionist movement the colored people throughout the state initiated a drumfire against the restriction. In February 1837 the Negroes of New York City, led by such abolitionist figures as Philip A. Bell, Samuel E. Cornish, Thomas Downing, Thomas L. Jennings, Thomas Van Rensselaer, and Henry Sipkins, held a meeting at which they drafted a petition to the state legislature to remove the Negro suffrage restriction. After the meeting the petition was kept at Phoenix Hall for three days in order to run up the number of signatures. At the end of this period of grace the document bore 620 names, 365 of them in the signers' own handwriting, one of which read, "Independence Roberts, born on 4th of July, 1776, in Philadelphia." Placed in a double envelope, the petition was taken to Albany by a special messenger and delivered in person to the mail guard at the state house. Reaching the legislature at the same time were similar petitions from Negroes in Oswego and Genessee counties and Albany.[6]

The legislature proved unresponsive, thus bringing upon itself the condemnation of a monster meeting of Negro young men in New York City on August 21, 1837, with speeches by Timothy Seaman, John J. Zuille, Henry Highland Garnet, and George T. Downing. The meeting authorized Charles B. Ray and Philip A. Bell to visit Negroes throughout the state urging them to deluge the legislature with petitions to abrogate the property requirement for Negro voting.[7]

The silence of the legislature did not crush the Negroes, since they had decided that if one petition failed, another would be presented. This drafting of petition after petition was the avowed object of the Association for the Political Improvement of the People of Color, formed in New York in July 1838. Two months later the association sent a supply of blank petitions to Utica for distribution at the New York State Anti-Slavery Society. With young Alexander Crummell as one of the secretaries at the Utica meeting and Theodore S. Wright as one of the featured speakers, the association felt that the petitions would not lack signers. In the following year the association held an August 1 meeting in New York City, at which petitions were circulated before and after the oration by Alexander Crummell.[8]

In the summer of 1840 the Negroes held a statewide convention at Albany, based on the proposition that "political disfranchisement is becoming more and more odious." With Austin Steward as president and William H. Topp, Charles L. Reason, and H. H. Garnet as secretaries, the convention drew up an address to the colored people of the commonwealth calling upon them to press for the ballot: "Let every man send in his remonstrance. Let petitions be scattered in every quarter."[9]

But if the colored people were aroused, the white voters of the state were indifferent, making no effort to remove the property proviso for Negroes. With the emergence of the Liberty party in the 1840's it was inevitable that the equal suffrage issue would come before the constitutional convention of 1846. This body referred the question to the electorate, with results that were hardly surprising. In November 1846 the property qualification for Negroes was retained by a vote of 224,000 to 85,000. It is to be noted that in addition to the race and color factor the Negro's political inclinations entered into this lob-sided tally. Negroes were Whiggish or Liberty party-ish and hence could hardly expect Democrats to vote for a measure that would add to the political strength of their opponents.

The pattern in New York did not change for the remainder of the prewar period, with Negroes pressing without success for equal suffrage. At a state convention held in Troy in September 1855 the delegates condemned political discrimination and proceeded to organize the New York State Suffrage Association. Stephen Myers was appointed lobbyist at Albany. In this capacity he attended the sessions of the legislature, buttonholing most of its members. In February 1856 Myers reported that two-thirds of the lawmakers were favorable to extending the franchise.[10] But either this figure was inflated, or a number of men changed their minds.

Four years later, during another presidential year, the issue was still high on the agenda of the New York Negroes. The state suffrage association was now joined by a number of local groups, including the New York County Suffrage Committee, the Brooklyn Elective Franchise Club, the Albany County Suffrage Club, and the Elective Franchise Club of Ithaca. By September 1860 there were forty-eight local suffrage clubs in New York City and eighteen in Brooklyn. But again the voters turned down the equal suffrage proposal. The negative vote was smaller in percentage than in 1846, but there was no ambiguity as to the result, 337,900 to 197,000. Sorrowfully the members of the state suffrage committee might have read again one of the lines appearing in a pre-election circular they had issued: "Our white countrymen do not know us. They are strangers to our characters, ignorant of our capacity, oblivious to our history and progress, and are misinformed as to the principles and ideas that control and guide us, as a people."[11]

The Negro in Pennsylvania had to undergo a political shock even greater than that of his fellows in New York. Down to 1838 many Negroes had voted in Pennsylvania, but this privilege was abrogated in that year when a constitutional convention added the word "white" to the suffrage requirement. During the extended debate the convention had received a number of petitions on the issue, two from groups of Negroes in Philadelphia and Luzerne calling for impartial suffrage.[12]

While the new constitution was before the voters the Negroes drew up a lengthy protest, an "Appeal of Forty Thousand Citizens Threatened With Disfranchisement, to the People of Pennsylvania." Largely the work of Robert Purvis, it told of the role of the Negro in the history of the state and described his progress and his present condition. It bore an abolitionist flavor:

> We freely acknowledge our brotherhood to the slave, and our interest in his welfare. Is this a crime for which we should be ignominiously punished? The very fact that we are deeply interested in our kindred in bonds shows that we are the right sort of stuff to make good citizens. Were we not so, we should better deserve a lodging in your penitentiaries than a franchise at your polls.[13]

Despite its erudition and its eloquence, the appeal did not change many minds. The anti-abolitionist outbreak at Pennsylvania Hall in May 1838, although not the work of the reformers, brought about an increase in sentiment against Negro voting. Hence, in October the new constitution disfranchising the colored man won decisive approval at the polls. The Negroes were dismayed, their mood deepened by the story of a white boy who seized the marbles of a colored boy, telling him, "You have no rights now." [14]

During the 1840's Pennsylvania Negroes kept the suffrage issue alive through county and state conventions. One of the latter, meeting at Harrisburg in December 1848, asked the white voters to petition the legislature, adding somewhat plaintively that "our petitions can only reach the Humanity of the Legislator, while yours will instruct him in a course of action." At the annual meetings of the Pennsylvania Anti-Slavery Society, Negro participants such as Purvis, Remond, J. J. G. Bias, and Thomas Van Rensselaer, invariably got in a word condemning the disfranchisement of the blacks. The Negro protest was also expressed in petitions and memorials sent to the state legislature, the number totaling eighty-one from 1839 to 1851.[15]

The unresponsiveness of the state legislature led Philadelphia Negroes to take the unusual step in 1855 of sending a petition on a state issue to Congress. This "Memorial of Thirty Thousand Disfranchised Citizens of Philadelphia to the Honorable Senate and House of Representatives" was a recital of the Negro's record of patriotism and good citizenship, his ownership of property, and his payment of taxes. But this appeal to the national legislature brought results as barren as those sent previously to the state capital at Harrisburg. Nearly twenty years of such legislative indifference had a dispiriting effect on some Negroes. At Philadelphia during the winter of 1856–57 two public meetings on equal suffrage drew small audiences of some forty each.[16]

In New Jersey and Connecticut Negroes held state conventions to obtain the suffrage. Such meetings followed a familiar pattern—the drafting of a document which listed the grievances of the Negroes, affirmed their right to vote, through residence, military service, or taxpaying, and appealed to the white electorate's sense of fair play. The result was negative in both states although in New Jersey the Judiciary Committee of the lower house brought out a favorable report.[17]

In the Midwest the Negro protest against political discrimination was voiced in Illinois, Iowa, Michigan, and Wisconsin. In Illinois the call to a state convention of colored citizens to be held at Alton in November 1856 stated the key issue in the opening sentence—"First: We complain of being taxed without the right to vote." In Ohio with its large black population the outcries were louder and more sustained than elsewhere in the region. Ohio Negroes held seven state conventions in the decade before the Civil War, six of them at Columbus and one at Cincinnati. One of the Columbus meetings was held in the legislative hall, the assembly having graciously granted the request by the Negroes.[18]

The most prominent of the participants in the Ohio conventions was J. Mercer Langston, offspring of a wealthy Virginia planter, graduate of Oberlin, and a practicing lawyer, having passed the state bar in 1850. Langston was a member of a small committee selected at the convention of 1851 to visit Governor Reuben Wood seeking his support in removing the Negro's political disability. The state convention of 1854 selected Langston to draw up an equal suffrage petition to the legislature. Langston's memorial was read at the state senate meeting on April 14, those who listened not finding it unworthy of their attention. In 1856 the State Central Committee of Colored People of Ohio appointed Langston as lecturer and agent to canvass the state in the interest of Negro suffrage, not only speaking but taking up collections and soliciting donations in the committee's name.[19]

But the idea of the black man as a voter was slow in winning converts. In 1849 Negroes had finally won the right to testify against whites in legal proceedings. But if Ohioans were ready for a measure of equality in the courts this was not the case at the polls.

To Negroes west of the Mississippi this issue of testifying against whites took priority even over the privilege of voting. In California the law depriving the Negro of his oath in court was the major topic to come before the statewide Negro conventions held in 1855, 1856, and 1857. At the first gathering, held in Sacramento, the forty-seven delegates from ten counties drafted an address to the people of the state clearly setting forth the problem: "You have enacted a law excluding our testimony in the courts of justice in this State, in cases of proceedings in wherein white persons are parties, thus openly encouraging and countenancing the vicious and dishonest to take advantage of us." [20]

The California petitioners were heartened by a message from Philadelphia Negroes who commended "their brethren on the Pacific coast" for their noble struggle for the rights of man. White Californians did not view the petition in quite this cosmic light. Like the people in the other nonslave states, Californians feared that the removal of restrictions on Negroes might lead to an increase in their numbers. In California, however, the already racially mixed population made it more difficult to discriminate against the Negro.[21] Hence in 1861 the law barring Negro testimony was repealed. But California was not ready to revise its policy of white manhood suffrage, its Negro voting restrictions remaining on the statute books until the Fifteenth Amendment in 1870. And, except for Wisconsin, this would be the case in all the other states where such restrictions existed.

The denial of the right to vote was discouraging to black abolitionists. Most of them, however, took an optimistic, long-range point of view. Jacob C. White, speaking at the closing exercises of the Philadelphia colored high school in May 1855, at which the governor of the state was the honored guest, stressed the point that although Negroes were "not recognized in the political arrangements of the Commonwealth," they were preparing themselves for a future day when citizenship in America would be based on manhood and not on color.[22]

In the viewpoint of the Negro abolitionists the whole struggle for human freedom embraced the rights of women. The legal and political discriminations against the colored man were shared by all women. Public opinion was in essence male opinion, and it had its fixed ideas about the role of women beyond the traditional categories of kitchen, church, and school. A joint convention of men and women abolitionists held in Berlin, Ohio, in September 1849 moved Jane G. Swisshelm to mock horror: "This is a precious state of affairs! Where are Mr. Masculine Prerogative, Mrs. Propriety and Miss Feminine Delicacy?" [23]

Negro reformers needed no one to tell them of the role of women in the antislavery crusade, particularly in fund raising. Hence when the woman's rights movement got under way in the 1840's it attracted support from the more perceptive Negroes. In New York few black leaders subscribed to Garrison's political views, but they shared his belief that women should be seen and heard in public life. At the first convention for equal rights for women in America, held in July 1848 at Seneca Falls, New York, Frederick Douglass gave a major address. He was the only man present who supported the suffrage resolution, seconding the motion of Elizabeth Cady Stanton that it was the duty of the women of the United States to obtain the sacred right of the elective franchise. The state-wide woman's rights convention scheduled for Rochester in November 1853 listed Douglass and J. McCune Smith among the signers of the call. At the meeting, Douglass was one of the featured speakers, Jermain W. Loguen was named a vice president, and the youthful, light-skinned William J. Watkins was appointed as one of the secretaries.[24]

Negro conventions held after 1848 generally seated women, although sometimes the delegates needed prodding. Women themselves were not loath to force the issue. At the Ohio state convention in 1849 the women, led by Jane P. Merritt, threatened to boycott the meetings unless they were given a voice in the proceedings, preferring not to remain as mute spectators.[25] At the 1855 convention at Philadelphia Mary A. Shadd was admitted after a spirited discussion, in which she took part.

Negro women abolitionists sensed the pivotal role of politics, particularly its relationship to slavery. In 1855 the Delaware Ladies Anti-Slavery Society of Delaware, Ohio, pointed out that Negroes were "subject to an atrocious and criminal system of political tutelage deliterious to the interest of the entire colored race and antagonistical to the political axioms of this republic." [26] And Negro women, like their white counterparts, wanted to exercise political power directly, not through their presumed influence on their husbands, brothers, and fathers.

Hence the Negro women abolitionists believed in equal suffrage not only between the races but between the sexes. Sojourner Truth was as much at home at a woman's rights meeting as at any other kind, her natural eloquence making one overlook her broken English. She invariably made a deep impression, although her listeners found it difficult to convey her language to a third party—"[one might] as well attempt to report the seven apocalyptic thunders," wrote J. Miller Mc-Kim.[27]

Frances Ellen Watkins was of comparable dedication in the battle for human rights but a contrast figure in appearance and style. Slender and graceful, with a soft and musical voice, Frances too could "take a deep hold on the human heart." In October 1857 the Pennsylvania Anti-Slavery Society hired her as lecturer and agent for Eastern Pennsylvania and New Jersey, and received glowing reports of her lectures until the termination of her appointment in May 1858. A reporter at Mount Holly called her the best speaker he had ever heard. A listener at Norristown, Pennsylvania, was just a shade less enthusiastic, rating her as the most eloquent woman he had ever heard except Lucy Stone.[28]

Frances, like Sojourner, had a little book to sell, but hers was not ghostwritten. Her *Poems on Various Subjects*, first published in 1854 and with a preface by William Lloyd Garrison, had a ballad simplicity and bore such titles as "Slave Auction," and "The Fugitive's Wife." Frances was one of the signers of the Constitution of the Ohio State Anti-Slavery Society, an offshoot of the state convention of Negroes held in Cincinnati in 1858. She pledged $10 to the new society and became a member of its committee to raise $500 for operating expenses.[29]

Charlotte Forten, like Frances, was frail, introspective,

deadly in earnest and of a literary bent which in her case
found its major expression in a diary. Charlotte joined the
Salem Female Anti-Slavery Society when she was seventeen.
She became a teacher at the Salem Normal School, of which
she was a graduate, and corresponded with Garrison and
Wendell Phillips. The latter, in a letter in January 1857, ap-
plauded her decision to stay in America and share the fight.
She owed it to her grandfather, he added, referring to James
Forten.[30]

A lyceum- and concert-goer, Charlotte attended a lecture,
"Fair Play for Women," given by George W. Curtis in Philadelphia in November 1858, going with her aunt, Harriet Purvis. The young Charlotte was delighted with Curtis, finding
his lecture as much abolitionist as suffragist. One winter day
in 1856 when the bitter weather prevented her getting out to a
reformist lecture, she was disconsolate, explaining in her
diary, "I crave anti-slavery food continually." A worshiper of
Charles Sumner, Charlotte walked on air one Saturday in
February 1858 when she received two large envelopes from
him, one of them bearing extracts from one of his speeches
and the other containing eight autographs of prominent persons in England and America.[31]

Woman suffrage, white or black, was not achieved in antebellum America and Negro manhood suffrage was limited.
But Negro abolitionists maintained their interest in politics,
realizing its importance in a country in which the voice of the
people was deified. And in this popular chorus the voice of the
Negro was not completely stilled. In some states the colored
man could vote and join political parties, and in all states he
could exercise the right of petition.

The Negro's role as a voter and party-worker was strongest
in New England and New York. The Negroes in Massachusetts had been politically active since the emergence of the

new abolitionists. A group of colored Bostonians attended a legislative hearing at the state house in March 1838 at which five white abolitionists, including Angelina Grimké, testified against slavery and on behalf of the free Negro. At a meeting held shortly thereafter, the Boston Negroes commended the state-house sergeant at arms for treating them courteously, and thanked their white friends who testified at the hearing. Four years later another breakthrough took place when Charles Lenox Remond appeared before a Massachusetts House of Representatives committee to protest against jim-crow on the railroads and steamboats. In his remarks Remond referred to the "elective franchise," saying that if the Negroes in Massachusetts had it he saw no reason why it should be denied in other states. A year later the Negroes of Boston petitioned the legislature to prohibit segregation in public transportation and repeal the law against intermarriage.[32]

At New Bedford the Negroes had a meeting in October 1839 pledging themselves to vote for no official, from governor down, who was not in favor of immediate abolition. A committee of eighty-three was appointed to visit the candidates for public office, putting to them a series of questions, of which the first two are typical: "Is Liberty the will of the Creator? Does Congress have the power to abolish slavery in the District of Columbia, and should such power be immediately exercised?" [33]

In Rhode Island the Negroes managed to retain equal suffrage despite an effort in 1841 to push through a new constitution which eliminated the property requirement for voting but also eliminated the Negro voter. Supported by resident Negroes like Alexander Crummell, a team of white abolitionists along with Frederick Douglass journeyed to the state late in 1841. The abolitionists and black supporters held a series of meetings, some of them broken up by mobs opposed to "nigger voting." [34] The constitution adopted in 1843, however, had no race or color qualification for voting. Negroes increasingly voted throughout the state, but, topped by the nearly four hundred other registrants in Providence, their numbers were not large enough to win concessions from the political parties.

It was in New York State that political activity among Negroes reached its peak, many of them being able to meet the property requirement. These qualified colored men were not likely to spurn a privilege like the ballot, particularly with the Negro press spurring them on. *Rights of All* urged its readers to get out and vote, admonishing them to make their choices carefully: "Set an example for the whites, who are already, too many of them, politically half crazy." Another editor advised unpropertied Negroes to save the money they spent on "perishable finery" at the clothing store in order to accumulate enough to enable them to go to the polls.[35]

The number of Negroes eligible to vote is not easy to determine. In New York City the figure reached 250 in 1838. Six years later there was a 1000 total for the state. In 1846 abolitionist Gerrit Smith set aside 120,000 acres for colored men (drunkards excluded), one of his purposes being the increase in the number of black voters. The Smith grantees eventually totaled 1985. By 1850 the list of qualified colored voters had risen to 1200 for New York City and environs. And whatever the figures they do not tell the whole story. Many Negroes followed the advice given by suffrage-seeking organizations: If denied the right to vote yourself, try to influence others to cast their ballots for the right candidates.[36]

Negroes eligible to vote needed no exhortation to exercise it. An organization calling itself the Colored Freeholders of the City and County of New York met periodically after 1838. At their first meeting, held in Philomathian Hall on October 29, 1838, they drafted two resolutions against slavery and one in support of Luther Bradish for lieutenant governor. Bradish had gone on record as favoring equal suffrage and passage of a law granting a jury trial to alleged fugitives. The public official that won the greatest admiration of the colored voter was Governor William H. Seward. A group of Negroes meeting in Union Hall in December 1842 sent him an address praising his antislavery stance—his refusal to render fugitives, his approval of the act establishing trial by jury in runaway slave cases, and the repeal of the nine months' residence law permitting slavery. In a gracious responding letter, Seward expressed his gratitude for the tribute.[37]

After 1840 the attention of the politically minded New York Negro was drawn to the new political parties that took an antislavery posture. Interest in these new alignments was felt no less by Negroes throughout the North. Hence while focusing attention on the relationship between Empire State Negroes and the new parties, it would be well on occasion to touch upon the wider scene.

The first of these new political groups bore a magic name to Negroes, the Liberty party. Founded in 1839 this body reflected the belief that the existing parties, Whigs and Democrats, could never strike a strong blow at slavery because their memberships counted hundreds of thousands of slave-owners. Hence only a new party could really push for measures repealing the fugitive slave laws, striking at slavery in the District of Columbia, prohibiting the domestic slave trade and excluding slavery from the territories. By 1839 most abolitionists west of Massachusetts were ready for independent political action. In April of the following year the new party selected James G. Birney and Thomas Earle, both active abolitionists, as its candidates for president and vice president.

One of the earliest responses to the new party's nominees came from a group of Albany Negroes meeting at the Baptist Church late in April, with Benjamin Paul in the chair. After the standard denunciation of the property qualification for Negro voting in New York, the group called upon all colored voters to sustain Birney and Earle in the coming election. The convention urged Negroes throughout the North to be politi-

cally active so as to "hasten the consummation of our disen-
thralment from partial and actual bondage." The new party
won the enthusiastic support of *The Colored American*, which
generally furnished an accurate barometer of Negro
thought.[38]

In the presidential election, Birney polled barely seven
thousand votes, but his followers were not to be discouraged.
Six months after the election the party's central nominating
committee met in New York to select the standard-bearers for
the 1844 campaign. The committee members included Theodore S. Wright, John J. Zuille, and Charles B. Ray. Among
Negroes the most ardent of the early Liberty party men was
Henry Highland Garnet. At the convention of the Massachusetts branch of the party, which was held in Boston in February 1842, Garnet delivered one of the major addresses. A defense of the principles and goals of the new party, Garnet's
speech was enthusiastically received, the Faneuil Hall audience constantly interrupting him with laughter, applause, and
cries of "hear, hear." The delegates also listened to a plea for
money from Lunsford Lane, raising $33 to help him purchase
a member of his family.[39]

Garnet took his Liberty party advocacy to the national convention of colored men held at Buffalo in August 1843. His
resolution endorsing the new party was supported by Theodore S. Wright, Charles B. Ray, and nearly fifty others. With
only seven dissenting votes the delegates gave their blessing to
the Liberty party, a circumstance that Garnet reported with
pride at the national meeting of the party held two weeks later
in the same city.

At this Buffalo convention of the Liberty party three Negroes took a prominent part. Garnet delivered an address on a
resolution he had proposed affirming that the new party was the
only one in the country that represented the true spirit of liberty. Samuel Ringgold Ward opened one of the sessions with
prayer and also delivered a formal address, and Charles B.

Ray served as one of the convention secretaries. Two of the party planks referred to the colored man, one extending a cordial welcome to him to join the party and another condemning racial discrimination as a relic of slavery.

Garnet and Henry Bibb took the field for the Liberty party in the election of 1844, the latter speaking mainly in Michigan. The party polled some sixty-two thousand votes, which was a considerable improvement over the results of the preceding presidential campaign. But Theodore S. Wright found reason for vexation because many Negroes still clung to the old parties.[40]

Support for the Liberty party of both Negroes and whites declined after the peak year of 1844. By the time of the next presidential campaign the party had split into two factions. But the greatest reason for its declining fortunes was the emergence in 1848 of a new party, the Free Soilers. This party, too, owed its existence to the slavery issue. Democrats and Whigs who opposed the extension of slavery in the territories met in Buffalo in the summer of 1848 and organized a new party with the proclaimed goals of free soil, free speech, free labor, and free men.

The question facing the Negro voter in 1848 was whether to support the badly enfeebled Liberty party or the seemingly vigorous Free-Soilers. The latter had chosen as its standard-bearer Martin Van Buren, a former president of whom Negroes had no fond memories. In his inaugural address eleven years earlier, he had announced his opposition to the abolition of slavery in the District of Columbia and his intention not to interfere with slavery wherever it existed. Samuel R. Ward took a strong stand against the Van Buren-led Free Soil party, but the great majority of Negroes took a half-a-loaf attitude, believing that it would be wiser to support the party that had a chance to win.

In New York the Free Soilers won more support from Negroes than any of the rival parties. They did much better in

Massachusetts, where some communities voted the ticket almost unanimously. This was not the case, however, in Rhode
Island. Here the Whigs issued a pamphlet reminding the
Negro that it was they who had fought six years earlier to
retain his right to vote.[41] Such peculiar and local considera-
tions operated against the Free Soilers in more than one state,
thus contributing to its failure to carry a single one of them
and to elect only five men to Congress.

The elections of 1848, while hardly cheering to Negroes,
had demonstrated that the old parties were splitting. This circumstance was viewed by the more optimistic as a proof of the
progress of the abolitionist crusade. And despite their outcome, the elections had whetted the Negro's interest in politics
and his desire to be a participant in its processes. This interest
tended to remain largely in the Free Soilers. This party numbered such friends of the colored people as Joshua Giddings,
Salmon P. Chase of Ohio, and Charles Sumner, Henry Wilson, and Charles Francis Adams of Massachusetts. In Ohio it
was the Free Soil party that championed Negro suffrage, and
in Massachusetts it was Free Soil men who had successfully
battled to remove discrimination in the marriage laws, in
transportation, and in the public schools.

Negroes attended the national convention of the Free Soil
party in August 1852 at Pittsburgh, held to select presidential
candidates. The speaker drawing the loudest applause was
Frederick Douglass, even though he emphasized that slavery
should be exterminated rather than merely contained, as the
Free Soilers advocated. Their party platform did not go that
far, and it was silent as to the discriminations against the free
Negro. But for national office the convention selected two men
highly regarded by the colored people, John P. Hale and
George W. Julian.

In the closing weeks of the campaign Free Soil Negroes
throughout New England held a series of rallies in Boston, all
characterized, according to William C. Nell, by great en-

thusiasm. At these gatherings such political figures as Hale, Sumner, Giddings, and Horace Mann were praised, and the two old parties were condemned. The speakers, including J. C. Beman of Connecticut and William J. Watkins and Jermain W. Loguen of New York, called upon the colored voter to sustain Free-Soilery and thereby advance the anti-slavery cause.[42]

A handful of Negroes, and not many more whites, remained with the Liberty party, headed by Gerrit Smith, the reformer-philanthropist. Smith, campaigning for Congress, won a seat, but on a local issue unrelated to slavery. Otherwise the elections brought little cheer to Negroes and abolitionists, the Free Soil vote being smaller than that of 1848.

Antislavery political parties, however, were far from having run their course, the greatest one of all coming into existence in 1854. In that year the Kansas-Nebraska Act, opening the door to slavery in territory where it had been prohibited since 1820, created a deep resentment in the North. "This Nebraska business is the great smasher in Syracuse, as elsewhere," wrote J. W. Loguen to Frederick Douglass, adding that the atrocious villainy of the author of the bill, Stephen A. Douglas, was doing a fine work for the slave, "but no thanks to him." A group of Philadelphia Negroes, headed by James McCrummell, held a meeting condemning the act on the grounds that slavery could not be legalized, and praising the congressmen who voted against it, Seward, Chase, Sumner, Giddings, Gerrit Smith, and Benjamin F. Wade.[43]

Negroes were not the only ones bitterly opposing the measure. Its passage prompted "Conscience" Whigs and antislavery Democrats to join with the Free Soilers to form a new party, the Republicans. Its ranks grew rapidly, spurred by the news of the bloody conflicts that accompanied the opening of Kansas.

Negroes as a whole hailed this newer and stronger party committed to the containment of slavery. But there were a few dozen colored voters who, like the Liberty party to which they belonged, refused fellowship with the Republicans. With a stubbornness almost unparalleled in politics, the Liberty party would not take itself out of existence. Despite its microscopic vote in 1852 the party scheduled two conventions in New York in 1853, the second of them at Canastota in October, with Jermain W. Loguen presiding.[44] A year later at Syracuse, thirty Liberty party diehards, among them Frederick Douglass, went through the ritual of nominating a candidate for governor and declaring that it was the right and duty of the federal government to do away with slavery.

The coming of the Republicans did force the Liberty party people to make one change, that of experimenting with a new name. The Radical Abolition party was organized in June 1855 at Syracuse, with J. McCune Smith as the presiding officer at the three-day convention. The party platform was indicated in the title of a lengthy statement drafted by the delegates, an "Exposition of the Constitutional Duty of the Federal Government to Abolish Slavery." The Radical Abolitionists held two subsequent conventions, one in Boston in October 1855 and the other at Syracuse in May 1856. Four Negro leaders took part in these gatherings, Smith, Douglass, Amos Beman, and J. W. Loguen.

The mass of Negro voters, however, made no effort to join the Radical Abolition party, despite its name. They felt that its chances of success were remote to the point of fantasy, a prediction that proved all too true. This attitude of "why waste your vote" even affected Frederick Douglass, who in mid-August 1856 announced that he was switching his support to the Republicans. Like the great majority of Americans, white or black, Douglass wanted his vote to count for something more than the affirmation of an abstract principle, however noble. Compromise was unavoidable if a political party hoped to attract enough voters to win at the polls. Negroes soothed their consciences by reasoning that the Republican party had a chance to win, that its victory would prevent any extension of slavery into the territories, and that such a policy of containment would cause slavery to die out for lack of breathing space.

The Republicans looked less drab to the Negro when contrasted with the only major alternative party, the Democrats. A group of Ohio Negroes meeting early in 1856 voiced its support of the Republicans because the opposing party was "the black-hearted apostle of American Slavery." Later in the year, Henry Highland Garnet took the same position in urging New York State's six thousand black voters to come out for the Republicans. Of all the things he hated to see, said Garnet, the worst was a black Democrat, although he had to admit that there were some colored men who were "so ignorant and misguided as to favor these avowed supporters of the enslavement of their race." [45] Negro support of the new party became even more solid after its opponents dubbed its followers as "Black Republicans."

Whatever one party might call another, the key issue in the election was slavery in the territories. The Republicans lost at the polls, but their candidate, John C. Frémont, did amass a popular vote of 1,340,000 as against James Buchanan's 1.838,000. Such a large vote for the candidate of a party only two years old certainly augured a promising future, an optimism shared by the Negroes.

Essentially their policy was a continuing attack on the Democrats. At a convention of Negroes in Troy in September 1858, the fifty-five delegates avowed that they were Radical abolitionists at heart but that their strong desire to defeat the Democrats would lead them to throw their support to the Republicans. The convention appointed William J. Watkins as a traveling solicitor to drum up Republican votes. A month later Watkins went to Cincinnati to attend the state convention of colored men. Here at Union Baptist Church he added his voice to that of John Mercer Langston and others to the effect that the Democratic party must be destroyed. Support for the Republicans, while strong, did not meet with the same unanimity, Peter H. Clark asserting that the rights of the Negro were no safer with the Republicans than with the Democrats.[46]

Negroes in the Northeast, like those in Ohio and New York, gave their support to the Republicans. A convention of New England Negroes meeting at Tremont Temple on August 1, 1859, with George T. Downing in the chair, gave its endorsement to the new party. The delegates voted, however, to press the Republicans to give their support to the black man's struggle for the right to vote. By so doing, they pointed out, the party would deserve the support of all who favored the cause of freedom.[47]

By election time in 1860 the Negro vote was almost solidly Republican. Their only possible rivals for black ballots, the Radical Abolitionists, were weaker, if possible, than in 1856. And, as in that year, the Republicans, although making no effort to win the colored vote, were attacked by the Democrats as being "nigger worshipers." Negroes, if only to strike back, almost had to support the Republicans. Thus did the colored man ally himself with a party that was not as much a workingman's party as the Democrats were. But he could scarcely join a party that villified him.

The victory of the Republicans in 1860 heartened the Negroes and the voting abolitionists. There was, however, a sense of frustration over the decisive defeat, previously noted, of the equal suffrage amendment in New York. "We were overshadowed and smothered by the Presidential struggle— over laid by Abraham Lincoln and Hannibal Hamlin," wrote Frederick Douglass. "The black baby of Negro Suffrage was thought too ugly to exhibit on so grand an occasion."[48] Hence, while the elections of 1860 were more favorable for the antislavery crusaders than in any preceding quadrennial campaign, it was evident that racial discrimination and its sustaining base of slavery still exerted a formidable influence.

In striking at slavery the abolitionists made use of a political instrument far more time-honored than the suffrage—the right to petition for a redress of grievances. Those whose voting privileges were restricted, as in the case of the black American, were particularly petition-minded. A state convention of Illinois Negroes, held in Alton in mid-November 1856, urged the colored people to avail themselves of the right to petition inasmuch as it was "the only constitutional guarantee now inviolate from the ruffianism of American Slavery." Two years later an Ohio convention of Negroes pointed out that the right to assemble and petition for a redress of grievances was one of the few rights left to colored people in the United States.[49]

Black Americans hardly needed any reminder of the right to petition, a practice they had been making use of since colonial and Revolutionary War times. And they needed even less advice as to what to petition for, having during the course of the eighteenth century sued either for their personal freedom or, as in the case of Paul Cuffe in Massachusetts in 1780, for the suffrage. The new century was hardly two days old when a petition from a group of Negroes from Philadelphia was brought before the House of Representatives. The petition, which had been circulated among Negroes by James Forten and churchmen Absalom Jones and Richard Allen, asked the House to adopt such measures "as shall in due course emancipate the whole of their brethren from their present situation." For a beginning step that might be taken, the petition mentioned a revision of the laws governing the slave trade and fugitive slaves. After two days of debate the members of the House overwhelmingly rejected the petition, alleging that it asked them to legislate on matters over which they had no control. One lone member voted for the measure, George Thatcher of Massachusetts, whose championship James Forten never forgot.[50]

With the coming of the new abolitionists after 1830, the use of the petition reached flood proportions. To put his name down on a long sheet of paper under a statement condemning slavery became second nature to a new-school abolitionist, even to a follower of Garrison who decried such political activity as voting or holding office. The massive abolition petition against slavery began in 1835 and, it is hardly necessary to add, with the full backing of the black abolitionists.

Three years earlier the Massachusetts General Colored Association, meeting in Boston, had voted to send a petition to Congress to abolish slavery in the District of Columbia. During the following spring at two meetings held at the African Masonic Hall in Boston, Maria W. Stewart gave an analysis of the Negro's problem and suggested a step for its solution. "Most of our color," she said, "have been taught to stand in fear of the white man from their earliest infancy, to work as soon as they can walk, and call 'master' before they could scarce lisp the name of 'mother.' " What should be done about changing things? "Let every man sign a petition to abolish slavery in the District of Columbia, and grant you the rights and privileges of common citizens." [51]

A few weeks later, on June 16, 1833, a petition was drafted in the name of twelve hundred Negroes of Providence, Rhode Island, and sent to Andrew Jackson. Reminding the Chief Executive of his commendation of the Negro troops under him at the Battle of New Orleans in January 1815, the Providence Negroes urged Jackson to free the slaves in the District of Columbia and in the territories of Arkansas and Florida, and entreated him not to forget "the million of our brethren and sisters still in slavery." [52]

Hundreds of abolitionist petitions were directed against the annexation of the Republic of Texas, which had won its independence from Mexico in 1836. If Texas came into the Union, it would come in, as abolitionists well knew, as a slave state. The New York Vigilance Society was one of the Negro groups that opposed the annexation. At the Broadway Tabernacle on August 1, 1837, the society opened a booth at which passers-by could sign a petition against the admission of Texas and against slavery in the District. A year earlier, at its first annual meeting, the American Moral Reform Society had gone on record as opposing Texas annexation. They had also thanked John Quincy Adams for having fought to maintain the right to petition, irrespective of color or condition.[53]

Although himself not an abolitionist, Adams had become an admired figure among them as a consequence of his fight against the "gag rule." First passed in the House of Representatives in May 1836, this was a measure declaring that all petitions relating to slavery should be laid on the table, not sent to a committee and reported back, as was customary. This measure backfired, however, since it struck at a basic constitutional right. Abolitionists became more petition-minded than ever. And Adams became their chief means of transmission, presenting petition after petition, despite the threats of his House colleagues to censure or expel him.

One of the largest petitions ever reaching the Washington office of Congressman Adams was an immense roll of paper about the size of a barrel. It bore 51,862 signatures, headed by the name, George Latimer. A runaway slave from Norfolk, Virginia, Latimer had been arrested and placed in a Boston jail in October 1842. Abolitionists and Negroes rallied to his defense, attempting to have him released by a writ of habeas corpus. When this proved unsuccessful the abolitionists held a mass meeting at Faneuil Hall on October 30, followed by a series of "Latimer meetings" throughout the state. "I have never known people so aroused before," wrote Samuel E. Sewall, legal counsel for Latimer and one of the speakers at the Faneuil Hall gathering.[54]

To co-ordinate the abolitionist protest a Latimer Committee was appointed, made up of Henry I. Bowditch, William F. Channing, and Frederick Cabot. This trio brought out a weekly, *The Latimer Weekly and North Star*. Another committee operation was the promotion of two monster petitions, one to the state legislature and another to the national legislature. The "Great Massachusetts Petition" called for a state law forbidding the use of public property or the services of public officials in the detention or arrest of any alleged fugitive. The "Great Petition to Congress" asked that such laws or amendments be passed as would separate the people of Massachusetts from all connection with slavery.[55]

The two Latimer petitions won the full support of Negroes. Indeed, five months before Latimer was arrested a group of Boston Negroes had pledged themselves to draft a petition to the incoming state legislature which would prohibit citizens and officials of Massachusetts from aiding slaveholders in seizing and returning fugitives. They also unanimously agreed to petition Congress to repeal the Fugitive Slave Law of 1793. Late in November, at a meeting held at the Belknap Street Baptist Church, a Negro gathering protested the imprisonment of Latimer and pledged themselves to support the two petitions being circulated by the Latimer Committee. At Hartford's Fifth Congregational Church, on November 17, 1842, the Reverend J. W. C. Pennington delivered a sermon on the Latimer case, "Covenants Involving Moral Wrong Not Obligatory Upon Man." Don't let Charles Dickens hear of the Latimer case, pleaded Pennington, lest he write an addendum to his *Notes on America*.[56]

If the Latimer case did not reach international proportions it was due to the uneasiness of James B. Gray, the owner of Latimer. Surprised by the depth of feeling which the case aroused throughout New England and fearful of the counter-charges launched by Latimer's legal advisers, Gray decided to sell him for $400. The abolitionists were highly pleased at this turn of events, but they did not propose to abandon their petition drive. By mid-February 1843 the two petitions were delivered to their respective destinations. The petition to the

Massachusetts legislature, bearing 64,526 signatures and weighing 150 pounds, was delivered at the state house on February 17, 1843, by Charles Francis Adams. Five weeks later the legislature passed a measure dubbed by the delighted abolitionists as the "Latimer Statute," because it was so closely modeled after their petition.

A similar fate eluded the companion petition that went to John Quincy Adams in Washington. This petition shared a common graveyard with such previous still-borns as the one from nine Negro women in Fredericksburg, Virginia, presented by Adams in February 1837, the petition from New York Negroes in June 1838 protesting against the treatment of American colored seamen in Cuba, and the petition by Boston Negroes in October 1842 bitterly complaining about the treatment given to black sailors in five Southern states. But if such petitions got nowhere, it was not the fault of those presenting them, and John Quincy Adams continued to receive expressions of high esteem from Negroes.[57]

His death in 1848, four years after the repeal of the "gag rule," was widely mourned by Negroes. Commemorative meetings were held by colored people in Detroit, Cincinnati, Buffalo, New York, and Philadelphia.[58] Adams had never been a professing abolitionist, and his bald and pot-bellied exterior hardly cast him in a heroic mold. But to Negroes he was a fearless advocate of the rights of man, and this was a breed none too numerous, as their experience had taught them.

To the various state legislatures in the North came petitions from Negro residents. As a rule these memorials dealt with discriminatory measures, impending or already enacted, against colored people. These petitions had one other thing in common—their instigators were almost invariably active abolitionists. For example, the eleven-page memorial sent to the Pennsylvania assembly in March 1832, protesting against a proposed bill severely limiting Negro migration to Pennsylvania, was planned at a meeting at which James C. McCrummell was chairman and Jacob C. White was secretary. The petition was worded by three men of equal reputation as black abolitionists—James Forten, Robert Purvis, and William Whipper.

In their petitions to state legislatures, then, Negroes were not addressing themselves solely to local or internal grievances. They were at the same time leveling their pieces at much bigger game—the jungle king of slavery.

Abolitionists found that political activity brought some gains. But it had its limitations. Petitions were of little good unless they were followed up. Voting for a winning candidate did not ensure the desired legislation. And even the law itself, particularly a new law, often turned out to be less binding than social and economic pressures. These strong pressures came to the fore in American life with a compelling urgency in the 1850's. And, with a twist that was not wholly surprising, they made their debut with a law relating to fugitive slaves.

IX

Protest's New Prophets

> *Thursday, May 25, 1854.* Did not intend to
> write this evening but another fugitive
> from bondage has been arrested like a
> criminal in the streets.
>
> Diary of Charlotte Forten

IT WAS the first time, this October 5, 1850, at twelve noon,
that New York Negroes had ever held a meeting in the public
park. But then there had never been so large a black audience
or so deeply moving an occasion. Five thousand people had
gathered to welcome home a fellow New Yorker who had been
gone hardly a week. Moreover, he was dressed as a laborer
and hence could hardly have been a community leader or
member of the black elite. But when the thirty-year-old porter
stood up, after being introduced by the presiding officer, the
audience cheered with deafening effect, drowning out the sob-
bing and the crying, some of which came from the guest of
honor himself.

For this man was a fugitive slave, James Hamlet, who had
been seized on the streets of New York nine days earlier. Hamlet had offered as his defense the fact that he was a free man,
having entitled himself to his freedom. But his line of reasoning lacked admissible legal precedent; in fact, the testimony of
an alleged fugitive was invalid by law. Hence, Hamlet had
been arrested and returned to his Baltimore mistress. A few

days later, New York Negroes held a mass meeting at Mother Zion Church, with many whites present, for the purpose of raising enough money to buy Hamlet. Amid great enthusiasm, the purchase price of $800 was raised, one Negro, Isaac Hollenbeck, starting things off with a donation of $100.

Now Hamlet was home again, no longer melancholy but restored to his family, friends, and job. Standing before the gathering in the park, Hamlet waved his dampened handkerchief, while a bevy of women gathered around his wife and child—"such kissing and crying never were seen," wrote a contemporary. When things quieted down, there were speeches by William P. Powell, Charles B. Ray, John Peter Thompson, and Robert Hamilton. But there was none from Hamlet, his heart too full. "He is a free man—that is a speech itself," explained Hamilton. The exercises closed with the singing of a hymn, and then Hamlet was hoisted in the air and borne on shoulders through the park and to his home.[1]

The Hamlet case was hardly a victory over slavery, for, as William P. Powell had remarked, it was brought about not by the irresistible genius of universal emancipation but by the irresistible genius of the almighty dollar. What gave the Hamlet case its dramatic impact was its timing—it took place a week after President Fillmore had signed into law a measure that shook the North: its subject, the fugitive slave.

One of five measures known collectively as the Compromise of 1850, the Fugitive Slave Law provoked an unprecedented hue and cry. The law denied both the testimony of the alleged runaway and his right to a trial by jury, and it assumed his guilt rather than his innocence. Such a measure could have been swallowed by Congress only because it was part of a package. For it violated the basic concepts of American law and the procedural guarantees of the Constitution. Hence, it recharged the emotional slavery debate, greatly widening the breach between the sections. In the North the measure was condemned and defied, and in the South this condemnation and defiance was regarded as an act of bad faith.

The Fugitive Slave Law gave to the abolitionists a weapon which they would exploit to the hilt. In this chorus of condemnation no voices were louder than those of the Negro. But long before the abolitionist attack could reach its full proportions many runaway slaves living in the North had decided to take to the road again, this time to Canada. The law was ex post facto, reaching back to fugitives who had almost forgotten that they had not always been free. Former runaways feared that the law might be enforced, a view sustained in some legal quarters that were friendly to the slave. Upon passage of the law, George T. Downing and William P. Powell had written William Jay asking his advice on its constitutionality and binding force. The former judge had little for their comfort: "You ask me how you shall secure yourselves from the kidnapper. God only knows." Jay urged the Negroes not to turn to violence, to leave the pistol and the bowie knife to "Southern ruffians and their Northern mercenaries." [2]

A group of New York Negroes sought the advice of another friendly figure, Congressman Thaddeus Stevens of Pennsylvania, as to the constitutionality of the new law. Stevens replied that he had little hope that the measure would not be upheld by the federal courts. Hence he could "advise nothing better than the subjects of it put themselves beyond its reach." [3]

Many fugitive slaves, apprehensive of their freedom in the land of the Fugitive Slave Law, made ready to take their departure. The black exodus touched every Northern city with more than a handful of Negroes. This embraced even Boston, with its tradition of challenging unpopular laws and defying the official charged with enforcing them. Forty former slaves bade farewell to Boston within sixty hours after the fugitive slave bill became law. The city's colored churches were particularly hard hit. The African Methodist Church lost 85 members and the much small Zion Methodist Church lost 10. The First Baptist Church lost 40 of its 125 enrollees. The congregation of the Twelfth Baptist Church quickly dwindled from 141 to 81, and two of its deacons were retained only because the members had raised $1300 to buy their freedom. Some of these departees to Canada were relatives of runaways, and a few might have been freeborn Negroes who felt jeopardized. But in Boston, as elsewhere, the Fugitive Slave Law revealed that the number of runaways was greater than most people would have thought.

For members taking flight the churches in upstate New York could match those in Boston. The Baptist Colored Church of Buffalo lost 130 members after the pastor told the congregation that he found gospel precedent for running away but none that warranted fighting. At the Colored Baptist Church of Rochester the Kentucky-born pastor was the first to quit the city, and he was soon followed by 112 members of his flock, leaving two behind.[4]

At Pittsburgh a group of 200 Negroes left for Canada a few days before the signing of the Fugitive Slave Law. They carried firearms, having vowed that they would die before being taken back into slavery. Pittsburgh lost an additional 800 Negroes, over half of whom were relatives of runaways. Another Pennsylvania city, Columbia, lost 487 of its 943 Negroes during the five-year span after the passage of the law. William Whipper assisted many of the Canada-bound emigrants, helping them to sell such possessions as they could not carry, particularly houses and real estate.[5] At both Columbia and Pittsburgh a runaway who had been taken into custody was purchased by Negroes, Whipper heading the effort of Columbia and John B. Vashon at Pittsburgh.

To most Negroes, outright defiance was a more emotionally satisfying response to the Fugitive Slave Law than flight outside the country or raising money to pay a master. Hence, Ne-

groes throughout the North held Anti-Fugitive Slave Law
meetings. On October 2, 1850, some 1500 black New Yorkers jammed into the Zion Chapel for a protest meeting. The
presiding officer, William P. Powell, set the tone in a series of
opening questions: "You are told to submit peacefully to the
laws; will you do so? (No, no.) You are told to kiss the mana-
cles that bind you; will you do so? (No, no, no.)" Other
speakers took up this refrain, which was reaffirmed by the formal resolutions utterly repudiating a law "so repugnant to
every principle of justice." Before the meeting adjourned, two
petitions condemning the law were circulated, one to the state
legislature and the other to Congress. A week later the Negroes of Elmira vowed that they would defy the Fugitive
Slave Law at the sacrifice of their lives.[6]

Negroes elsewhere voiced similar sentiments. Ten days
after the Fugitive Slave Law went into operation a group of
Pittsburgh Negroes held a meeting at the public square. They
condemned the Pennsylvania congressmen who had supported
the "Slave Bill," which they declared to be a deadly blow at
liberty. The most stirring remarks came from Martin R. Delany, who said that he hoped that the ground would refuse his
body if a slaveholder crossed his threshold and he did not lay
him a lifeless corpse at his feet. An even more impassioned
statement came from Robert Purvis, presiding at the annual
meeting of the Pennsylvania Anti-Slavery Society at West
Chester on October 17, 1850. His eyes flashing, Purvis declared that "should any wretch enter my dwelling, any pale-
faced spectre among ye, to execute this law on me or mine, I'll
seek his life, I'll shed his blood." Parker Pillsbury, deeply
moved by the outburst, wrote that the Fugitive Slave Law was
revealed in all its horror when it could move a man like Purvis
"to such extremity." [7]

Negroes elsewhere shared the defiant mood of Delany and
Purvis. New York Negroes held a meeting which sanctioned
forcible resistance to the Fugitive Slave Law, the chairman

appointing a committee to assist endangered runaways. Less than a week after the passage of the measure, a "large and enthusiastic" group of Negroes met at Quinn Chapel in Chicago and proceeded to organize the Liberty Association. Forty-two men, working in teams, were to patrol the city, spying for possible slave-hunters. At Zanesville, Ohio, a group of Muskingum County Negroes met in November 1850 and formally declared that if they heard of anyone being arrested as a fugitive they would "leave our several employments" to come to his assistance. Two months later at a statewide meeting of colored citizens at Columbus the Fugitive Slave Law was denounced as "an outrage upon humanity." [8]

Boston Negroes held a protest meeting of a "resolute and enthusiastic character" at the Belknap Street Church on October 4, 1850. Following a series of addresses "of a most emphatic type," a resolution was adopted pledging its sponsors to resist unto death any attempt upon their liberties. But some of the fugitives who were present expressed the wish for a large-scale public expression of support.[9] These former slaves were apprehensive, having witnessed the departure, and anticipating the impending departure, of others of their kind.

Ten days later such a reassurance meeting was held at Faneuil Hall, an appropriate site. The call to the meeting had been signed by Josiah Quincy, former mayor of Boston, and 340 other white abolitionists. With hundreds milling outside the packed hall, the meeting allayed any fears as to abolitionist support in defying the law. On the platform the presiding officer, Charles Francis Adams, was flanked by Richard Henry Dana, substituting for the ailing Josiah Quincy, Theodore Parker, Wendell Phillip, Frederick Douglass, Charles Lenox Remond, and runaways William and Ellen Craft.

After stating the purpose of the meeting, Adams called upon Douglass, "to state the condition of the colored people under this new act of oppression." Arising amid an ovation, the much-sought-after orator and former slave did not mince words. Boston Negroes, he said, had vowed to die rather than return to bondage: "We must be prepared should this law be put into operation to see the streets of Boston running with blood." As if to bear out his assertion, Douglass recited the stories of fugitives who had exhibited unusual daring and courage. Then he asked the audience whether it would permit slaveholders to seize a Negro in Boston. Faneuil Hall's rafters echoed to the cry of "No." Douglass closed on a personal note, saying that a rumor had reached Rochester, where he lived, that a group of slave-hunters were after him and would visit his home. He had resolved to meet them and "as his house was rather small, and the party probably rather large, he went up to a trapdoor in the attic, in order to receive them one at a time." [10]

This forceful address set the tone for the remaining speeches and actions. Two resolutions were adopted: one calling for the repeal of the Fugitive Slave Law and the other proclaiming that Constitution or no Constitution, "We will not allow a fugitive slave to be taken from Massachusetts." A fifty-member Committee of Vigilance was empowered to set up an office to give advice and assistance to fugitive slaves. "I am happy to state," wrote Douglass the following morning, "that the public meeting held here last night had done much toward quieting the colored people." [11]

As it turned out, this optimism was shattered by an occurrence the very next day. Two agents of Dr. Robert Collins of Macon, Georgia, owner of William and Ellen Craft, had arrived in Boston and obtained warrants for their arrest. Wrote Douglass in a hurried dispatch to his weekly, "Mr. Craft is armed and resolved to stand his ground, and in less than an hour blood may flow in the streets of Boston." [12]

No blood was shed, but not because Craft was unarmed. The clergyman, Theodore Parker, had inspected his weapons, although confessing that it was rather a new business for him. But Parker's analysis bore a professional ring:

His powder had a good kernel, and he kept it dry; his pistols were of excellent proof, the barrels true and clean; the trigger went easy; the caps would not hang fire at the snap. I tested his poinard; the blade had a good temper, stiff enough, yet springy withal; the point was sharp.[13]

When Henry I. Bowditch offered to drive Craft across town the former slave agreed upon condition that Bowditch arm himself. The two drove in Bowditch's buggy, Craft with a revolver in one hand and a pistol in the other.[14]

The two agents of Collins were told that they had better get out of Boston, and one of them heeded the advice. However, the Crafts decided that they, too, would leave. Upon the advice of well-wishers they hastened out of the country, having received $250 from the Boston Vigilance Committee to pay their passage to England. But the attending excitement did not die down; the Craft's episode proved to be but one in a highly dramatic series involving the rendition of runaways.

Defiance of the Fugitive Slave Law became a new commandment to abolitionists throughout the North. The rescue of slaves who had been taken in custody did not begin in 1850, however. It was something that Negroes had been doing for nearly two decades. In the early summer of 1833 a group of Detroit Negroes rescued two slaves, wounding the sheriff in the process and leading the mayor to issue a call for federal troops. In the following spring, several Negroes in Philadelphia were sent to the penitentiary for an attempt to seize a slave from the police, the court having authorized his delivery to his master.[15]

Late in July 1836 Boston was the scene of a rescue which came to be known as the "Abolition Riot." Two slaves, Eliza Small and Polly Ann Bates, were claimed as runaway slaves belonging to John B. Morris of Baltimore and brought to court. While the attorney for Morris was addressing the judge, someone in the spectator's section shouted, "Go, go." Whereupon some colored people rushed to the bench and bore the prisoners down the courthouse steps and shoved them into a waiting carriage. A colored woman "of great size," who scrubbed floors for a living, threw her arms around the neck of one officer, immobilizing him.[16] Eliza and Polly were never recaptured, and their abettors went scot-free, although Sheriff C. P. Sumner, father of Charles Sumner, was criticized for permitting such a breach of the peace.

In Chicago in October 1846, while the case of two runaway slaves from Missouri was in progress in court, a crowd of Negroes and their white sympathizers gathered around the officers and carried the slaves away. At Pittsburgh a year later a group of Negroes seized a runaway from two Virginia constables who had placed him under arrest.[17]

Up to 1850 the rescuing of fugitive slaves had been a business conducted almost exclusively by Negroes. The Fugitive Slave Law of that year brought an influx of new blood into the work. This the Negro abolitionists welcomed heartily. But they did not use it as an excuse to retire to the sidelines. The Shadrach rescue is a case in point.

An employee at the Cornhill Coffee House in Boston, Fred Wilkins, or Shadrach as he was popularly known, was seized at noon on February 15, 1851, and rushed to the courthouse with his waiter's apron still on. The news spread as if with wings, the Negro residential section being nearby. Five lawyers, including Robert Morris, a Negro, had just succeeded in obtaining a court delay to prepare for the defense when the rescue took place. A group of some fifty Negroes pressed into the courtroom, lifted Shadrach in the air, and bore him to the street. His clothes half torn off, Shadrach was placed in a carriage and soon the rescued and the rescuers were moving away "like a black squall." There was no pursuit, the seizure having been so sudden and unexpected.

Taking refuge in Canada, Shadrach was beyond the reach of American law. But some of his rescuers did not escape legal action. On February 18, 1851, President Fillmore issued a special proclamation ordering that proceedings be commenced against the "aiders or abettors in this flagitious offense." Robert Morris and Lewis Hayden were among those indicted for complicity in the rescue. Neither was ever sentenced. On June 16, 1851, the jury trying Hayden reported that it had been unable to reach a verdict. Five months later the Morris case came to an end. The federal authorities had tried to charge him with treason but the grand jury had him bound over for a misdemeanor. On November 11, 1851, the jury that heard the case, *United States v. Robert Morris*, returned a verdict of not guilty.

Boston had two cases of runaways being sent back to slavery, but in each instance the Fugitive Slave Law won a clouded victory at best. Early in April 1851, while the abolitionists were still in the pleasant afterglow of the Shadrach rescue, Thomas Sims, a fugitive from Georgia, was seized. Sims was rushed to the courthouse, a gloomy, granite building that the federal authorities had to use as a jail, Massachusetts law preventing the use of state facilities for fugitive slave purposes. Legal efforts to free Sims were unsuccessful.

A plot to effect his escape was equally abortive. Leonard A. Grimes visited Sims and told him that a mattress would be placed outside his window at a certain hour and that he was to jump and land on it and be spirited away. But before the scheme could be put into operation the courthouse authorities put bars on every window. Taking additional precautions, especially to secure the doorways, they placed an iron chain around the building, already encircled by a hundred policemen.

Shortly before sunrise on April 13, Sims was marched to the Long Wharf to be shipped back to slavery. Despite the early hour one hundred abolitionists were present, marching solemnly behind a cordon of policemen three times their number. As Sims, tear-streaked but erect, marched up the gangplank, someone cried out, "Sims, preach liberty to the slaves." [18] The sorrowing abolitionists made their way back to the antislavery office, pausing on State Street at the spot where the black Crispus Attucks fell in the Boston Massacre of March 5, 1770, an event signaling the Revolutionary War.

Sims was gone but he left behind more than the coat he wore on the day he was seized, as prized as it became among abolitionists. His seizure gave to the recently reorganized Vigilance Committee a reason for being, thus attracting new supporters and swelling its coffers. Many of its meetings were held at the home of Lewis Hayden. In 1851 the committee assisted sixty-nine fugitives of record. It had on its payroll forty-nine Negroes who harbored slaves pending their final disposition.[19] John S. Rock, then practicing medicine rather than law, was paid by the committee for his services to sick fugitives.

Despite the efforts of Boston abolitionists, white and black, a runaway slave was taken from the city in the spring of 1854. This was the celebrated Anthony Burns, who had learned to read and write in slavery, having had a kindly disposed master. Late in May 1854 Burns was arrested as a fugitive slave and put in irons. Two days later an attempt was made to storm the courthouse and seize Burns, but the attack was repulsed, one of the deputies, however, being shot and killed. During the following week, while the city awaited the commissioner's decision, feeling ran high. "Beg our colored friends to bear and forbear," wrote John Greenleaf Whittier. "Oh let them beware of violence." The black people thronged around the courthouse, showing their sympathy by watching around the clock.[20]

Burns needed sympathy, as United States Commissioner Edward G. Loring had returned a verdict in favor of his master. Richard Henry Dana and Leonard Grimes hastened to the courthouse to be with the prisoner and attempt to raise his spirits. Later that day many shops were hung in black, and a huge coffin was strung over State Street. "Our worst fears are realized," wrote sixteen-year-old Charlotte Forten in her diary for June 2, 1854. "A cloud seems hanging over me, over all our persecuted race, which nothing can dispel." [21]

One thing remained—to get Burns from the courthouse to the wharf to be put aboard a revenue cutter that was bound for Virginia. From the courthouse door a loaded gun was mounted and from the courthouse to the wharf the streets were lined with police. In the center of the armed posse marched Burns. He had expected to have Dana and Grimes walking beside him but the marshal of the posse had gone back on his word to permit such an arrangement.

Fifty thousand spectators witnessed the procession as it made its way past buildings draped in black. One of these viewers was a good-looking young Negro girl whose teeth were clenched and whose eyes were tearful. Samuel Gridley Howe attempted to console her, saying that Burns would not be hurt. "Hurt!" she said, "I cry for shame that he will not kill himself!—oh! why is he not man enough to kill himself!" [22]

Charlotte Forten expressed the belief that very few clergymen would speak against "the cruel outrage on humanity" represented by the rendition of Burns. The fearless Theodore Parker could be numbered in that select company, preaching a sermon which asserted that "in the wicked week of 1854" Massachusetts was one of the inferior counties of Virginia and Boston but a suburb of Alexandria. It is hardly surprising that when William J. Watkins had heard Parker six months earlier he had come to the conclusion that no man preached more truth.[23]

The rendition of Anthony Burns left the abolitionists frustrated and angry. But its sequel was more to their liking. The revulsion of feeling throughout Massachusetts prompted the legislature to pass a more comprehensive personal liberty law in 1855, one which practically made the Fugitive Slave Law a dead letter in the Bay State. Public opinion was changing, with abolitionists coming to be regarded less as traitors and more as patriots.

Moreover, Burns remained a slave for less than a year. His new master, unlike his predecessor, was willing to set him at liberty for a price. With money raised in abolitionist circles, Leonard A. Grimes went to Baltimore to complete the transaction and accompanied Burns back to the free states and a joyous welcome. Shortly thereafter he entered Oberlin, where he remained for two years before enrolling at the Fairmount Theological Seminary at Cincinnati.[24]

Except in the far West the defiance of the Fugitive Slave Law was widespread. The locale of slave rescues ranged from Massachusetts to the Middle Atlantic States and those bordering the Great Lakes and known collectively as the Old Northwest. Three representative examples of slave recaptures may be briefly noted, including the typical role played by black activists.

In New York the most celebrated instance of the law's defiance was the rescue of William Henry on October 1, 1851, at Syracuse. A muscular mulatto who went by the name "Jerry," he was known to be a runaway, but his conduct had been above reproach and his employer, C. P. Williston, had found no complaint with his work as a cooper. Seized and taken to the federal commissioner's office, Jerry was in the process of being indicted when he slipped his guard and dashed out of the building and down the street. But, being manacled, he was caught by the police, and after a stiff fight the battered and disheveled prisoner was returned to the commissioner's office.

The news of the incident spread rapidly, and within a few hours the abolitionists had formulated a rescue plan. Shortly after eight o'clock that evening a group of men dashed into the police office, overwhelmed the guards by sheer numbers, battered down the door to the room Jerry was in, and took him. The first persons reaching him were two Negroes, Peter Hollenbeck and William Gray, the latter a runaway. Jerry was first taken to the home of a colored man, where his shackles were removed. Then, to avoid suspicion, he was removed to the home of a white friend. Here he remained in hiding for five days before beginning his journey to Kingston, Ontario.[25]

Someone had to face the music, and the federal government proceeded to indict eighteen of the rescuers. Samuel Ringgold Ward, who claimed to have assisted in filing off Jerry's chains, hastened to Montreal. From this retreat he wrote to George Whipple of the American Missionary Association offering his services in the Canadian field.[26] Another equally well-known black abolitionist, Jermain W. Loguen, also made his way to Her Majesty's dominions. Loguen took the step in response to his wife's urgings. Two months later, on December 2, 1851, he wrote to Governor Hunt requesting protection should he return to Syracuse.

Along with Loguen four other Negroes were indicted, Prince Jackson, William Thompson, Harrison Allen, and Enoch Reed. Only three of the eighteen rescuers were put on trial, and only one of these, Enoch Reed, was found guilty. He died pending an appeal which he would have undoubtedly won.[27]

The Jerry rescue, in common with others of its kind, had great significance to abolitionists. They did not propose to let it die. Annually until the Civil War the reformers in western

New York commemorated October 1 as Jerry Rescue Day. At the first anniversary, typical of those which followed, some twenty-five hundred abolitionists came together, including William H. Topp, Frederick Douglass, William G. Allen, and the short-time emigrant, Jermain W. Loguen. White participants included Daniel Drayton of the *Pearl*, Samuel J. May, William Lloyd Garrison, and suffragists Lucretia Mott and young Lucy Stone. The speeches that lacked eloquence were not wanting in earnestness. Perhaps the palm went to a practiced scene-stealer. "Frederick Douglass gave us some of the thunder of the Gods," wrote William G. Allen. "Some say that his was the speech of the morning, but I must confess that my heart palpitated toward Lucy," added that ever gallant youthful professor of belles-lettres.[28]

The attempted rendition of Jerry took place less than a month before the far more upsetting and highly publicized "Christiana Riot," the first defiance of the Fugitive Slave Law resulting in bloodshed. To Christiana, a town in southern Pennsylvania, came Edward Gorsuch on September 11, 1851, from bordering Maryland in search of his four escaped slaves. Gorsuch and his party of six went to the home of William Parker, whom he suspected of harboring one or more of the fugitives. Himself a runaway from Maryland, Parker was in no mood to release an alleged slave, a feeling shared by the other Negroes in the town. Still vivid in their memory was the midnight seizure of a Negro six months previously, his abductors, a slave-hunting band known as the Gag Gang, having produced no warrant.

When Gorsuch demanded that Parker permit him to enter the house, the latter's wife, Eliza Ann, herself a former runaway, blew a large dinner horn, a signal which summoned some two dozen Negroes to the scene. Soon an exchange of shots took place, resulting in the death of Gorsuch and the wounding of his son. Thereupon the outnumbered besiegers, already in no mood to press matters, withdrew.

Forty-five marines and a civil posse of fifty men were dispatched to restore order. The acting Secretary of State, W. S. Derrick, assured the governor of Maryland that the President deplored this violation of the rights of the citizens of his state and that the federal government would exercise all its powers in bringing the offenders to book. Thirty-eight persons, thirty-five of them Negroes, were arrested on the charge of treason. Missing among these was Parker and the Gorsuch slaves, all safe by then in Canada.[29]

Negroes throughout the country held meetings to raise money for legal counsel for the defendants, to make their stay in prison more comfortable and to provide relief for their families. At Philadelphia in the space of four months a Special Vigilance Committee in behalf of the Christiana Sufferers raised $663.41, of which $250 came from Negro contributors in San Francisco. In two successive weeks the Negroes of New York City held meetings with such speakers as Charles B. Ray, J. McCune Smith, William P. Powell, William J. Wilson, J. W. C. Pennington, and white Lewis W. Paine, who had spent six years in a Georgia prison for giving assistance to a runaway. A meeting of Negroes at Columbus, Ohio, late in September 1851, hailed the "victorious heroes at the battle of Christiana." At a meeting of the colored citizens of Chicago the prosperous tailor, John Jones, was appointed chairman of a committee to receive donations, the Ladies of Chicago Mutual Protection Society subscribing $10 on the spot.[30]

The defendants spent three months in jail, but none was found guilty of the charge of treason; indeed, the cases were dropped after the first one resulted in an acquittal. Again the abolitionists had won a large measure of popular sympathy. There would be no annual observance of the Christiana affair, but its site became something of a shrine. When William

Wells Brown came to Christiana in 1858 to deliver an August
First lecture, he visited the Parker house and the spot where
Gorsuch fell. Brown came away with the impression that no
master would ever come there again in pursuit of his fugitive
slave.[31]

Ohio's most dramatic confrontation between those on the
opposite sides of the Fugitive Slave Law was the Oberlin-
Wellington rescue case. John Price, living at Oberlin, was
seized in September 1858 as a runaway slave and rushed to
Wellington, nine miles away, to await a southbound train.
Learning of the act, some fifty Oberlin citizens and college
students hastened to Wellington and freed the captive, sending him on to Canada. Warrants were issued against thirty-
seven of the resuers, including twelve Negroes. Only two of
the accused were put to trial, one of them being Charles H.
Langston, the thin-visaged, thirty-eight-year-old brother of
John Mercer Langston.

The jury found Charles guilty. Permitted by the judge to
make a statement before sentence was passed, Langston delivered an impassioned address before the crowded courtroom,
the spectators breaking out in cheers and clapping and the
judge threatening to clear the chambers unless it stopped.
Langston asserted that it was ridiculous to say that a law taking away a man's liberty was constitutional; he charged the
judge, jury, and his court-appointed legal counsel with being
prejudiced, and he alluded to his father's service under Lafay-
ette in the Revolutionary War. It was, wrote brother John
Mercer Langston, a "speech in the interest of the abolition
cause." But it deeply impressed the judge, as he admitted in
giving Langston the minimum sentence of twenty days in jail
and $100 fine, plus the costs of the suit. Even so, the verdict
provoked widespread protest, capped by a monster meeting in
Cleveland on May 24, 1859. Langston served his time, re-

suming his duties as secretary of the Ohio Anti-Slavery Society upon his release.[32]

Langston and his fellow defendants had won a large measure of public sympathy. They had always been assured of support in Negro circles, a convention of colored men of Ohio sending a vote of thanks to those who had "rescued John Price from the bloody hands of a heartless slaveholder and the ruffian Deputy United States Marshal and his mercenary posse." [33]

Langston was not alone in serving a sentence for defying the Fugitive Slave Law. In Philadelphia in March 1860, a group of Negroes rushed upon a carriage moving toward the Baltimore depot and bearing back to slavery a recaptured runaway, Moses Horner. But in this instance the tables were turned, the rescuers themselves being seized. Arrested and charged with obstructing the law and rioting, each of the five —Alfred M. Green, St. Clair Burley, Jeremiah Buck, Basil Hall, and Richard Williams—was fined $25 and given a thirty-day sentence.

Two days after the seizures a mass meeting was held at the Philadelphia Institute expressing sympathy for those attempting to rescue Moses Horner, "alleged fugitive." A little later Frances Ellen Watkins sounded a widely held sentiment in praising the imprisoned men, assuring them that it was a privilege to do the humblest deed for freedom.[34]

Such moral support may have had some influence on the men serving time. Alfred M. Green sent a long letter to John C. Bowers, addressed from "Cherry Hill Prison, Summer Retreat," saying that although he was being well treated under the circumstances, he was lonely, seeing no one except for the jailer three times a day. But, concluded Green, he was sustained by the reflection that God was just and that His retributive powers would one day "be meted out on this guilty, hypocritical and ungodly nation." [35]

The jail sentence of the Moses Horner Five, like that of the

others charged with the same offense, simply added to the out-
cry against the Fugitive Slave Law. Thus had this unpopular
measure enabled the abolitionists to bring hundreds of thousands around to their way of thinking. This enactment dramatized the fugitive slave issue, giving to the Negro-originated
runaway rescue work a much greater increase in strength and
scope, although with little change in basic principle.

Although destined to strengthen greatly the abolitionist
cause, the Fugitive Slave Law of 1850 did cause many Negroes to re-examine the whole matter of leaving the United
States. In April 1852 the staunch abolitionist, James G.
Birney, in a letter to Frederick Douglass, expressed the belief
that Negroes would do well to go elsewhere inasmuch as they
could not hope to enjoy their just rights in America.[36] By
1852 this point of view was meeting with a less frigid reception among Negroes, perhaps one quarter of them having
reached an open mind on colonization.

This new receptiveness to an old idea had its notable converts. Foremost among these was Martin R. Delany. Remaining harshly critical of the American Colonization Society,
Delany nonetheless came to share its pessimism about the Negro's future in America. In his book, *The Condition, Elevation, Emigration, and Destiny of the Colored People of the
United States, Politically Considered*, published in 1852, he
reprinted in full the entire ten sections of the Fugitive Slave
Law of 1850, as an illustration of the plight of the Negro.
The remedy for prejudice and discrimination in America was
departure therefrom, wrote Delany: "That there have been
people in all ages under certain circumstances, that may be
benefited by emigration, will be admitted; and that there are
circumstances under which emigration is absolutely necessary
to their political elevation, cannot be disputed."

Delany was joined by young H. Ford Douglas of Illinois,

whose views were eloquently stated at a National Emigration Congress held in Cleveland in August 1854. Is not the history of the world the history of emigration, he asked? Asserting that moving away was the best resort of an oppressed people, Douglas stated that he was willing to forget the enduring names of home and country and, as an unwilling exile, seek on other shores the freedoms denied him in the land of his birth.[37]

James Theodore Holly was an associate of Delany and young Douglas in advancing emigration. A shoemaker by trade, Holly had by the private study of theology become rector of St. Luke's Church in New Haven. In 1850 he was in friendly correspondence with the American Colonization Society and was therefore ready to support the thrust for emigration following the Fugitive Slave Law. Holly held that even if the American Negro won political rights it would do him little good because he would still face "a social proscription stronger than conventional legislation." [38]

One of emigration's greatest proselytes was the influential Henry Highland Garnet, whose conversion antedated the Fugitive Slave Law. "I hesitate not to say that my mind of late has greatly changed in regard to the American Colonization scheme," he wrote on January 21, 1848. "I would rather see a man free in Liberia than a slave in the United States." A year later he said that he favored colonization to any country that promised freedom and enfranchisement to the Negro.[39]

Like Garnet, some emigrationists expressed an open mind as to which country the Negro might go. The National Emigration Convention of 1854 had appointed agents to investigate the possibilities of Haiti, Central America, and the Niger Valley. But most emigrationists had some special place or region that in their opinion held special advantages.

Liberia had its drum-beaters, including Garnet himself. It had become independent in 1847, thus adding to its appeal. Two years later Garnet expressed the opinion that Liberia would not only be a success but that it would become the Empire State of Africa.[40] With the demise in 1858 of the National Emigration Convention it is hardly surprising that Garnet would become the founder and president of the African Civilization Society, with the avowed purpose of bringing about "the civilization and chrisitanization" of the Dark Continent.

Many emigrationists expressed a preference for the American tropics rather than faraway Liberia. The foremost exponent of intertropical colonization was James T. Holly, who held that Negroes "have the most inveterate prejudice against being separated from the New World." Journeying to Haiti in the summer of 1855, Holly met with a cordial reception and received glowing promises as to the treatment of prospective emigrants. He returned to America a lover of Haiti for life. He told Negro audiences in Connecticut, Ohio, and Michigan that it was their duty to link their destiny with their heroic brethren in that independent island.

If Holly found few emigrationists who shared his enthusiasm it was in part due to the superior allure of Canada. In the three months following the passage of the Fugitive Slave Law some three thousand Negroes fled to Canada, and in the ten years after 1850 the number reached over fifteen thousand. Canada had its black supporters, including runaways like Henry Bibb and Samuel Ringgold Ward. But it also won the approval of free Negroes like H. Ford Douglas, William H. Day, and William Whipper, the last asserting that many black men were getting along well in Canada and were thereby "doing a more practical anti-slavery work than they were capable of performing in the States." [41]

The chief protagonist of Canadian emigration was Mary Ann Shadd, daughter of abolitionist Abraham Shadd. Slender and somewhat tall, Miss Shadd combined an attractive femininity with an imperious manner, a combination enabling her to overawe a hostile audience or to outstare a segregation-minded streetcar conductor. To let Negro Americans know about conditions in Canada, Miss Shadd published *The Provincial Freeman* from 1854 to 1858, with headquarters first at Toronto and later at Chatham. The *Freeman* was a well-edited weekly, with due note for its predilection to contrast the alleged progress of the Negro in Canada with his alleged stagnation in the United States. In promoting emigration Miss Shadd made frequent trips to Northern cities, holding lectures, seeking subscribers to the weekly, and soliciting funds. At Shiloh Church in Philadelphia on November 19, 1855, Eilzabeth Taylor Greenfield (the "Black Swan") gave a benefit concert for Miss Shadd, paying the piano accompanist herself and scheduling a larger repetoire than usual because of the inclusion of a group of antislavery songs.[42]

Although sincere and not easily misled, Miss Shadd in her speeches and writings gave an overly optimistic assessment of the Negro's lot in Canada. Indeed, the formation of many all-Negro communities there, a development to which Miss Shadd objected, was in part a normal reaction of a people who felt discriminated against or unwanted. And, of course, all-Negro settlements also stemmed from the related aim of proving that the black man was not inferior, that given a chance he could develop to the fullest the talents that were his. Thus a successful communal experiment would affirm the abolitionist contention that the Negro was fit for something more than a slave. That such experiments were, with one exception, short-lived stemmed from many causes. But crucial among them, however dimly perceived at the time, was the necessity for "changing white attitudes as well as black." [43]

The emergence of emigrationist sentiment in the 1850's inevitably encountered opposition. During the thirties and forties Negro leaders had continued to denounce the American Colonization Society, climaxed by a two-day session at Shiloh Presbyterian Church in New York in April 1849. The meeting was called to refute the charge allegedly made in England by a member of the colonization society to the effect that the Negro people now gave it their support. At the two-day meeting an imposing roster of speakers gave testimony to the contrary, among them Boston Crummell, J. W. Pennington, Ransom F. Wake, William F. Powell, Charles B. Ray, Henry Bibb, Charles Reason, George T. Downing, Frederick Douglass, and Charles Lenox Remond. But the American Colonization Society had scarcely needed his reminder of its unpopularity among Negroes; one of its branches had publicly noted that, although Negroes in Philadelphia had held a celebration when the French Republic outlawed slavery in its West Indies possessions, no Negro group anywhere had held a celebration when Liberia became independent.[44]

In the spring of 1851 John Jones of Chicago wrote that no convention of colored men "for sixteen or twenty years" had failed to condemn emigration. But, he added, "the enemy still lives." Hence the Negroes continued their attack, adding no argument that was new although voicing more doubt as to the validity of calling Africa their home. "What do I know of Africa?" queried William H. Topp of Albany, at the annual meeting of the Pennsylvania Anti-Slavery in 1852. "I am part Indian and part German." A year earlier a group of New York Negroes stated that they did not trace their ancestors to Africa alone—"We trace it to Englishmen, Irishmen, Scotchmen; to the German; to the Asiatic, as well as to Africa. The best blood of Virginia courses through our veins." [45]

The Negro's opposition to emigration embraced those who seemed to sanction it. Late in 1852 Governor Washington Hunt of New York, in a message to the state legislature, recommended that an appropriation be made to the American Colonization Society. New York City Negroes went into action, calling meetings on January 8 and January 13 at which they decided to send a delegation to Albany to visit Hunt. On January 20 George T. Downing, William H. Topp, and Stephen Myers went to Hunt's office. Wishing to be thought friendly to the colored people, Hunt received them in a gracious fashion and listened to their carefully prepared objections to his proposals. The delegates unquestionably made a favorable impression on the governor, and they left with the feeling that if a bill appropriating money for colonization ever reached his desk he would never sign it.[46]

To Negroes opposing colonization Harriet Beecher Stowe posed a somewhat more difficult and delicate problem than that of Governor Hunt. For while Mrs. Stowe's *Uncle Tom's Cabin* was written fundamentally from an abolitionist point of view, and while it had "fired up" many slaves to make the dash for liberty, upon the word of no less an authority than William Still,[47] nevertheless the book had a great flaw. George Harris, one of its leading characters, had remarked that the desire and yearning of his soul was for "an African nationality," and under such a compulsive influence Harris had sailed for Liberia.

At the annual meeting of the American and Foreign Anti-Slavery Society in New York in May 1853, George T. Downing and Charles B. Ray expressed regret that Mrs. Stowe had ever written the chapter favoring colonization, Ray adding that he hoped that something could be done to counteract its influence. Downing later reaffirmed his regret that Mrs. Stowe left one of her main characters in Africa, "in fact, the only one that really betrays any other than the subservient, submissive, Uncle Tom spirit, which has been the cause of so much disrespect felt for the colored man." From a correspondent of a Negro weekly came an even more strongly worded condemnation: "Uncle Tom must be killed, George Harris exiled! Heaven for dead Negroes! Liberia for living mulattoes. Neither can live on the American continent. Death or banishment is our doom, say the Slaveocrats, the Colonizationists, and, save the mark—Mrs. Stowe!!"[48]

Leonard W. Bacon, a New Haven Congregationalist minister, who himself had once favored colonization, came to Mrs. Stowe's defense. He asserted that she had told him that if she had to write *Uncle Tom's Cabin* again "she would not send George Harris to Liberia." [49] Negroes were mollified by this explanation, but they wondered why it had not come from Mrs. Stowe herself, one who was hardly reticent or word-shy.

Going beyond the destination of George Harris, William G. Allen attacked his concept of African nationality, terming it "sheer nonsense." Professor Allen gave Harriet a little lecture: "Nations worthy of the name are only produced by a fusion of races." Although Americans rolled their eyes and went into pretended fits at the mere mention of amalgamation, he continued, this country was the most interbred under the sun: "Indeed, fusion of races seems to be a trait distinctive of Americans." [50]

In the decade before the Civil War the high point of Negro objection to colonization came in 1855 at the national convention of colored men at Philadelphia. Here a letter was read from Jacob Handy of Baltimore in support of emigration. Not a single delegate spoke in favor of the Handy's proposal, several of them saying that his letter should be returned unanswered. Going further, George T. Downing moving that the letter be burned, thus saving the three-cent postage to mail it back. By a vote of 33 to 20, the delegates sustained Downing's stand, the burning of unpopular documents not being without precedent in abolitionist circles. Subsequently, however, this action was rescinded, the delegates deciding to return the letter. [51]

In the late fifties the Negro leaders who opposed colonization centered their fire on the African Civilization Society. The fight was bitter and personal, Henry Highland Garnet, the society's president, reveling in a battle, no matter how badly outnumbered. His opposition embraced influential black abolitionists like Downing, Purvis, Remond, John S. Rock, and William C. Nell, to name but a few.

But some of these anticolonizationists began to waver a bit —Frederick Douglass, for example. In September 1859 he had emphatically denied that he had emigrationist leanings,[52] but a year later his mood was less adamant. In the spring of 1861 he accepted an invitation from the Haitian government to visit the island, all expenses paid. He was on the point of sailing when the news came that the people of Charleston, South Carolina, had fired on Fort Sumter. This event changed Douglass's plans, as it did to those of millions of other Americans. Douglass immediately called off the trip to Haiti. War had come, and to him, as to other antislavery crusaders, war just might turn out to be abolitionism by other means.

X

Shock Therapy and Crisis

Come thou, Sweet Freedom, best gift of God
to man! Not in a storm of fire and blood
I ask it, but still, at all events,
and all hazards, come.

William G. Allen, October 6, 1852

THE INTEREST that many Negroes showed in colonization in the fifties stemmed basically from the discriminations against them in the land of their birth. In the case of emigration to Africa there was an additional motive—a feeling of identity based on color and ancestry. As a result many Negroes came to view the land of their fathers in a fresh light, discarding the shibboleths as to its backwardness and stagnation. But such a more positive attitude toward Africa was far short of any Pan-Negro movement or black hands-across-the-sea. For the lure of Africa could never compare with that of an America in which slavery had been wiped out and its twin offspring— prejudice and discrimination—put on the run.

On the surface of things, such a brightening day was hardly on the horizon when Frederick Douglass made his plans to take a trip to Haiti. But by 1860 America was close to a civil war. This country's institutions, secular and religious, had failed to bring about the emancipation of the slaves without bloodshed. The power structure was unable to cope with slavery because slavery itself had become a key component of the power structure. Since American institutions therefore lacked the strength or will to subdue slavery, other and more revolutionary techniques would begin to take hold of men's minds. Thus in the two decades prior to 1860 the notion of an armed confrontation mounted in intensity, however inapparent on the surface. On the eve of the Civil War, then, the idea of physical violence to free the slave was far from new. Since the time of Nat Turner this idea of a showdown by force of arms had been a recurring theme in Negro thought. Black fire-eaters did not go out of style with David Walker. But for a time their tones were muted because black people had taken on new hope with the coming of the new abolitionists.

These new friends of the Negro were strongly pacifist in method, no matter how forthright in language. They proposed to rely on reason and moral truth, opposing any efforts by the slave to obtain his rights by physical force. In their famous Declaration of Sentiments, issued December 4, 1833, the new abolitionists made their position clear: "We reject and entreat the oppressed to reject the use of all carnal weapons for deliverance from bondage; relying solely upon those which are spiritual and mighty through God to the pulling down of strongholds." Five years later, the influential James G. Birney assured a Southern inquirer that he did not know of a single abolitionist who would incite the slaves to insurrections.[1]

The new abolitionists were pacifists, a stance fully supported by William Lloyd Garrison, a name revered among Negroes. Garrison wielded great influence among Negroes down to 1840. Harriet Martineau asserted in 1837 that Garrison's strong hold on the Negro people was the explanation "that no blood has been shed from the time his voice began to be heard until now." [2] After the abolitionist split in 1840 Garrison's influence among Negroes waned outside of New England and even there his word was no longer gospel although affection for him remained constant.

In the 1840's it was a Garrisonian, Charles Lenox Remond,

who first voiced unpacific thoughts. In the British Isles to attend the World Anti-Slavery Convention of 1840, Remond told the Glasgow Anti-Slavery Society that he would welcome a war between the United States and England over the Canadian boundary inasmuch as such a development would bring about the freedom of the slaves. Remond was rebuked by *The Anti-Slavery Standard*, which called his language "hardly in accordance with the character of primitive abolitionism." In a later address to the Hiberian Anti-Slavery Society, the undeterred Remond said that the dissolution of the American Union would lead the outraged slaves to turn upon their then friendless and weakened torturers, measuring arms with them.[3]

A year later the possibility of having to bear arms for the United States brought a cool response from a Negro weekly in New York, the *People's Press*. The United States and England were in dispute over the *Creole*, a ship which, like the *Amistad*, had been seized by its slaves, but which had put into port at Nassau. A diplomatic argument was inevitable, with America's Secretary of State, Daniel Webster, saying that she would demand indemnification. Negroes had little sympathy with any efforts made to repossess the 135 slaves of the *Creole*. Hence the *People's Press* pointed out that since the previous military services of black Americans had been repaid with chains and slavery, they should maintain an organized neutrality if war came. Such a position would be held until the laws, federal and state, should make the Negro a free and equal citizen.[4]

A note of militancy was sounded at a meeting called by Negroes in Troy, New York, in March 1842 to discuss the decision of the Supreme Court in *Prigg v. Pennsylvania*. The ruling of the court did need a word of explanation. For although it held that a state law could not restrain a master in seizing his slave, it also declared that the state authorities were not bound to assist in such seizures. After weighing the

decision the Negroes meeting at Troy passed a series of resolutions, one of which expressed a full concurrence "with the
statement of Patrick Henry, and solemnly declare that we will
have liberty, or we shall have death." [5]

At the Troy meeting the chairman of the five-man committee drafting the resolutions was Henry Highland Garnet, then
a local clergyman. This was the man, the grandson of a Man-
dingo chieftan and warrior, who the following year delivered
the most forthright call for a slave uprising ever heard in
antebellum America. It took place at a national convention for
black men in Buffalo in August 1843. Although then having
appeared on the public platform only three years, Garnet already had a reputation as an orator, particularly for having
"the power to fire up his auditors in such a way as to make
every man feel like daring to do."

To an audience including the more than seventy delegates
and scores of white visitors, the twenty-seven-year-old Garnet
delivered "An Address to the Slaves of the United States." The
time has come, brethren, when you must act for yourselves,
said Garnet. There was little hope of obtaining freedom without some shedding of blood. The way would not be easy but
"you will not be compelled to spend much time in order to
become inured to hardships."

As the audience listened, some in tears and others with fists
clenched, Garnet proceeded to hold up some examples of a
slave who struck a blow for freedom—Denmark Vesey of
South Carolina, "patriotic Nathaniel Turner," Joseph Cinque
of the *Amistad*, and Madison Washington of the *Creole*.
Garnet brought his remarks to a close with a sustained exhortation, reading in part as follows: "Brethren, arise, arise.
Strike for your lives and liberties. Now is the day and hour.
Let every slave throughout the land do this and the days of
slavery are numbered. *Rather die free-men than live to be
slaves*. Remember that you are four millions." [6]

When Garnet finished it would have been risky, according

to a Buffalo reporter, for any slaveholder to have been present.[7] The deeply moved delegates, recovering from the powerful outburst, proceeded to give it an unprecedented amount of attention. Those opposing it included William Wells Brown, Frederick Douglass and Amos G. Beman, the last named speaking for over an hour. The convention turned the address over to a revision committee to soften its language, but even this toned-down version was rejected, although by a single vote.

Garnet's address hardly sat well with white abolitionists, particularly the Garrisonians. The latter called attention to the 1833 Declaration of Sentiments abjuring the use of force. They asked Garnet whether he, as a clergyman, found the gospel in harmony with his address to the slaves. Maria Weston Chapman deplored the kind of advice that Garnet had been getting: "Trust not in counsels that lead you to the shedding of blood." [8]

In a sharp reply to Mrs. Chapman, Garnet said that she wished him to think as she did, thus reducing him again to the level of the slave. Rejecting her contention that he had received bad advice, he retorted that he was capable of thinking on the subject of human rights without any help "from the men of the West or the women of the East." Be assured, he concluded, "that there is one black American who dares to speak boldly on the subject of universal liberty." [9]

Despite the criticisms of the Garrisonian press, Garnet's address to the slaves left its stamp on Negro thought. A national convention of Negroes at Troy in October 1847, the first since the Buffalo meeting four years earlier, did disapprove of physical violence—"we frown down any attempt to confide in brute force as a reformatory instrumentality." But a few months later Garnet published his 1843 address, combining it with a sketch of David Walker and the text of his forceful "Appeal to the Colored Citizens of the World." In January 1849 a convention of the Negroes of Ohio passed a resolution recommending that five hundred copies of this 1848 Garnet publication "be obtained in the name of the Convention and gratuitously distributed." [10] This resolution was not carried out but the militant spirit it reflected is unmistakable.

Five months later Frederick Douglass gave a speech at Boston, one which indicated that he had abandoned the pacific stance he took at the Buffalo convention six years earlier. To a packed audience at Faneuil Hall, Douglass closed a lengthy address with the remark that he would welcome the news that the slaves had risen and "that the sable arms which have been engaged in beautifying and adorning the South were engaged in spreading death and devastation there." Although this remark occasioned "marked sensation," Douglass continued in the same vein. Saying that a state of war existed in the South, he asserted that Americans should welcome a successful slave uprising just as they had recently hailed the news that the French citizens had overthrown the monarchy. Douglass took his seat amid great applause but not without some hissing.[11]

With the coming of the 1850's the militant tone among Negroes grew louder, spurred by the Fugitive Slave Law and their growing belief that liberty and slavery could not escape a head-on collision. By the summer of 1853 the clergyman Jermain W. Loguen was of the opinion that slavery would be done away with either by agitation or bloodshed, adding ominously, "and I sometimes think that I care not which." A year later H. Ford Douglas declared that he could join a foreign enemy and fight against the United States without being a traitor inasmuch as "it treats me as a stranger and an alien." In 1856 John S. Rock urged Negroes to undertake some daring or desperate enterprise in order to demonstrate their courage. Rock had been stung by a remark of Theodore Parker to the effect that if Margaret Garner, an escaped slave who put one of her daughters to death when facing recapture, had been Anglo-Saxon, the 400,000 white men in Ohio would have arisen in her defense.[12]

Believing that a sectional war over slavery was likely to come, the Negro of the 1850's gave increasing attention to the question of bearing arms. In 1847 the delegates at the Troy national convention had debated that a proposal to "recommend to our people the propriety of instructing their sons in the art of war." This motion was lost, but within a half-dozen years a changed attitude had become manifest. A group of New York Negroes, meeting at the Shiloh Presbyterian Church in April 1851, took the position that a knowledge of the use of defensive weapons was necessary inasmuch as all history taught that every people should be prepared to defend themselves. Hence the convention urged the young men of New York, Williamsburg, and Brooklyn to organize military companies. Frederick Douglass subsequently pointed out that if a knowledge of firearms was desirable in any people, it was desirable in the Negro. William J. Wilson of Brooklyn wrote that he heartily favored the introduction of the science of military tactics among colored people.[13]

A state convention of Ohio Negroes in 1857 urged Negroes to form military companies where it was practical and where they could not be enrolled with whites. This was the overriding problem, Negroes being barred from the state militia by a congressional act of 1792. Our federal government, observed abolitionist William Jay, was probably the only one in the world which forbade a portion of its subjects to take part in the national defense on account of the tincture of their skin.[14]

Barred from the state militia, Negroes had formed military companies of their own. These outfits were largely ceremonial, parading on August 1 or at the grand opening of a church or school. But without state or federal support, Negro militia companies were bound to remain small and indifferently equipped. Hence in 1855 Rhode Island blacks were pleased when the legislature granted to the newly organized Providence military company of Negroes the right to make use of state arms. The legislators felt that they had done as much as they could; certainly they had done more than any other state would do.

It was in Massachusetts that the Negroes made the most sustained effort to win state support for a colored military unit. In May 1852 Robert Morris and Charles Lenox Remond appeared before the Military Committee of the state legislature bearing petitions for the establishment of a Negro company. Ten months later Morris was back before the legislature, this time accompanied by William J. Watkins. The two spokesmen presented petitions signed by 65 Negroes after which they recited the role played by the Negro in the American Revolution and the War of 1812.[15]

In 1855 the Massasoit Guards, organized the preceding year in Boston, asked Governor Henry J. Gardiner for a loan of a stack of arms and equipment. Gardiner replied that his attorney general had advised him that he had no power to comply with the request. Evidently, added Gardiner, the framers of the Militia Act of 1792 were unmindful of the services of the Negro in the Revolutionary War. The Guards thereupon announced that for the time being they would seek by subscription to raise the necessary funds. As if to attract donors, they also announced that their organization was open to all, one member assuring a reporter "that he believed that white men were as good as colored men if they behaved themselves." [16] But the Guards never got state support. Moreover, in 1859 a bill authorizing Negroes to join the militia was vetoed by Governor N. P. Banks as unconstitutional, and his veto was sustained.

The militant spirit among Negroes was fanned full sail in 1857 by the Dred Scott decision in which the Supreme Court opened the territories to slavery. The decision was additionally repugnant to Negroes inasmuch as it denied their citizenship, proclaiming that at the time this country was founded the Negro had no rights which the white man was bound to respect. "Your national ship is rotten and sinking, why not leave it," counseled Mary Ann Shadd Cary from Chatham, Ontario. John Peck of Pittsburgh advised his fellow Negroes to leave the country, and clergyman Benjamin S. Tanner announced that he was going to "remove to Canada in the name of God." [17] But aside from a handful of departees, most Negro leaders reacted by staging indignation meetings.

Some of the speakers at these meetings took the philosophic point of view that the Dred Scott decision might be a blessing in disguise, since, in the words of William Still, "great evils must be consummated that good might come." [18] To be a true reformer is to take obstacles in stride, hence many abolitionists found comfort in the belief that the Dred Scott decision was so monstrous as to boomerang against slavery, making for its ultimate downfall.

But to abolitionist orators the presentation of philosophical viewpoints in measured tones was hardly in a class with the heady language of invective and name-calling. At a Dred Scott indignation meeting at Philadelphia's Israel Church on April 10, 1857, with James M.Bustill presiding, Robert Purvis thundered that he owed no allegiance to a government founded upon the position that a black man had no rights that a white man was bound to respect. A month later, at the annual meeting of the American Anti-Slavery Society in New York, Frederick Douglass characterized the decision as a "judicial incarnation of wolfishness," the product of "the Slaveholding wing of the Supreme Court." [19]

The Taney decision took the center stage at the convention of the colored citizens of Massachusetts, held at New Bedford on August 2, 1858. Robert Morris said that the decision should be trampled upon and that he doubted whether the Massachusetts courts would enforce it. Joshua B. Smith, who in 1847 had fled from his North Carolina master, told the

gathering that he could not respect a Supreme Court that
would "so infamously take from him his rights." Charles
Lenox Remond, a more practiced denouncer, proclaimed that
he was prepared to spit upon the ruling by Judge Taney. He
wanted no long resolution, added Remond, only a short one
"saying that we *defy* the Dred Scott decision."

The wrought-up Remond was far from finished. He moved
that a committee be appointed to prepare an address to the
slaves inviting them to rebel. He said that he did not wish to
see the people on the platform turn pale at his proposal but to
rise and talk. The first person to rise was Josiah Henson, made
famous as the man after whom Mrs. Stowe had modelled her
chief character, Uncle Tom. Henson said that he doubted that
the time was ripe for such a step. As for turning pale, Henson
declared that he had never turned pale in his life. ("Father
Henson is a very black man," added the reporter, parentheti-
cally.)

In a thrust at Remond's courage, Henson voiced the opinion
that "if the shooting time came, Remond would be found out
of the question." When Remond was able to get the floor
again, he denied that he would skulk in time of danger: "He
only regretted that he had not a spear with which he could
transfix all the slaveholders at once." Following a "spirited discussion," the Remond proposal was voted down by a "small
majority." [20]

A convention of New England Negroes meeting in Boston
in August 1859 called the decision of Taney and his "slaveholding associates" a disregard for all historical verity, a defiant contempt of state sovereignty, and a wanton perversion
of the Constitution. The speeches by Garrison, Remond,
Loguen, John S. Rock, and others were all characterized by "a
radical anti-slavery sentiment," although, according to a Negro weekly, "an allusion to colored barbers and their refusal to
shave men of their own complexion, produced a little discord-
ance." [21]

The most novel and long-continued means of protesting the Dred Scott decision took place in Boston where, beginning in 1858, Negro abolitionists held a Crispus Attucks Day. The first to die in the Boston Massacre of March 5, 1770, Attucks had impeccable credentials as a martyr for American liberty. Others might forget him, but not black Bostonians. In 1851 seven of them, including William C. Nell and Lewis Hayden, had sent an unsuccessful petition to the state legislature asking that $1500 be appropriated for the erection of a monument to the memory of Attucks.

The meeting held at Faneuil Hall on March 5, 1858, in protest to the Taney decision, was a feast of sight and sound. The hall was decorated for the occasion. In front of the speaker's rostrum was an exhibit of Revolutionary War relics, which included a small cup allegedly owned by Attucks, a picture of Washington crossing the Delaware in which black Prince Whipple was seen pulling the stroke oar, and a banner presented by Governor John Hancock to a Negro military company, the Bucks of America. The meeting was graced by original songs, one of them by Charlotte Forten, who journeyed from Salem to be on hand. A hymn by Frances Ellen Watkins, "Freedom's Battle," was delivered by the Attucks Glee Club. This youthful quintet included Edward M. Bannister and George L. Ruffin, both destined for fame, one as a painter and the other as a judge.

With William C. Nell presiding, the speakers included Theodore Parker, Garrison, Phillips, and John S. Rock. A letter was read from Thomas Wentworth Higginson lauding the role played by Negroes in the slave rescue cases in Boston and divulging that the first man to enter the courthouse door in an attempt to rescue Anthony Burns was a Negro, "contrary to general supposition." In his speech Wendell Phillips outdid himself as far as his predominantly Negro audience was concerned. After glorifying Attucks, he urged his black listeners to show valor in life so that when their deeds became known, people would say, "Oh, yes, they have always been a brave, gallant people! Was there not an Attucks in '70?" [22]

Of the speeches the most militant came from John S. Rock. Refuting the charge that the Negro was docile, he predicted that "sooner or later the clashing of arms will be heard in this country and the black man's services will be needed." The race-conscious Rock also recurred to the theme that black was beautiful: "When I contrast the fine, tough muscular system, the rich beautiful color, the full broad features of the Negro, with the delicate physical organization, wan color and lank hair of the Caucasian, I am inclined to believe that when the white man was created, nature was pretty well exhausted." [23]

Fifth of March commemorations would be held in Boston every year until the ratification of the Fifteenth Amendment in 1870. Eighteen years later the city and state authorities appropriated a total of $13,000 to erect a Crispus Attucks monument on the Boston Common. In 1932, as a result of the efforts of Boston Negroes, the Massachusetts legislature passed an act ordering the governor to issue annually a proclamation "calling for a proper observance on March fifth of the anniversary of the Boston Massacre." [24]

The annual observance of Crispus Attucks Day had begun in 1858 as a protest against the Dred Scott decision. But its meaning was more of an affirmation than of a remonstrance. For it was an evidence that the spirit of the American Revolution, of which Attucks was a conspicuous symbol, was still alive, not having run its course by 1858 or, as it turned out, by 1888 or 1932.

Throughout the North the strong denunciation of the Dred Scott decision did much to raise the threshold of incipient violence. Certainly, among Negroes the spirit of militancy became more pervasive and insistent. At a convention of Ohio Negroes in 1858, William H. Day, after reviewing the plight of the colored people, declared that resistance by force of arms was their right and duty. John I. Gaines, a boat-storekeeper from Cincinnati, criticized Day as being impractical, Negroes being "a weak, enslaved and ignorant people." [25]

But however impractical, Negro public speakers were preparing their addresses around highly militant figures and themes. James T. Holly lauded Toussaint L'Overture, Haitian liberator, in a speech entitled, "The Auspicious Dawn of Negro Rule." Holly ended his lecture with the assertion that it was far better "that his sable countrymen should be *dead freemen than living slaves*." J. Sella Martin, pastor of the Joy Street Baptist Church in Boston, drew large audiences for his prepared address on a Baptist exhorter of an earlier day, Nat Turner.[26] Blunt-spoken William J. Watkins toured the abolitionist circuit with a lecture on the "irrepressible conflict."

The new climate of impending physical confrontation inevitably produced its own energizers. Of the abolitionist figures thrust up by the undercurrents of violence, one stands in a class by himself—John Brown of Osawatomie. To Brown, slavery itself was a species of warfare, demanding a counter resort to arms. Brown's daring sweep into Virginia in October 1859, his capture and his execution constituted a national shock from which there would be no recovery. Abolitionists hitherto of a pacifist orientation found reason to reverse themselves as the whole atmosphere became charged.

Brown's relationships with Negroes had been close, continuous, and on a peer basis, a pattern which no other white reformer could boast. Apparently no Negro who ever knew Brown ever said anything in criticism of his attitude or behavior toward colored people. Brown's attitude toward slavery and his grim and forceful response to it were shaped by many things, of which his own personal experiences with Negroes was not the least.

The reciprocal relations between John Brown and the blacks began long before five of them accompanied him to Harpers Ferry and four of them to his doom. Brown's interest in colored people dated back to 1834 when he proposed "to get at least one Negro boy or youth, and bring him up as we do our own." Fifteen years later Brown moved his family to North Elba, New York, expressly to settle among Negroes, most of them recipients of land grants from Gerrit Smith. Brown attempted to assist his Negro neighbors in business matters, and he invited them to his weekly sessions in the study of the Bible. Richard Henry Dana, paying a farewell call to John Brown at North Elba on a morning in late June 1849, noted that at the breakfast table eating with the family were the hired hands, including three Negroes.[27]

Brown's attempt to spur Negroes on led him in 1848 to contribute a lengthy article to the *Ram's Horn*, a short-lived weekly. Entitled "Sambo's Mistakes," this article lampoons the habits of the Negro. Brown felt that the colored people were not doing all that they themselves could do in self-improvement. Hence in "Sambo's Mistakes" he makes his points by posing as a Negro who is offering to his fellows the benefit of his experience in life. A typical passage reads as follows:

> Another error of my riper years has been, that when any meeting of colored people has been called in order to consider any important matter of general interest, I have been so eager to display my spouting talents, and so tenacious of some trifling theory or other that I have adopted, that I have generally lost all sight of the business hand, consumed the time disputing about things of no moment, and thereby defeated entirely many important measures calculated to promote the general welfare; but I am happy to say I can see in a minute where I missed it.
>
> Another small error of my life (for I never committed great blunders) has been that I never would (for the sake of union in the furtherance of the most vital interests of our race) yield

any minor point of difference. In this way I have always had to act with but a few, or more frequently alone, and could accomplish nothing worth living for; but I have one comfort, I can see in a minute where I missed it.[28]

If few men knew the Negro's shortcomings as perceptively as Brown, there were even fewer who were as distressed by color prejudice as he. One of his followers relates that while walking in Boston in April 1857 Brown was greatly annoyed at the rude language addressed to a colored girl, language of the type, Brown said, that would not have been directed to a white girl. Entering the Massasoit House in Chicago for breakfast on April 25, 1858, Brown was told that the Negro member of his party, Richard Richardson, a fugitive slave, could not be served. Brown marched out, although not before subjecting the proprietor to "a little bit of terse logic." [29]

Aside from his equalitarian principles, Brown was interested in the welfare of the colored people because he had something for them to do. His all-consuming passion was the abolition of slavery, an end which he proposed to accomplish be enlisting a semi-militaristic group of followers ready for direct action. Brown's role for the Negro was implicit in an organization he formed in January 1851 at Springfield, Massachusetts, the United States League of Gileadites. Formed to resist the Fugitive Slave Law, the Gileadites pledged themselves to go armed and to shoot to kill,[30] a pattern of conduct that would characterize Brown's later operations in Kansas and at Harpers Ferry. The forty-four colored men and women who signed the agreement apparently had little call for action. Moreover, in March 1851, Brown, the original man-in-motion, left for Ohio.

Brown was interested in recruiting Negro leaders and the black rank and file. Prominent figures sought out by Brown included Frederick Douglass, Martin R. Delany, Stephen Smith, Jermain W. Loguen, Henry Highland Garnet, William Still, and Charles H. Langston. His contacts with Douglass, whom he desperately wished to win over, stretched over a longer time-span and were more numerous than with any other Negro leader. Brown's acquaintance with Douglass went back to the spring of 1848 when the latter, at Brown's request, visited him at Springfield. In the spring of 1858 Brown paid two visits to the Douglass home in Rochester, New York, one of them extending over a period of two weeks. While a guest of Douglass, Brown met a fugitive slave, Shields Green, who would accompany him to Harpers Ferry.

Shortly before Brown got ready to make his raid into Virginia he arranged to meet Douglass at Chambersburg, Pennsylvania, some twenty miles from the site of the planned foray. Douglass brought a letter for Brown from Mrs. J. N. Gloucester, a Brooklyn woman of means, with $25 enclosed. Douglass was accompanied by Shields Green, the two of them being led to Brown's hideout by Harry Watson, a Negro underground railroad operator at Chambersburg. For three days Brown tried to persuade Douglass to join the expedition. Douglass steadfastly refused, discretion having formed his decision.

Not a single other Negro leader would join Brown, all of them considering his venture imprudent. On May 17, 1859, Brown wrote to Loguen: "I will just whisper in your private ear that I have no doubt you will soon have a call from God to minister at a different location." [31] Despite the language, the Negro clergyman remained unconvinced. Loguen, like other Negroes, admired Brown for his antislavery exploits in Kansas and his daring excursion into Missouri in which he had freed eleven slaves by a show of force. However, as much as they revered Brown for his courage, Negro leaders thought that the proposed seizure of Harpers Ferry was inordinately risky, if not foolhardy.

Brown's most ambitious attempt to enlist the Negro rank and file was the holding of a convention at Chatham, Ontario, in early May, 1858. Brown's own party of twelve was present,

as were thirty-four Negroes. These included the presiding
officer, a Negro clergyman, William C. Munroe, the poet
James Madison Bell, and Martin R. Delany, the last named
then practicing medicine at Chatham, having come at the urgent personal invitation of Brown himself.[32] The chief work of
the convention was the adoption of a provisional constitution
of the United States, a document which avowed the Declaration of Independence and condemned slavery.

The Chatham convention lacked follow-up. With Brown
gone and with no action of any kind forthcoming for more
nearly seventeen months, the enthusiasm of the Chatham
signers abated, never to be rekindled. But at Chatham, Brown
for the first time had met Harriet Tubman. He had thought of
her as the shepherd of the slaves that he would shake loose.
Brown's tête-à-tête with Harriet confirmed his already high
opinion of her. But neither she nor Delany would be with him
at Harpers Ferry. Brown, however, had not left Chatham
empty-handed. A young printer's devil, Osborn Perry Anderson, had been impressed by the convention and by its con-
vener; he would be the only black survivor of Harpers Ferry.

By the autumn of 1859 Brown was ready to seize the government arsenal at Harpers Ferry, a prelude to establishing a
stronghold in the mountains and thus liberating the slaves on
a mounting scale of operations. Late in the night of October
16 Brown moved into the town, leaving three of his party at
the Kennedy Farm, the base of operations in Maryland.
Marching into the darkened Harpers Ferry behind Brown
were eighteen followers, five of them Negroes, Osborne Perry
Anderson, Shields Green, Dangerfield Newby, like Green an
escaped slave, and two recruits from Oberlin, Ohio—John
A. Copeland, Jr., and Lewis S. Leary, his uncle. Copeland, a
former student in the preparatory department at Oberlin College and the most articulate of the five, had joined Brown "to

assist in giving that freedom to at least a few of my poor and enslaved brethren who have been most foully and unjustly deprived of their liberty." [33]

John Brown was hardly a battlefield tactician; lacking a clear and definite plan of campaign, his raid was quickly suppressed. The first of the five fatalities inflicted by Brown's men was on a free Negro, Heywood Shepherd, baggage master of the train depot, a contretemps which seemed to set the stage for a military fiasco. Ten of Brown's band were killed, Newby first and Leary later. Copeland and Green were among the seven who were captured, and Anderson was among the five who escaped.

Brown and his captured followers were imprisoned in Charleston. Brown was tried first, and on October 31 the jury returned with a verdict of guilty. Two days later the judge pronounced a sentence of death by hanging. During the thirty-day interval between the sentence and the execution, Brown bore himself with fortitude and serenity.

Brown's inner peace was not shared by his countrymen, particularly those in the North. For his act, however rash and wrongheaded, had dramatized the issue of slavery, forcing neutrals to abandon their fence-sitting posture and giving to the abolitionists a martyr figure of unprecedented proportions. Charles H. Langston, like half a dozen white abolitionists, felt the necessity of issuing a "card of denial" stating that he had had no hand in the Harpers Ferry affair. "But what shall I deny," added Langston. "I cannot deny that I feel the very deepest sympathy with the immortal John Brown in his heroic and daring effort to free the slaves." [34] Langston's sentiment of sympathy and esteem mirrored the reaction of the overwhelming majority of black Americans.

During Brown's month in jail innumerable prayer and sympathy meetings were held throughout the North. None were more fervent than those called by Negroes. *The Weekly Anglo-African* for November 5 carried a guest editorial by

James W. C. Pennington entitled, "Pray for John Brown." Such advice was hardly needed. On the day after Brown was sentenced a group of Providence Negroes, meeting at the Zion Church, expressed their full sympathy for Captain John Brown. Despite their "abhorrence to bloodshed and civil war," they referred to Brown as "hero, philanthropist and unflinching champion of liberty," and pledged themselves to send up their prayers to Almighty God on his behalf. A group of Chicago Negroes, meeting later that month, drafted a letter to Brown assuring him of their deep sympathy and their intention to contribute material aid to his family: "How could we be so ungrateful as to do less for one who has suffered, bled, and now ready to die for the cause?" [35] At the Siloam Presbyterian Church in Brooklyn, a prayer meeting cutting across denominational lines was led by the pastor, A. N. Freeman, assisted by fellow clergymen Henry Highland Garnet, James N. Gloucester, and Amos G. Beman.

Colored women sent letters of esteem to the jailed Brown. A group of Brooklyn matrons wrote that they would ever hold him in their remembrance, considering him a model of true patriotism because he sacrificed everything for his country's sake. From Kendalville, Indiana, Frances Ellen Watkins sent a letter on behalf of the slave women, an admixture of Christian faith in the future and symbolic references to the past— "You have rocked the bloody Bastile," and, "The hemlock is distilled with victory when it is pressed to the lips of Socrates." A group of women from New York, Brooklyn, and Williamsburg sent Mrs. Brown a letter on November 23, its content summarized in the lines, "Fear not, beloved sister. Trust in the God of Jacob." [36]

As John Brown stepped from the jail on the last morning of his life, "no little slave-child was held up for the benison of his lips, for none but soldiers were near and the street was full of marching men." However, as Brown was led to the gallows, a slave woman said, "God bless you, old man; if I could help you, I would." Brown went to his death with dignity, and the day concluded, wrote one who was present, "with the calm & quiet of a New England Sabbath." [37]

If December 2, 1859, was also a quiet day in abolitionist circles, it was due to the nature of its observance. Throughout the North reformers held prayer meetings or meetings with a religious orientation. At Boston, where all Negro businesses were closed, the colored people, wearing arm bands of black crepe, held three prayer meetings—morning, afternoon, and night—at Leonard Grimes's Twelfth Baptist Church. Many persons stayed from one meeting to the next, not needing to go out for meals on a day of widespread fasting. One of these all-day sojourners was Lydia Maria Child, who had journeyed from Wayland, fifteen miles away, to spend the solemn day with Negroes.[38] She therefore had to miss the much larger meeting at Tremont Temple arranged by the white abolitionists but with Negroes attending in large numbers and with J. Sella Martin as one of the featured speakers. But perhaps it was just as well that Mrs. Child did not go to the crowded Temple, for thousands were turned away.

Martyr Day, as some black abolitionists called it, was appropriately observed by New York Negroes at a meeting at Shiloh Church beginning at ten in the morning and with a period of silent prayer at noon. Of the six clergymen on the program, William Goodell, the only white speaker, differed from two of his colleagues on one point. When James N. Gloucester endorsed John Brown's course, Goodell dissented on the grounds that the weapons of the abolitionists were moral and religious rather than carnal. Sampson White took issue, informing Goodell that George Washington, whom Americans revered, had not taken the position that "our weapons are not carnal" when he led the new nation in its struggle against English oppression. Washington and the Americans of his day had acted on the premise that "resistance to tyrants was obedience to God." White, somewhat carried away, said that he had an arm which he felt duty-bound to use when his God-given rights were invaded.[39]

Philadelphia Negroes, like those in Boston, observed Martyr Day by closing down their businesses. Public prayer meetings were held at two churches—Shiloh and Union Baptist. Hundreds of colored men and women went to National Hall to hear Robert Purvis and white William Furness. Pittsburgh's black community held a meeting addressed by native son George Vashon. At Detroit the colored people gathered at the Second Baptist Church where they passed a resolution vowing to venerate Brown's character, regarding him as "our temporal leader whose name will never die."

On Martyr Day at Cleveland the two thousand who managed to get into crowded Melodeon Hall included almost as many whites as blacks, with almost as many equally mixed milling around outside, unable to get in. Judges and members of the state legislature were among the platform guests flanking the presiding officer, Charles H. Langston. The walls were draped in black and the stage was hung with large-lettered, framed quotations from John Brown's writings and conversations.[40] Negroes in lesser towns throughout the North —from Worcester, Massachusetts, to Galesburg, Ohio— likewise paused on December 2, 1859, to honor John Brown on the day of his death.

Negroes felt that they had an especial obligation to assist in the efforts to give financial aid to John Brown's widow. Their donations would not be large, but they would represent a more widespread giving than their modest totals might indicate. The John Brown Relief Fund of New Haven raised $12.75 for Mary Brown. Philadelphia Negroes sent her $150 and the recently formed John Brown Liberty League of Detroit donated $25. Some Negroes, such as Francis Ellen Watkins, sent personal contributions. Mrs. Brown's letters of acknowledgement were brief, but gracious and inspirational.[41]

The sympathy that Negroes felt for Mrs. Brown extended to Mrs. Mary Leary, widow of Lewis S. Leary. The wife and seven children of the other Negro who fell at Harpers Ferry, Dangerfield Newby, were in slavery, and neither of the two Negroes who were hanged, John A. Copeland or Shields Green, was married. Boston Negroes raised $40 for Mrs. Leary and her child, and $10 to go toward erecting a monument to the memory of the heroes of Harpers Ferry. The colored women in Brooklyn and New York sent Mrs. Leary a total of $140, bringing from her the reply that her loss had been great but she hoped that her husband and his associates had not died in vain in their "attack on that great evil—American Slavery."[42]

Negroes did not wait for history to pass the verdict on John Brown. He was the greatest man of the nineteenth century, ran a resolution adopted by a group of New Bedford Negroes two days after he mounted the scaffold. This evaluation was echoed by Frederick Douglass in a letter to Brown's associate, James Redpath, on June 29, 1860. Brown's portrait graced the wall of the Purvis diningroom at Byberry, Pennsylvania; in Troy, New York, the black children pooled their pennies so that they might buy a picture of him for their school. A Negro weekly compared him with Nat Turner, discovering that both were idealistic, Bible-nurtured, tenacious of purpose, swayed by spiritual impulses, and calm and heroic in prison.[43]

The evaluation of Brown by Negroes was uncritical, since he perhaps "was worth more for hanging than anything else." But as prophets, Negroes did better. For with the ensuing rapid current of national events Brown's fate became a rallying cry and his name a legend. It is true, wrote John A. Copeland, as he sat in the jail awaiting the hangman's noose, that the outbreak at Harpers Ferry did not give immediate freedom to the slave but it was the prelude to that event.[44]

On the eve of the Civil War the abolitionists lost John Brown, but they regained Charles Sumner. The Massachusetts senator had been the victim of a physical assault which, like the John Brown raid, bespoke the mounting violence of the times. On May 22, 1856, as Sumner sat reading his mail in the nearly empty Senate chamber, a congressman from South Carolina, Preston S. Brooks, belabored him on the head with a heavy cane. Brooks had bitterly resented a verbal attack which Sumner had made two days earlier against his uncle, Senator Andrew Pickens Butler, in a Senate speech which at once became famous under the title, "The Crime Against Kansas." Brooks's cane felled Sumner, bleeding and unconscious, to the floor. Reformers throughout the North were shocked, Negroes throughout the North holding protest meetings.

By mid-1860 Sumner, now become by martyrdom a truly important figure, was ready once more to answer the roll call. On June 4, after an absence of nearly fifty months from the Senate chamber, he arose to deliver a speech. He "took the floor at ten minutes past twelve, and spoke until a little after four." Sumner's was "the eloquence of industry rather than the eloquence of inspiration," wrote one of his Negro admirers, Archibald H. Grimké. "He requires space and he requires time." Doubtless on this occasion Sumner felt that his subject, "The Barbarism of Slavery," warranted extended treatment. The essence of the address, however, may be briefly stated: slavery was a "Upas Tree with all its gigantic poison."

In the esteem of black Americans, Sumner already was second to none in national politics. For this maiden effort on his return to the Senate, Negro leaders showered him with "a profusion of epistolary plaudits." From Robert Morris, who had worked with him in 1849 on the separate schools issue in Boston, came a letter of thanks "in behalf of the colored young men of Boston." Another lawyer, John S. Rock, later to be admitted, on motion of Sumner, to the bar of the United States Supreme Court, sent word, "Your immortal speech has sent a thrill of joy to all lovers of Freedom everywhere." A colored citizen of New Bedford who had, upon his own testimony, "faithfully devoted more than 20 years of his brief life to the elevation of his race," assured the senator that the gratitude of the colored people was incalculable.

However phrased, all of the letters expressed complete approval. Ebenezer D. Bassett, principal of the Institute for Colored Youth at Philadelphia, and later to become the first Negro to represent the United States at Port-au-Prince, Haiti, informed Sumner that the speech was unequalled by anything in the oratory of modern times. Bassett, as one with a reputation as a classical scholar, felt emboldened to place Sumner's effort "side by side with the matchless *De Corona* of Demosthenes." From Philadelphia also came word from William Still, "You have effectually laid the axe at the root of the tree." At near-by Byberry Robert Purvis had posted a note—Sumner's speech had stirred within him "the deepest emotions." H. O. Wagoner, venturing to "speak in the name or in the behalf of the seven or eight thousand colored people of the State of Illinois," return heartfelt thanks for the "ever-memorable services which you have just rendered in the Senate of the United States to the cause of my enslaved and down-trodden fellow-countrymen. . . ." Could the poor slave, continued Wagoner, know the substance of that speech and the circumstances under which it was given, "in the very face of the Slave Power,—I say could the slaves be made to comprehend fully all this, it would thrill their very souls with emotions of joy unspeakable."

"The right word has been uttered," intoned Frederick

Douglass. "You spoke to the Senate and the nation, but you have a nobler and a mightier audience. The civilized world will hear you, and rejoice at the tremendous exposure of meanness, brutality, blood-guiltiness, hell-black iniquity, and barbarism of American Slavery." [45] Terming it the most anti-slavery speech ever made in the Senate Hall of the United States, *Douglass' Monthly* carried it in full.[46] Francis Ellen Watkins caught the mood, turning out some lines whose spirit may be sampled from the opening and closing stanzas:

> Thank God that thou hast spoken
> Words earnest, true and brave;
> The lightning of thy lips has smote
> The fetters of the slave.
>
> Thy words were not soft echoes,
> Thy tones no syren song;
> They fell as battle-axes
> Upon our giant wrong.[47]

Although fulsomely praised by Negroes, Sumner's speech drew bitter comments in the North where the prevailing sentiment was far less hostile toward slavery than his. Less than five months after the address, however, Abraham Lincoln was elected to the Presidency and a rapprochement between the sections became all but impossible. Less than seven weeks after the Republican victory, South Carolina officially dissolved its union with "the other States of North America."

Seeking to convince the South that her institutions, particularly slavery, were not endangered, conciliators in both houses of Congress tried to find a pacifying formula. Their efforts provoked a heated public discussion which in turn made for an increased hostility toward the colored man, who was held to be the source of all discord. "The *everlasting negro* is the rock upon which the Ship of State must split," ran an angry, widely reprinted editorial in a Providence daily. "Will the people stand for this much longer? Will they make the Negro their god?" [48]

The possibility of a rapprochment between the North and the South dismayed the Negro. "All compromises now are as new wine to old bottles, new cloth to old garments," editorialized *Douglass' Monthly*. "To attempt them as a means of peace between freedom and slavery is as to attempt to reverse irreversible law." [49] Negro leaders were apprehensive lest the road to sectional reconcilation become the last resting ground for freedom. But such fears of a "sell out" solution by the North, or any kind of peaceful settlement, proved premature. Six weeks after Lincoln took office Fort Sumter was fired upon, compromise measures, like the Union itself, having proved unable to cope with slavery.

"Our National Sin has found us out," ran an editorial in *Douglass' Monthly* for May 1861. In this Old Testament sense, war had indeed come as sort of an atonement for a fall from grace, an act of redemption, no matter how untoward its expression. But in a sense less retributive and more peculiarly American, the Civil War was a phase of the continual striving for the goals for which this country had been conceived. The downfall of slavery would thus bring additional strength for the tasks ahead. Viewed in this light, the abolitionist crusade itself was but a continuing phase of the revolution of 1776, an attempt to put into practice the doctrine of man's essential equality.

"We have good cause to be grateful to the slave for the benefit we have received to *ourselves*, in working for *him*," wrote Abby Kelley. "In striving to strike *his* chains off, we found, most surely, that *we* were manacled ourselves." [50] Miss Kelley's sentiment bespoke a largeness of mind and of spirit. But, written in 1838, it did not fully encompass the role of the black American in the abolitionist crusade. More than an unhappy pawn, he had known that he must work to forge his own freedom. And to this task he had brought special skills. The struggle to make man free was a grim business, but he was accustomed to grim businesses. The struggle to make men free might entail armed resistance, but he was crisis-oriented from birth. To the extent that America had a revolutionary tradition, he was its protagonist no less than its symbol.

Note on Bibliographical Literature

ALL STUDENTS of the abolitionist movement are indebted to Dwight L. Dumond for his comprehensive, *A Bibliography of Antislavery in America*. Dumond's entries are not annotated, but many of them, notably the pamphlets, bear lengthy, descriptive titles. A few items have escaped Dumond's careful attention, particularly if the conventions held by Negroes be considered of abolitionist kidney. A model for the other states, the excellent *New Jersey and the Negro: A Bibliography, 1715–1966* (New Jersey Library Association, Trenton, 1967), includes a number of citations dealing with the slavery controversy, many of them relating to matters by no means confined to New Jersey. Louis Filler's thoroughly researched *The Crusade Against Slavery* (New York, 1960) has a highly useful annotated bibliography designed for both the scholar and the general reader. In the fine essay on sources in his *North of Slavery: The Free Negro in the United States, 1790–1860*, Leon F. Litwack devotes one heading to white abolitionists and another to black abolitionists, in the latter emphasizing the significant role of the antebellum Negro conventions. Two works which do not list a separate bibliography but whose footnote entries are richly suggestive are Larry Gara, *The Liberty Line: The Legend of the Underground Railroad* (Lexington, Kentucky, 1961) and Charles H. Wesley, *Neglected History: Essays in Negro History by a College President* (Wilberforce, Ohio, 1965), chapters 3, 4, 5.

Generous samplings of abolitionist writings have been made available in book form, most of these titles being found in the large libraries. Leading the lot for the black abolitionist is Carter G. Woodson, *The Mind of the Negro As Reflected by Letters Written During the Crisis, 1800–1860*. Sixty-nine of these 254 Negro-written letters relate to antislavery matters directly, with most of the remaining ones having some peripheral relevance. Of almost equal importance are the first two volumes of Philip S. Foner's massive four-volume work, *The Life and Writings of Frederick Douglass* (New York, 1950–55), a treasure-house of first-hand information not only about Douglass but about the whole freedom impulse in America during the two decades preceding the Civil War.

Of the white abolitionists the writings of William Lloyd Garrison would, not unexpectedly, contain numerous references to the Negro, such being the case in Francis J. Garrison and Wendell P. Garrison, *William Lloyd Garrison, 1805–1879: The Story of His Life Told by His Children* (4 vols., New York, 1885–89). Light is thrown on the black abolitionist in Gilbert H. Barnes and Dwight L. Dumond, *Letters of Theodore Dwight Weld, Angelina Grimké Weld, and Sarah Grimké, 1822–1844* (2 vols., New York, 1934), a work made all the more valuable by the meticulous scholarship of its editors. If Dwight L. Dumond, ed., *Letters of James Gillespie Birney, 1831–1857* (2 vols., New York, 1938) is of lesser value for the Negro abolitionist, it is because Birney has fewer contacts with black reformers than did Weld and the Grimké sisters.

Annie H. Abel and Frank J. Klingberg, eds., *A Side-Light on Anglo–American Relations, 1839–1858 Furnished by the Correspondence of Lewis Tappan and Others with the British and Foreign Anti-Slavery Society* (Lancaster, Pa., 1927), while describing the community of interests held by British and American reformers include a number of references to Negro abolitionists, references are made readily evident by a detailed index. Herbert Aptheker's, *A Documentary History of the Negro People in the United States* (New York, 1951) includes a section on the abolitionist era containing 135 entries. Arranged chronologically and with helpful headnotes, Aptheker's selections are rich both in their range of subject matter and their type of source materials. *Negro Orators and Their Orations* (Washington, 1925), edited by the great pioneer in black history, Carter G. Woodson, contains twenty-eight declamations for the antebellum period. In an easy narrative style generally missing from his histories, Woodson links one document with the next while simultaneously presenting a thumb-nail sketch of the orator and the setting of his address.

Notes

CHAPTER I

1. *The Emancipator* (New York), June 30, 1835.
2. *Annals of Congress*, Thirteenth Congress, first and second sessions, May 24, 1813, to Apr. 18, 1814, 569–72, 601, 861–63. *Biography of the Rev. Robert Finley*, D.D. (2nd ed., Phila., 1875), 126; hereafter cited as *Biography of Finley*. For Negro removal sentiment in post-Revolutionary America, see Winthrop D. Jordan, *White over Black* (Chapel Hill, 1968), 546–69.
3. *Biography of Finley*, 123.
4. *Niles' Register* (Baltimore), Nov. 27, 1819. Edward Needles, *An Historical Memoir of the Pennsylvania Society for the Abolition of Slavery; the Relief of Free Negroes Unlawfully Held in Bondage and for Improving the Condition of the African Race* (Phila., 1848), 66; hereafter cited as *Memoir of Pennsylvania Society*.
5. *Freedom's Journal* (New York), June 8, 1827, Jan. 31, 1829; *Rights of All* (New York), June 12, 1829.
6. Carter G. Woodson, *Negro Orators and Their Orations* (Washington, D.C., 1925), 80, hereafter cited as *Negro Orators*.
7. *The Liberator* (Boston), Feb. 27, 1833. For Mrs. Stewart, see Lillian O'Connor, *Pioneer Woman Orators* (New York, 1954), 53–55, and Eleanor Flexner, *Century of Struggle: The Woman's Rights Movement in the United States* (Cambridge, Mass., 1959), 44–45. Jesse Torrey, *The American Slave Trade* (London, 1822), 118.
8. *The Genius of Universal Emancipation* (Baltimore), Feb. 24, 1827. Russwurm to Gurley, Feb. 24, 1829, May 7, 1829, American Colonization Society Manuscripts, Library of Congress.
9. Columbia, Harrisburg, Lewiston, Philadelphia, Pittsburgh and York in Pennsylvania; Hartford, Lyme, Middletown, and New Haven, Connecticut; Boston, Nantucket, and New Bedford, Massachusetts; Brooklyn, Catskill, and

New York, New York; Newport and Providence, Rhode Island; Trenton and Wilmington, Delaware and Baltimore and Washington.

10. *Minutes of the Fifth Annual Convention for the Improvement of the Free People of Colour in the United States, Held by Adjournments in the Wesley Church, Philadelphia, from the First to the Fifth of June, Inclusive, 1835* (Phila., 1835), 15.

11. Harriet Martineau, *The Martyr Age of the United States of America, with an Appeal in Behalf of Oberlin Institute* (Newcastle-upon-Tyne, 1840), 2; hereafter cited as *Martyr Age.*

12. For antislavery sentiment among the early Quakers, see David Brion Davis, *The Problem of Slavery in Western Culture* (Ithaca, 1966), 291–332.

13. *Genius of Universal Emancipation,* Oct. 13, 1827.

14. Edward R. Turner, *The Negro in Pennsylvania* (Washington, D.C., 1911), 220. *Correspondence Between the Hon. F. H. Elmore . . . and James G. Birney* (New York, 1838), 8.

15. *The American Convention for Promoting the Abolition of Slavery to the Free People of Colour in the United States, Philadelphia, 1829* (Phila., 1829), 5. *Minutes of the Proceedings of the Ninth American Convention for Promoting the Abolition of Slavery and Improving the Condition of the African Race, January 9–13, 1804* (Phila., 1804), 33.

16. Channing to Webster, May 14, 1828, in *The Works of Daniel Webster* (ninth ed., 6 vols., Boston, 1856), V, 367.

17. *Minutes of the Proceedings of a Special Meeting of the Fifteenth American Convention for Promoting the Abolition of Slavery, and Improving the Condition of the African Race, Assembled at Philadelphia, December 10–15, 1818* (Phila., 1818), 39. Minutes of the Proceedings of a Convention of Delegates from the Abolition Societies, 1798, in "Documents: The Appeal of the American Convention of Abolition Societies," *The Journal of Negro History,* April 1921 (VI), 213. Early Lee Fox, *The American Colonization Society, 1817–1840* (Baltimore, 1919), 181.

18. Andrews to Gurley, June 28, 1828, Nov. 6, 1828, Jan. 9, 1829, American Colonization Society Manuscripts. Moore to Gurley, Apr. 9, 1829. Ibid. Russwurm to Gurley, July 24, 1829. Ibid.

19. *Minutes of the American Convention for Promoting the Abolition of Slavery and Improving the Condition of the African Race, January 9, 1804* (Phila., 1804), 13. The list of members from 1775 to 1859 may be found in *Act of Incorporation of the Pennsylvania Society for Promoting the Abolition of Slavery* (Phila., 1860), 13–36.

20. *Minutes of the Nineteenth Session of the American Convention for Promoting the Abolition of Slavery and Improving the Condition of the African Race, October 4, 1825* (Phila., 1825), 8. For the African school, see Charles C. Andrews, *History of the New York African Free-School* (New York, 1830). Turner, *Negro in Pennsylvania*, 131.

21. For a qualifying point of view, see Arthur Zilversmit, *The First Emancipation: The Abolition of Slavery in the North* (Chicago, 1967), 226–29.

22. Needles, *Memoir of Pennsylvania Society*, 64.

23. *Proceedings of the Anti-Slavery Convention Assembled at Philadelphia, December 4, 5, 6, 1833* (New York, 1833), 15.

24. George W. Julian, "The Genesis of Modern Abolitionism," *The International Review* (New York), June 1882 (XII), 533–54.

25. *Emancipator*, Feb. 3, 1835. Thomas Wentworth Higginson, *Contemporaries* (Boston, 1899), 69. *Sixteenth Annual Report of the Massachusetts Anti-Slavery Society, January 26–27 1848* (Boston, 1848), 89. The Phillips quotation and the reference to Webster, Clay, and Calhoun are in *Twenty-First Annual Report of the Massachusetts Anti-Slavery Society, January 26–27, 1853* (Boston, 1853), 107, 92.

26. On this whole point, see Gordon Esley Finney, "The Anti-slavery Movement in the South, 1787–1836: Its Rise and Decline and Contribution to Abolitionism in the West," Ph.D. dissertation, Duke University, 1962.

27. For this document and an analysis of its setting and its meaning, see Herbert Aptheker, *One Continual Cry* (New York, 1965).

28. *Freedom's Journal*, Oct. 3, 1828; Oct. 24, 1828.

29. Aptheker, *One Continual Cry*, 137.

30. Martineau, *Martyr Age*, 11. *Genius of Universal Emancipation*, Apr. 1830. *Niles' Register*, Mar. 27, 1830, and see Clement Eaton, "A Dangerous Pamphlet in the Old South," *The Journal of Southern History*, 1936 (II), 323–34. *The African Repository* (Washington, D.C.), Mar. 1830 (VI), 29. Samuel J. May, *Some Recollections of our Antislavery Conflict* (Boston, 1869), 133; hereafter cited as *Some Recollections*.

31. See, for example, Kenneth Stampp, "The Fate of the Southern Anti-Slavery Movement," *Journal of Negro History*, Jan. 1943 (XXVIII), 10–22.

32. In *The North Star* (Rochester), Nov. 10, 1848.

33. *Frederick Douglass' Paper* (Rochester), Jan. 26, 1854.

34. *Liberator*, Jan. 1, 1831.

35. William Lloyd Garrison, *An Address Delivered Before the Free People of Color in Philadelphia, New York and other cities during the month of June 1831* (Boston, 1831), preface. W. P. Garrison and F. J. Garrison, *Life of William Lloyd Garrison* (4 vols., New York, 1885–89), I, 258; hereafter cited as *Life of Garrison*.

36. Lewis Tappan, *The Life of Arthur Tappan* (New York, 1870), 136. *Proceedings of a Crowded Meeting of the Colored People of Boston Assembled July 15, 1846, for the Purpose of Bidding Farewell to William Lloyd Garrison on His Departure for England* (Dublin, 1846), 11. *Liberator*, Jan. 31, 1851. Garrison and Garrison, *Life of Garrison*, I, 432.

37. "Letters of William Lloyd Garrison to John B. Vashon," *Journal of Negro History*, Jan. 1927 (XII), 35, 36. *The Abolitionist* (Boston), Dec. 1833, 192.

38. *Liberator*, June 1, 1833; Feb. 16, 1832; Mar. 30, 1833.

39. Garrison to Tappan, Dec. 17, 1835, Lewis Tappan Papers, Library of Congress.

40. Garrison and Garrison, *Life of Garrison*, I, 428. "Letters of Garrison to Vashon," 40. *Proceedings of the Anti-Slavery Meeting Held in Stacy Hall, Boston, on the Twentieth Anniversary of the Mob of October 21, 1835* (Boston, 1855), 20.

41. *Liberator*, Oct. 20, 1832. Garrison and Garrison. *Life of Garrison*, II, 356.

42. *Liberator*, Jan. 2, 1832. *Emancipator*, Sept. 14, 1833.

43. *Liberator*, July 16, 1831. Lydia Maria Child, "William Lloyd Garrison," *The Atlantic Monthly* (Boston), Aug. 1879 (XLIV), 234.

CHAPTER II

1. Ira V. Brown, "Miller McKim and Pennsylvania Abolitionism," *Pennsylvania History*, Jan. 1963 (XXX), 57.

2. John Greenleaf Whittier, "The Antislavery Convention of 1833," *Atlantic Monthly*, Feb. 1874 (XXXIII), 169.

3. *Abolitionist*, Dec. 1833. For the discrimination against Barbadoes, see *Liberator*, Dec. 8, 1833.

4. Ibid. Dec. 21, 1833.

5. Ibid Mar. 1, 1834. Ibid. Feb. 15, 1834. For the meeting in upstate New York, see *Proceedings of the New York Anti-Slavery Convention Held at Utica, October 21, and New York Anti-Slavery Society, Held at Peterboro, October 22, 1835* (Utica, 1835).

6. *Weekly Advocate* (New York), Feb. 25, 1837. *The Colored American* (New York), Jan. 27, 1838. *Liberator*, July 13, 1838.

7. Garrison and Garrison, *Life of Garrison*, I, 417. *The Independent* (New York), Nov. 15, 1906 (LXI), 1139.

8. For Sarah Forten's poem, see William C. Nell, *The Colored Patriots of the American Revolution* (Boston, 1855), 351.

9. *Proceedings of the Anti-Slavery Convention of American Women, Held in Philadelphia, May 15, 16, 17, and 18, 1838* (Phila., 1838), *passim*.

10. *Proceedings of the Third Anti-Slavery Convention of American Women, Held in Philadelphia, May 1, 2, 3, 1839* (Phila., 1839), 8.

11. *Liberator*, Nov. 17, 1832.

12. Ibid. July 5, 1834; June 21, 1834; May 27, 1834; Feb. 5, 1834; June 14, 1834. For the Middletown women, see *Emancipator*, Apr. 15, 1834, and also Horatio T. Strother, *The Underground Railroad in Connecticut* (Middletown, 1962), 154.

13. *Colored American*, Mar. 13, 1837. *Emancipator*, Mar. 9, 1837. *Colored American*, June 16, 1838.

14. *The Anti-Slavery Offering and Picknick* (Boston), May 1842, 65.

15. *Liberator*, Dec. 26, 1835. Ibid. May 17, 1834, and Feb. 15, 1834. *Emancipator*, Dec. 23, 1834. *Colored American*, Dec. 23, 1834.

16. *Colored American*, Nov. 23, 1839. Ibid. Sept. 1, 1838, and Oct. 20, 1838. *Emancipator*, Jan. 3, 1839. *Second Annual Report of the Massachusetts Anti-Slavery Society, January 22, 1839* (Boston, 1839), 15.

17. Beman to S. S. Jocelyn, Mar. 7, 1859, in American Missionary Association (A.M.A.) Papers, Fisk University, Nashville, Tenn. *Liberator*, June 1, 1833. *Abolitionist*, Aug. 1833, 128.

18. *Abolitionist*, Dec. 1833, 192. Ibid Nov. 1833, 176. Donations of November 1834 compiled from *The Anti-Slavery Record* (New York), Jan. 1835, and donations from Boston and New York Negroes compiled from *Anti-Slavery Record*, May, June, Aug., Sept., Oct., and Nov. 1836.

19. *Liberator*, Feb. 7, 1835. *Eighth Annual Report of the Board of Managers of the Massachusetts Anti-Slavery Society, January 22, 1840* (Boston, 1840), xlviii. *Anti-Slavery Record*, Nov. 1836.

20. *Correspondence between the Hon. F. H. Elmore . . . and J. G. Birney*, 17.

21. *Liberator*, Feb. 7, 1835. *Rights of All*, Oct. 9, 1829. *Emancipator*, July 13, 1833. *Emancipator*, Jan. 13, 20, 27, Feb. 3, 10, 17. *Herald of Freedom*, Mar. 16, 1839. *The*

Northern Star and Freeman's Advocate (Albany), Dec. 2, 1842.

22. Minutes of Pennsylvania Society for Promoting the Abolition of Slavery, 1827–1847 (The Historical Society of Pennsylvania, Philadelphia), 66. *Colored American*, Mar. 11, 1837. *Herald of Freedom*, Mar. 19, 1838. *Colored American*, Sept. 29, 1838, *Emancipator and Free American* (Boston), May 26, 1842. *Colored American*, Sept. 2, 1837. *Northern Star and Freeman's Advocate*, Jan. 2, 1843.

23. *Liberator*, Mar. 7 and 21, 1835. *Herald of Freedom*, June 9, 1838. Ibid. May 24, 1839. *The National Anti-Slavery Standard* (New York), June 11, 1840. *Oberlin Evangelist* (Oberlin, Ohio), June 3, 1840.

24. Samuel Ringgold Ward at the tenth annual meeting of the American and Foreign Anti-Slavery Society at New York in 1850 in *Annual Report of the American and Foreign Anti-Slavery Society at New York, May 1850* (New York, 1850), 22.

25. *Proceedings of the New England Anti-Slavery Convention Held in Boston, May 24, 25, 26, 1836* (Boston, 1836), 70.

26. *The Pennsylvania Freeman* (Phila.), Oct. 16, 1852.

27. *Poems by a Slave* (Phila., 1837), 7.

28. *Emancipator*, Nov. 11, 1841. *The National Era* (Washington, D. C.), July 19, 1847.

29. *Liberator*, Sept. 6, 1834.

30. Ibid. June 15, 1840.

31. *The Philanthropist* (Cincinnati, Ohio), Sept. 25, 1838. *Right and Wrong in Boston: Report of the Boston Female Anti-Slavery Society . . . for 1835* (Boston, 1836), 3. For the unpopularity of the abolitionists, see Lorman Ratner, "Northern Concern for Social Order as Cause for Rejecting Anti-Slavery, 1831–1840," *The Historian*, Nov. 1965 (XXVIII), 1–18.

32. Vincent Y. Bowditch, ed., *Life and Correspondence of Henry Ingersoll Bowditch* (2 vols., Boston, 1902), I, 101; hereafter cited as *Henry Ingersoll Bowditch*. For Ticknor, see

Van Wyck Brooks, *The Flowering of New England, 1815–1865* (New York, 1937), 330–33 and *passim*. Octavius B. Frothingham, *Theodore Parker* (Boston, 1874), 393. May, *Some Recollections*, 288.

33. William S. Heywood, ed., *Autobiography of Adin Ballou, 1803–1890* (Lowell, Mass., 1896), 282. Bayard Tuckerman, *William Jay and the Constitutional Movement for the Abolition of Slavery* (New York, 1893), 122. Lowell to C. F. Briggs, Mar. 26, 1848, in Charles Eliot Norton, ed., *Letters of James Russell Lowell* (2 vols., New York, 1894), I, 125.

34. *Liberator*, June 28, 1834. *Niles' Weekly Register* (Baltimore), July 19, 1834.

35. *Herald of Freedom*, Oct. 31, 1838.

36. *The Education of Henry Adams* (Boston, 1917), 42.

37. *The Anti-Slavery Bugle* (Salem, Ohio), May 18, 1850. John F. Hume, *The Abolitionists* (New York, 1905), 112. W. Freeman Galpin, "Samuel Joseph May, 'God's Chore Boy,'" *New York History*, Apr. 1946 (XXI), 143 and May, *Some Recollections*, 153. Dwight L. Dumond, *Anti-Slavery Origins of the Civil War in the United States* (Ann Arbor, 1939), 58. For examples of mob violence against abolitionists, see William Goodell, *Slavery and Anti-Slavery* (New York, 1853), 404–7.

38. Theodore Lyman, III, *Papers Relating to the Garrison Mob* (Cambridge, Mass., 1870), 4.

39. *Colored American*, Nov. 25, 1837. Ibid. Dec. 2, 1837. *Emancipator*, Dec. 21, 1837. *Colored American*, Jan. 20, 1838.

40. *Colored American*, Mar. 4, 1837. Jocelyn to Gurley, Oct. 5, 1829, American Colonization Society Papers.

41. *Proceedings of the Pennsylvania Convention to Organize a State Anti-Slavery Society at Harrisburg, January 31, February 1, 2, 3* (Phila., 1837), 53. *Colored American*, July 15, 1839. Sarah Forten to Angelina Grimké, Apr. 15, 1837, in Gilbert H. Barnes and Dwight L. Dumond, eds., *Letters of Theodore Dwight Weld, Angelina Grimké Weld and Sarah Grimké, 1822–1844* (2 vols., New York, 1934), I, 379; hereafter cited *Weld-Grimké Letters*.

CHAPTER III

1. *Liberator*, Sept. 22, 1837. Ibid. Nov. 14, 1837.

2. Ibid. Dec. 20, 1834.

3. Ibid. May 10, 1839. Ibid. June 14, 1839. *Eighth Annual Report of the Board of Managers of the Massachusetts Anti-Slavery Society, January 22, 1840* (Boston, 1840), 36–37. *Liberator*, June 14, 1839.

4. *Herald of Freedom*, Mar. 8, 1839. *Colored American*, Sept. 28, 1839.

5. Totals compiled from names listed in *Emancipator*, May 29, 1840.

6. *Standard*, Sept. 23, 1841.

7. *Emancipator*, May 22, 1840. Ray to Birney, May 20, 1840, *Weld-Grimké Letters*, I, 578.

8. *Liberator*, May 22, 1840. Ibid. June 5, 1840.

9. *Herald of Freedom*, Aug. 6, 1841. Ibid. Aug. 10, 1839. Ibid. Jan. 8, 1841, and Jan. 15, 1841.

10. Woodson, *Negro Orators*, 91. *The Friend of Man* (Utica), Mar. 14, 1838. *Standard*, July 2, 1840. Martin B. Duberman, *James Russell Lowell* (Boston, 1966), 185.

11. *Colored American*, May 18, 1838. J. M. Smith to Gerrit Smith, Mar. 1, 1855, in Gerrit Smith Miller Collection, Syracuse University. *Northern Star and Freeman's Advocate*, Mar. 3, 1842.

12. *The Works of Charles Follen* (5 vols., Boston, 1841), I, 627–28. Malcolm R. Lovell, *Two Quaker Sisters: Elizabeth Buffum Chace and Lucy Buffum Lovell* (New York, 1937), 119–20. Minute Book of the Junior Anti-Slavery Society of the City and County of Philadelphia, 1836–1846, Historical Society of Pennsylvania.

13. *Northern Star and Freeman's Advocate*, Mar. 3, 1842. Sarah H. Southwick, *Reminiscences of Early Anti-Slavery Days* (Cambridge, Mass., 1893), 29. *Fifth Annual Report of the Massachusetts Anti-Slavery Society, January 25, 1837* (Boston, 1837), xxxix.

14. See, for example, *Address of the People of Color in the City of New York, By Members of The Executive Committee of the American Anti-Slavery Society* (New York, 1834), 5–6.

15. *Proceedings of the Convention which Formed the Maine Union in Behalf of the Colored Race* (Portland, 1835). Apparently this was a short-lived organization. Dwight L. Dumond's comprehensive compilation of printed anti-slavery literature, *A Bibliography of Antislavery in America* (Ann Arbor, 1961), lists a single entry for it.

16. *Herald of Freedom*, June 1, 1839. *Liberator*, Nov. 17, 1832. *Colored American*, Sept. 1, 1838. *Northern Star and Freeman's Advocate*, Mar. 3, 1842, and Mar. 31, 1842.

17. Tappan to Reason, July 11, 1840, Tappan Papers, Library of Congress.

18. *Colored American*, Nov. 25, 1837. *Philanthropist*, May 26, 1841.

19. *Exposition of the Objects and Plans of the American Union for the Relief and Improvement of the Colored Race* (Boston, 1835).

20. Garrison and Garrison, *Life of Garrison*, I, 174.

21. Weld to Tappan, Feb. 22, 1836, *Weld-Grimké Letters*, I, 263–65. Tappan's memorandum under date of Mar. 2, 1836, is found in the Tappan Papers.

22. *Weekly Advocate*, Feb. 18, 1837.

23. *Emancipator*, Aug. 5, 1837. William Yates, *Rights of Colored Men to Suffrage, Citizenship and Trial by Jury, Being a Book of Facts, Arguments, and Authorities, Historical Notices and Sketches of Debates—with Notes* (Phila., 1838). *Emancipator*, Dec. 29, 1836.

24. *Emancipator*, July 6, 1837. *Colored American*, Oct. 27, 1838.

25. For this report in full, see *Colored American*, June 22, 1839, or *Emancipator*, June 6, 1839.

26. *Liberator*, Jan. 31, 1851.

27. Charles K. Whipple, *The Non-Resistance Principle: With Peculiar Application to the Help of Slaves by Abolitionists* (Boston, 1860).

28. For this whole topic, see the path-breaking study by Howard H. Bell, "A Survey of the Colored Convention Movement, 1830–1861," unpublished doctoral dissertation, Northwestern University, 1953.

29. Goodell, *Slavery and Anti-Slavery*, 561.

30. *Emancipator*, June 12, 1840.

31. For August meetings, see *Standard*, Oct. 1, 1840. Whipper and Purvis to Ruggles, Aug. 22, 1840, in *Standard*, Sept. 10, 1840.

32. Ray's remarks in *Standard*, July 16, 1840. *Standard*'s position in its issue of June 18, 1840. Ward to *Standard*, June 27, 1840, in *Standard*, July 2, 1840.

33. "An Address to the Colored People of the United States," in *North Star*, Sept. 29, 1848. For Purvis declining a sixth term, see *Thirteenth Annual Report Presented to the Pennsylvania Anti-Slavery Society by Its Executive Committee, October 15, 1850* (Phila., 1850), 55.

34. Frederick Douglass, *North Star*, Oct. 19, 1849. *Standard*, Jan. 13, *Bugle*, Aug. 18, 1849. *Herald of Freedom*, June 30, 1838.

35. *Emancipator*, Aug. 12, 1834. Remond to Garrison, Sept. 21, 1840, in *Liberator*, Oct. 23, 1840. *The Weekly Anglo-African* (New York), Sept. 10, 1859. William C. Nell, *The Colored Patriots of the American Revolution* (Boston, 1855), 246; hereafter cited as *Colored Patriots*.

36. Douglass at Harrisburg in Garrison and Garrison, *Life of Garrison*, III, 192. *Douglass' Monthly* (Rochester), Apr. 1859, 2. Remond to Phillips, Apr. 5, 1845, in *Liberator*, Apr. 18, 1845.

37. *Liberator*, Feb. 14, 1844. *Colored American*, Sept. 15, 1838.

38. *North Star*, Dec. 15, 1848.

39. Charles Francis Adams, ed., *Memoirs of John Quincy Adams* (12 vols., Phila., 1874–77), X, 30. *Proceedings of the New England Anti-Slavery Convention, Boston, May 24, 25, 26, 1836* (Boston, 1836), 30.

40. Needles, *Memoir of Pennsylvania Society*, 95.

41. *Proceedings of the Ohio Anti-Slavery Convention Held at Putnam April 22, 23, 24, 1835* [n.p.n.d.], 34–35.

42. Weld to Tappan, Mar. 18, 1834, in *Weld-Grimké Letters*, I, 134–35. Sylvestre C. Watkins, Sr., "Some Early Illinois Free Negroes," *Journal of the Illinois State Historical Society*, Autumn 1963 (LVI), 499. William T. Catto, *A Semi-Centenary Discourse Delivered in the First African Presbyterian Church, Philadelphia, on the Fourth Sabbath of May, 1857* (Phila., 1857), 12. Edward Ingle, *The Negro in the District of Columbia* (Baltimore, 1893), 13. Allan Peskin, ed., *North into Freedom: The Autobiography of John Malvin, Free Negro, 1795–1880* (Cleveland, 1966), 52. Hannah F. Lee, ed., *Memoir of Pierre Toussaint* (Boston, 1854), 22. *Emancipator and Free American*, Sept. 14, 1842. William G. Hawkins, *Lunsford Lane* (Boston, 1863), 199. *Emancipator and Free American*, Nov. 3, 1842.

43. *Philanthropist*, Oct. 28, 1836. For Hester Lane, see Lydia Maria Child's short sketch in *Standard*, Sept. 23, 1841, also Lewis Tappan's remarks in *Proceedings of the Pennsylvania Convention to Organize a State Anti-Slavery Society at Harrisburg, January 31, February 1, 2, 3*, 74, and E. S. Abdy, *Journal of a Residence and Tour in the United States of North America, From April, 1833, to October, 1834* (2 vols., London, 1835), II, 32–33.

44. Minute Book, Annual Report of the Western Anti-Slavery Society for 1857, Library of Congress. *Liberator*, June 7, 1850.

45. *The Liberty Tree* (Chicago), July 1, 1846. Undated newspaper clipping in Tappan Newspaper Clippings, Howard University Library.

46. *National Era*, June 3, 1847. *Oberlin Evangelist*, July 17, 1844. *The Blackstone Chronicle* (Blackstone, Mass.), Apr. 1848.

47. Vernon Loggins, *The Negro Author* (New York, 1931), 158. See also W. Edward Farrison, "William Wells Brown: America's First Negro Man of Letters," *Phylon*, First Quarter 1948 (IX), 13–33.

48. For Brown's account of the escape, see *Liberator*, Jan. 12, 1849.

49. Collins to Garrison, Jan. 18, 1841, in *Liberator*, Jan. 29, 1841.

50. *Herald of Freedom*, Feb. 11, 1842. New York *Tribune*, May 28, 1842.

51. Samuel Ringgold Ward, *Autobiography of a Fugitive Negro: His Anti-Slavery Labours in the United States, Canada & England* (London, 1855), vi. John Spencer Bassett, *Anti-Slavery Leaders of North Carolina* (Baltimore, 1898), 61. On the Williams narrative, see *Emancipator*, Aug. 30, 1838, and Oct. 25, 1838, and *Philanthropist*, Oct. 30, 1838, and Nov. 6, 1838. For this whole topic, see Charles H. Nichols, *Many Thousands Gone: The Ex-Slaves' Account of Their Freedom and Bondage* (Leiden, 1963).

52. *North Star*, Apr. 21, 1848. *Liberator*, June 6, 1845. Tappan to Douglass, Dec. 21, 1855, Tappan Papers.

53. Boston *Chronotype*, in *Bugle*, Nov. 3, 1849. Furness to editor of *Standard*, Mar. 9, 1854, in *Pennsylvania Freeman* (Philadelphia), Mar. 23, 1854.

54. Douglass to his former master, Sept. 22, 1848, in *Liberator*, Sept. 14, 1849.

55. Mrs. Stowe's appraisal of slave narratives in *Douglass' Paper*, Mar. 14, 1856, copied from *The Independent*. Frederick Law Olmsted, *A Journey in the Seaboard States* (2 vols., New York, 1904), I, 198–99.

CHAPTER IV

1. For Payne's remarks see Douglas C. Stange, "Document: Bishop Alexander Payne's Protestation of American Slavery," *Journal of Negro History*, Jan. 1967 (LII), 59–64.

2. Delany to Douglass, Jan. 16, 1849. *North Star*, Feb. 16, 1849.

3. John Mercer Langston, *Selected Lectures and Addresses* (Washington, D. C., 1883), 135.

4. *Pennsylvania Freeman*, Aug. 12, 1847. *The Minutes of the Christian Anti-Slavery Convention Assembled April 17–20, 1850* (Cincinnati, 1850), 66–68.

5. *Liberator*, July 14, 1832. *Emancipator*, June 25, 1840. Emma Lou Thornbrough, *The Negro in Indiana Before 1900* (Indianapolis, 1957), 151; hereafter cited as *Negro in Indiana*.

6. Sermon preached on occasion of death of Williams in William Douglass, *Sermon Preached in the African Protestant Episcopal Church of St. Thomas* (Phila., 1854), 248. *Colored American*, Sept. 28, 1839. *Proceedings of the General Anti-Slavery Convention Called by the Committee of the British and Foreign Anti-Slavery Society, and Held in London from Tuesday, June 13 to Tuesday, June 20, 1843* (London, 1843), 208.

7. *Philanthropist*, Sept. 22, 1840. The Session Book of the First Colored Presbyterian Church, Washington City, Howard University Library, 3.

8. William Douglass, *Annals of the First African Church in the United States of America, Now Styled the African Episcopal Church of St. Thomas* (Phila, 1862), 94.

9. *Fourteenth Annual Report of the Pennsylvania Anti-Slavery Society, October 7, 1851* (Phila., 1851), 44. For a contemporary defense of the Quakers, see *A Brief Statement of the Rise and Progress of the Testimony of the Religious Society of Friends Against Slavery and the Slave Trade* (published by direction of the Yearly Meeting, Phila., 1843), especially page 57.

10. *Douglass' Paper*, Apr. 13, 1855. *Proceedings of the General Anti-Slavery Convention Called by the Committee of the British and Foreign Anti-Slavery Society, and Held in London from Tuesday, June 13 to Tuesday, June 20, 1843*, 208.

11. S. Douglass to William Bassett, Dec. 1837, in *Weld-Grimké Letters*, II, 830.

12. Ibid. II, 831. Thomas E. Drake, *The Quakers and Slavery in America* (New Haven, 1950), 118. *A Tribute to the Memory of Thomas Shipley by Robert Purvis, Delivered at St. Thomas' Church, Nov. 23d, 1836* (Phila., 1836). Purvis to Garrison, Sept. 19, 1836, *Human Rights* (New York), Oct. 1836.

13. *Colored American*, Aug. 4, 1838. *Liberator*, Oct. 18, 1839. *Pennsylvania Freeman*, July 10, 1852.
14. *Genius of Universal Emancipation*, Feb. 1831. Ibid. May 1831.
15. Ibid. May, 1831. Ibid. Aug. 1831.
16. *Freedom's Journal*, Oct. 19, 1827.
17. *Colored American*, July 27, 1838. Ibid. Feb. 2, 1839. Clifton Herman Johnson, "The American Missionary Association, 1846–1861," doctoral dissertation, University of North Carolina, 1958, 59.
18. *Liberator*, Apr. 5, 1834. Benjamin Thomas, *Theodore Weld: Crusader for Freedom* (New Brunswick, N. J., 1950), 162.
19. William Still, *The Underground Railroad* (Phila., 1872), 759. *Douglass' Paper*, June 29, 1855. White's lecture in Leon Gardiner Collection of Negro History, Historical Society of Pennsylvania.
20. *Colored American*, Sept. 28, 1839. *Philanthropist*, Dec. 9, 1840.
21. Ibid. May 19, 1841. *Emancipator*, June 17, 1841.
22. The trial of the *Amistad* captives is covered in great detail in the pages of *The Emancipator*, highlighted by long, on-the-scene reports from Joshua Leavitt. *Philanthropist*, May 5, 1841.
23. *Emancipator*, July 29, 1841. Joseph Sturge, *A Visit to the United States in 1841* (London, 1842), xlvii, xlix.
24. Johnson, "American Missionary Association, 1846–1861" 58–59.
25. *The American Missionary Association: Its Missionaries, Teachers, and History* (New York, 1869), 9–10.
26. *The American Missionary* (New York), Oct. 1846 (I), 1.
27. Ibid. Aug. 1848 (III), 76. Beman to S. S. Jocelyn, Mar. 7, 1859, A.M.A. Papers. Beman to Lewis Tappan, Jan. 16, 1860, Ibid. Charles B. Ray to Jocelyn, Mar. 19, 1848, Ibid.
28. For the A.M.A. in Kentucky and North Carolina, see Fletcher M. Green, "Northern Missionary Activities in the South,"

Journal of Southern History, May 1955 (XXI), 156–61. For Scott, see Donald G. Mathews, "Orange Scott: The Methodist Evangelist as Revolutionary," in Martin B. Duberman, ed., *The Antislavery Vanguard* (Princeton, 1965), 71–101.

29. James W. C. Pennington, *A Sermon Preached Before the Third Presbytery of New York in the Thirteenth Street Presbyterian Church, July 3, 1853* (New York, 1854), 14. On this meeting, see *Minutes of the Christian Anti-Slavery Convention Assembled April 17th–20th, 1850, Cincinnati, Ohio* (Cincinnati, 1850).

30. Andrew E. Murray, *Presbyterians and the Negro—A History* (Phila., 1966), 103–18.

31. *Emancipator*, Feb. 3, 1835. Leavitt to his mother, May 10, 1842, Joshua Leavitt Papers, Library of Congress.

32. *Douglass' Paper*, June 10, 1852. Ibid. Sept. 23, 1853.

33. Ibid. Sept. 12, 1856. For the meeting at Cincinnati, see Daniel A. Payne, *History of the African Meahodist Episcopal Church* (Nashville, 1891), 335–45.

34. *Emancipator*, Nov. 16, 1837. Douglass to Sydney Gay, Aug. 7, 1847, *Standard*, Aug. 19, 1847. *Liberator*, Dec. 31, 1852. Watkins to McKim, Dec. 2, 1857, in The John B. and Mary Estlin Papers, 1840–1884 (British Records Relating to America in Microfilm, Microfilm Publication). Parker Pillsbury, *Acts of the Anti-Slavery Apostles* (Boston, 1884), 338; hereafter cited as *Anti-Slavery Apostles*.

35. *North Star*, Apr. 27, 1849. Ibid. Dec. 8, 1848.

36. *Rights of All*, May 29, 1829. Fredrika Bremer, *The Homes of the New World* (2 vols., New York, 1853), I, 491.

37. Laura S. Haviland, *A Woman's Life Work, Including Thirty Year's Service on the Underground Railroad and in the War* (Grand Rapids, Mich., 1881), 161; hereafter cited as *Woman's Life Work*. Miles Mark Fisher, "Negro Churches in Illinois," *Journal of Illinois Historical Society*, Autumn 1963 (LVI), 554.

38. *Colored American*, Mar. 4, 1837.

39. *North Star*, Apr. 28, 1848.

40. *Emancipator*, Nov. 16, 1837. *Douglass' Paper*, Mar. 9, 1855.

41. *Colored American,* Mar. 4, 1837. *Emancipator,* Aug. 24, 1837.
42. *Correspondence between the Hon. F. H. Elmore . . . and James G. Birney,* 47.
43. *Weekly Advocate,* Feb. 18, 1837. *Colored American,* May 27, 1837. Ibid. July 8, 1837. Ibid. Sept. 30, 1837. Ibid. June 27, 1839.
44. Benjamin Quarles, *Frederick Douglass* (Washington, D. C., 1948), 88–95.
45. *The Provincial Freeman* (Chatham, Ontario), Feb. 28, 1857. *Colored American,* Sept. 29, 1838. *The Impartial Citizen* (Boston), Sept. 27, 1851. Russwurm to R. R. Gurley, Apr. 8, 1829, American Colonization Society Papers.
46. *Philanthropist,* Oct. 9, 1838. Still to Shadd, Mar. 13, 1855, in *Provincial Freeman,* Mar. 24, 1855.
47. Ibid. Mar. 28, 1857.
48. *Oberlin Evangelist,* Sept. 27, 1848.

CHAPTER V

1. *Herald of Freedom,* Aug. 8, 1835.
2. John S. Tyson, *Elisha Tyson, The Philanthropist* (Baltimore, 1825), 126–31. *Letters and Addresses by George Thompson During His Mission in the United States From October 1, 1834 to November 27, 1835* (Boston, 1837), 16. "An Address to Free Colored Americans," *Anti-Slavery Convention of American Women, New York, May 9–12, 1837* (New York, 1837), 6. *Proceedings of the Pennsylvania Convention Assembled to Organize a State Anti-Slavery Society at Harrisburg, on the 31st of January and 1st, 2d and 3d of February 1837* (Phila., 1837), 79–83.
3. Richard Allen, *The Life Experience and Gospel Labors of the Rt. Rev. Richard Allen* (Nashville, 1954), 73–74. *Liberator,* Apr. 4, 1851.
4. *Aliened American* (Cleveland), Apr. 9, 1853. *The New York Times,* May 11, 1855.
5. *National Reformer,* in *Emancipator,* Mar. 12, 1840.

6. Loguen to Douglass, Aug. 5, 1853, *Douglass' Paper*, Aug. 12, 1853. *Liberator*, Jan. 21, 1834. White manuscript in Leon Gardiner Collection. *Herald of Freedom*, July 20, 1839.

7. *Minutes and Proceedings of the First Annual Meeting of the American Moral Reform Society . . . 1837* (Phila., 1837), 27. Howard H. Bell, "Some Reform Interests of the Negro During the 1850's as Reflected in State Conventions," *Phylon*, Summer 1960 (XXI), 178.

8. *Emancipator*, Nov. 16, 1837.

9. *Liberator*, Apr. 13, 1833.

10. *Rights of All*, May 29, 1829. *Liberator*, Dec. 3, 1831.

11. *Emancipator*, May 10, 1836. *Northern Star and Freeman's Advocate*, Apr. 7, 1842. Ibid. Dec. 8, 1842.

12. *North Star*, Nov. 24, 1848.

13. *Philanthropist*, July 21, 1840.

14. *Bugle*, Feb. 23, 1849. Ibid. May 18, 1849. *Official Proceedings of the Ohio State Convention of Colored Freemen, Held in Columbus, January 19–21, 1853* (Columbus, 1853), 5.

15. *Liberator*, Aug. 7, 1845.

16. For letter, see *Emancipator*, May 5, 1835.

17. *Standard*, July 9, 1846. *North Star*, June 2, 1848. Ibid. Sept. 15, 1848.

18. *Bugle*, Aug. 10, 1850. Ibid. Jan. 14, 1854.

19. For the disorder, see *Standard*, Aug. 11 and Aug. 25, 1842, and *Emancipator and Free American*, Aug. 11, 1842.

20. *Colored American*, Mar. 18, 1837. *Emancipator*, Jan. 28, 1841. Joseph W. Wilson, *Sketches of the Higher Classes of Colored Society in Philadelphia* (Phila., 1841), 62; hereafter cited as *Sketches of the Higher Classes*. Harold D. Langley, "The Negro in the Navy and Merchant Marine Service, 1798–1860," *Journal of Negro History*, Oct. 1967 (LII), 285.

21. *Rights of All*, Oct. 9, 1829. Robert Purvis, *Remarks on the Life and Character of James Forten, Delivered at Bethel Church, March 30, 1842* (Phila., 1842), 17. *North Star*, Mar. 10, 1848.

22. *Emancipator and Free American*, Sept. 8, 1842.

23. *Laws of the Sons of the African Society, Instituted at Boston, Anno Domini, 1798* (Boston, 1802), 1.

24. *Genius*, Mar. 31, 1827. *Pennsylvania Abolition Society Facts on Beneficial Societies, 1823–1838* (Historical Society of Pennsylvania). *A Statistical Inquiry into the Condition of the People of Color of Philadelphia* (Phila., 1849), 22. New York *Tribune*, Feb. 24, 1844.

25. A. H. Payne, "The Negro in New York Prior to 1860," *The Howard Review*, Jan. 1921 (I), 57. *Emancipator*, Nov. 9, 1837. *Weekly Advocate*, Feb. 11, 1837.

26. *Anglo-African*, Sept. 10, 1859. *Minutes and Proceedings of the First Annual Meeting of the American Moral Reform Society . . . 1837*, 5–6. *Douglass' Paper*, Oct. 6, 1854.

27. *Address and Constitution of the Phoenix Society of New York and of the Auxiliary Ward Associations* (New York, 1833).

28. Edmund Quincy, *Introductory Lecture Delivered before the Adelphic Union, November 19, 1838* (Boston, 1839). *Standard*, Nov. 28, 1844.

29. *Liberator*, Dec. 10, 1831. *Northern Star and Freeman's Advocate*, Jan. 2, 1843.

30. *Genius*, May 1833. Wilson, *Sketches of the Higher Classes*, 26. *Douglass' Paper*, Sept. 22, 1854. J. McCune Smith to editor of New York *Tribune*, Feb. 6, 1844, in New York *Tribune*, Feb. 24, 1844. *Emancipator*, Nov. 9, 1835.

31. *Colored American*, June 30, 1838. Officer roster of Gilbert Lyceum in Leon Gardiner Collection.

32. *Liberator*, Dec. 3, 1831. *Genius*, Mar. 1832. *Pennsylvania Abolition Society Facts on Beneficial Societies, 1823–1838*. *Anglo-African Weekly*, Apr. 14, 1860.

33. *Liberator*, Apr. 19, 1834.

34. Dorothy B. Porter, "The Organized Educational Activities of Negro Literary Societies, 1828–1846," *Journal of Negro Education*, Oct. 1936 (V), 575. *Douglass' Paper*, May 18, 1855. Smith to Douglass, Dec. 28, 1858, in Calendar of the Writings of Frederick Douglass in the Frederick Douglass Memorial Home, Anacostia Heights, Washington, D. C., reel no. 8.

35. *Freedom's Journal*, June 1, 1827. For the number of early
    schools, see also *Genius*, Feb. 23, 1828. For a rounded dis-
    cussion of the struggle for educational opportunities for
    Negroes in pre-Civil War times, see Leon Litwack, *North
    of Slavery: The Free Negro in the United States 1790–
    1860* (Chicago, 1961), 113–52; hereafter cited as *North
    of Slavery*.

36. *First Annual Convention of the People of Color*, 7.

37. *Niles' Weekly*, Oct. 1, 1831.

38. For three lengthy, contemporary letters from Miss Crandall
    to S. S. Jocelyn describing her ordeal, see "Documents:
    Abolition Letters Collected by Captain Arthur B. Spin-
    garn," *Journal of Negro History*, Jan. 1933 (XVII), 80–
    84. For this whole episode, see May, *Some Recollections*,
    39–72.

39. *Herald of Freedom*, Aug. 22, 1835.

40. *Genius*, May 1832. Harry E. Davis, "Early Colored Residents
    of Cleveland," *Phylon*, Third Quarter, 1943 (IV), 238.
    Julian S. Rammelkamp, "The Providence Negro Commu-
    nity, 1820–1842," *Rhode Island History*, Jan. 1948
    (VIII), 27. *Emancipator*, Sept. 29, 1836. *Philanthropist*,
    Dec. 6, 1836. Garrett to Edinburgh Ladies' New Anti-
    Slavery Association, Nov. 28, 1857, in *Report of Edin-
    burgh Ladies' New Association for 1856 and 1857* (Edin-
    burgh, 1858), 33. *Weekly Anglo-African*, Aug. 13, 1859.

41. Thaddeus M. Harris, *Discourse before the African Society in
    Boston, July 15, 1822* (Boston, 1822), 26. *Douglass' Pa-
    per*, Dec. 7, 1855. *Philanthropist*, Oct. 6, 1840.

42. *African Repository*, May 1858 (XXXIV), 153, and Car-
    ter G. Woodson, *The Education of the Negro Prior to
    1861* (Washington, D.C., 1919), 270–71; hereafter cited
    as *Education of the Negro*. Daniel A. Payne, *History of the
    African Methodist Episcopal Church* (Nashville, 1891),
    276. *Pennsylvania Freeman*, July 31, 1852.

43. *Report to the Primary School Committee, June 15, 1846, on
    the Petition of Sundry Colored Persons for the Abolition of
    the Schools for Colored Children. With the Solicitor's Opin-
    ion* (Boston, 1846). *Report of the Minority of the Com-*

mittee of the Primary School Board on the Caste Schools of Boston (Boston, 1846).

44. *Report of a Special Committee of the Grammar School Board, Presented August 29, 1849, on the Petition of Sundry Colored Persons Praying for the Abolition of the Smith School* (Boston, 1849). On this whole case, see Leonard W. Levy and Harlan B. Phillips, "The *Roberts* Case: Source of the 'Separate but Equal' Doctrine," *American Historical Review*, Apr. 1951 (LVI), 510–18.

45. *Proceedings of the Presentation Meeting Held in Boston, December 17, 1855*, (Boston, 1855) 24.

46. *Proceedings of the New England Anti-Slavery Convention, Held in Boston, May 24, 25, 26, 1836* (Boston, 1836), 54, 57.

47. Hugh Hawkins, "Edward Jones, 1826: First American Negro College Graduate?" *Amherst Alumni News*, Winter 1962, 20. Russwurm's graduation oration is carried in the *Genius of Universal Emancipation*, Oct. 14, 1826.

48. G. Frederick Wright, *Charles Grandison Finney* (Boston, 1891), 135. *Memoirs of Charles G. Finney* (New York, 1876), 352.

49. *Oberlin Evangelist*, in *Emancipator and Freedom's Advocate*, Sept. 8, 1842. Daniel A. Payne, *The Semi-Centenary and the Retrospection of the African Methodist Episcopal Church in the United States of America* (Baltimore, 1866), 65. *Proceedings of the General Anti-Slavery Convention Called by the Committee of the British and Foreign Anti-Slavery Society, and Held in London from Tuesday, June 13 to Tuesday, June 20, 1843*, 206. Robert S. Fletcher, *A History of Oberlin College* (2 vols., Oberlin, 1943), II, 536.

50. For Allen at Oneida, see Lewis Tappan to Gerrit Smith, Oct. 16, 1839, in Tappan Papers. Reeve is found in *Standard*, July 10, 1858.

51. Nell, *Colored Patriots*, 10. Ralph V. Harlow, *Gerrit Smith* (New York, 1939), 231–32.

CHAPTER VI

1. Harrisburgh *Daily Telegraph*, in *Weekly Anglo-African*, Aug. 6, 1859.

2. On this whole topic, see Thomas Franklin Harwood, "Great Britain and American Antislavery," doctoral dissertation, University of Texas, 1959.

3. Peter Williams, *An Oration on the Abolition of the Slave Trade; Delivered in the African Church, in the City of New York, January 1, 1808* (New York, 1808), *passim*. Henry Sipkins, *An Oration on the Abolition of the Slave Trade; Delivered in the African Church, in the City of New York, January 2, 1809. William Hamilton, "An Address to the New York African Society for Mutual Relief, Delivered in the Universality Church, January 2, 1809"* (typescript copy, Arthur Schomburg Collection, New York Public Library). Joseph Sidney, *An Oration Commemorative of the Abolition of the Slave Trade in the United States; Delivered Before the Wilberforce Philanthropic Association, in the City of New York on the Second of January, 1809* (New York, 1809).

4. *Freedom's Journal*, Apr. 27, 1827.

5. Ibid. July 6, 1827, and Oct. 12, 1827.

6. New York *Daily Advertiser*, in *Genius of Universal Emancipation*, July 14, 1827. See also *A Memorial Discourse by Henry Highland Garnet delivered in the House of Representatives, Washington, D. C., with an Introduction by James McCune Smith* (Phila., 1865), 24-25.

7. *Freedom's Journal*, Apr. 20, 1827. Paul's address is found in *Genius of Universal Emancipation*, Sept. 8, 1827.

8. Ibid. July 27, 1827, and Sept. 8, 1827. See also Howard W. Coles, *The Cradle of Freedom* (Rochester, 1942), 22-26.

9. The Cooperstown, New Haven, and Fredericksburg celebrations are in *Freedom's Journal*, July 13, 1827; the Baltimore celebration is in *Freedom's Journal*, July 20, 1827.

10. *Douglass' Paper*, July 18, 1856.

11. Watkins's musing in *Genius*, July 1831. *Colored American*, July 21, 1838. *Douglass' Paper*, July 6, 1855.

12. *Liberator*, Dec. 1, 1832. *Weekly Anglo-African*, July 23, 1859.

13. *Liberator*, Aug. 30, 1834. *Emancipator*, Aug. 24, 1837.

14. *Colored American*, Aug. 25, 1838.

15. Ibid. Aug. 18, 1838. Ibid. Sept. 15, 1838. New York meeting in *Philanthropist*, Aug. 21, 1838, with Garrison's speech there in *Colored American*, Aug. 18, 1838.

16. *Emancipator*, July 12, 1838. Marian R. Studley, "An 'August First' in 1844," *New England Quarterly*, Dec. 1943 (XVI), 568. *Colored American*, July 29, 1837. *Emancipator and Free American*, Aug. 17, 1843.

17. *Liberator*, Aug. 15, 1852. *Douglass' Paper*, Aug. 10, 1855. *Liberator*, Aug. 20, 1858. *Weekly Anglo-African*, Aug. 6, 1859.

18. *Liberator*, Aug. 20, 1858.

19. *Standard*, Aug. 12, 1854. Herman R. Muelder, *Fighters for Freedom* (New York, 1959), 219. *Douglass' Paper*, Aug. 15, 1856, and Aug. 10, 1855. *Liberator*, Aug. 6, 1858. *Life of William J. Brown of Providence* (Providence, 1883), 131.

20. *Douglass' Paper*, July 21, 1854. *Bugle*, Aug. 10, 1849. *The New York Times*, Aug. 2, 1855.

21. *Colored American*, Aug. 24, 1839. *Douglass' Paper*, Aug. 26, 1853. *Liberator*, Aug. 6, 1858.

22. *Douglass' Paper*, July 21, 1854. Ibid. Sept. 25, 1855.

23. *Colored American*, Sept. 28, 1839.

24. Ibid. Aug. 17, 1839. Thornbrough, *Negro in Indiana*, 144, n. 41.

25. Pillsbury, *Anti-Slavery Apostles*, 326.

26. *Douglass' Paper*, Aug. 6, 1856. *Anglo-African*, Aug. 6, 1859. *The Columbian*, in *Douglass' Paper*, Aug. 25, 1854.

27. *Douglass' Paper*, Apr. 21, 1854. Eva B. Dykes, *The Negro in English Romantic Thought* (Washington, D. C., 1942), 89. *The Edinburgh Review*, July 1813 (XXI), 473.

28. Adams, *Works*, III, 570.

29. Charles Stuart, *Remarks on the Colony of Liberia and the American Colonization Society. With Some Account of the Settlement of Coloured People at Wilberforce, Upper Canada* (London, 1832), 16.

30. *Liberator*, June 22, 1833.

31. *Second Annual Report of the New England Anti-Slavery Society, January 15, 1834* (Boston, 1834), 47. For a fuller description of Paul's trip, see William H. Pease and Jane Pease, *Black Utopia: Negro Communal Experiments in America* (Madison, Wis., 1963), 58–61; hereafter cited as *Black Utopia*.

32. For Purvis's passport difficulties, see *Standard*, Aug. 23, 1849, and also Joseph Boromé, "Robert Purvis and His Early Challenge to American Racism," *Negro History Bulletin*, May 1967 (XXX), 9. *Liberator*, Aug. 23, 1834. Ibid. Nov. 15, 1834.

33. Burleigh, Diary: Journal of the Little Things of Life, August 1, 1844–March 5, 1845 (Historical Society of Pennsylvania), entry of Sept. 20, 1844.

34. Frederick B. Tolles, ed., *Slavery and "The Woman Question": Lucretia Mott's Diary of Her Visit to Great Britain to Attend the World's Anti-Slavery Convention of 1840* (Haverford, Pa., 1952), 45.

35. *Liberator*, May 21, 1841. *Herald of Freedom*, Mar. 5, 1841.

36. *Abolitionist*, Feb. 1833 (I), 28.

37. *Anti-Slavery Reporter*, July 1, 1840. *Liberator*, Sept. 25, 1840.

38. *Emancipator and Free American*, May 12, 1832. For Irish American coolness to abolitionism, see Madeleine Hooke Rice, *American Catholic Opinion in the Slavery Controversy* (New York, 1944), 83. Nell's remarks are in *North Star*, Dec. 3, 1847.

39. Sarah Pugh to Mary Estlin, Mar. 7, 1853, in Estlin Papers. Sarah Pugh to Mary Estlin, Nov. 29, 1853, in Estlin Papers.

40. *Three Years' Female Anti-Slavery Effort in Britain and America, Being a Report of the Proceedings of the Glasgow Ladies Auxiliary Emancipation Society Since Its Formation in January 1831* (Glasgow, 1837), 21.

41. *Emancipator and Free American*, Sept. 14, 1843. Ibid. Sept. 21, 1843. Garrison to Helen Garrison, Sept. 3, 1846, William Lloyd Garrison Manuscripts, Boston Public Library. *Report of a Public Meeting Held at Finsbury Chapel, Moorfields, to Receive Frederick Douglass, the American Slave* (London, 1846), 77.

42. M. W. Chapman to Garrison, Aug. 29, 1849, in *Standard*, Sept. 20, 1849. Ibid. Feb. 7, 1850. *Liberator*, June 17, 1850.

43. *Mercury* in *Liberator*, Jan. 24, 1851. Ibid. Feb. 14, 1851. *Proceedings of the American Anti-Slavery Society at Its Second Decade, December 3, 4, 5, 1853* (New York, 1854), 153. *Liberator*, May 9, 1851.

44. *British Banner* in *Pennsylvania Freeman*, Aug. 25, 1853.

45. *Proceedings of the American Anti-Slavery Society at Its Second Decade*, 154. *Liberator*, May 5, 1854. *Standard*, Dec. 26, 1857. *Liberator*, July 22, 1853. *Anti-Slavery Reporter* (London), July 1, 1863.

46. Letter from Maria to Sarah in Estlin Papers.

47. *Minutes of the Bristol and Clifton Ladies Anti-Slavery Society*, Aug. 15, 1859, in Estlin Papers.

48. *Anti-Slavery Advocate* (London), Apr. 1859.

49. For the gist of her remarks at Edinburgh see *Liberator*, Nov. 16, 1860. *Annual Report of the Leeds Young Men's Anti-Slavery Society for the Year Ending December 1860* (Leeds, 1861), 6.

50. For Delany in London, see Benjamin Quarles, "Ministers Without Portfolio," *Journal of Negro History*, Jan. 1954 (XXXIX), 36–39, also Frank A. Rollin, *Life and Public Services of Martin R. Delany* (Boston, 1883), 127; hereafter cited as *Martin R. Delany*.

51. *Report of the Proceedings of the Anti-Slavery Conference and Public Meeting, Held at Manchester on the 1st of August, 1854, in Commemoration of West India Emancipation* (London, 1854), 35.

52. *Liberator*, Oct. 19, 1833. *Emancipator*, Oct. 19, 1833. *Liberator*, Oct. 12, 1833.

53. *The Man: The Hero: The Christian! A Eulogy on the Life and Character of Thomas Clarkson: Delivered in the City*

of New York, December, 1846. By the Rev. Alexander
Crummell, Together with Freedom, A Poem, Read on the
Same Occasion by Charles L. Reason (New York, 1847),
43.

CHAPTER VII

1. Still to J. M. McKim, Aug. 8, 1850, in *Bugle*, Nov. 9, 1850.
   See also the interesting article, Robert Brent Toplin, "Peter
   Still Versus the Peculiar Institution," *Civil War History*,
   Dec. 1967 (XIII), 340–49.
2. L. Maria Child, *Isaac T. Hopper: A True Life* (Boston,
   1853), 209.
3. Fred Landon, "A Daring Canadian Abolitionist," *Michigan
   History Magazine*, July-Oct. 1921 (V), 370.
4. Birney to Tappan, Feb. 27, 1837, Dwight L. Dumond, ed.,
   Letters of James Gillespie Birney (2 vols., New York,
   1938), I, 376. Benjamin G. Merkel, "The Underground
   Railroad and the Missouri Borders, 1840–1860," *Missouri
   Historical Review*, Apr. 1943 (XXXVII), 278. Rush R.
   Sloane, "The Underground Railroad of the Firelands,"
   Magazine of Western History, May 1888 (VIII), 38. E.
   Delorus Preston, Jr., "The Underground Railroad in Northwest Ohio," *Journal of Negro History*, Oct. 1932 (XVII),
   411.
5. Wilbur H. Siebert, *The Underground Railroad from Slavery
   to Freedom* (New York, 1898), 32; hereafter cited as
   Underground Railroad. Ibid. 151. Ibid. 403–36.
6. Earl Conrad, *Harriet Tubman* (Washington, D. C., 1943),
   232. Mary Thacher Higginson, ed., *Letters and Journals
   of Thomas Wentworth Higginson, 1846–1906* (New
   York, 1921), 81.
7. Siebert, *Underground Railroad*, 70. Ibid. 296.
8. Wilbur Siebert, "The Underground Railroad in Massachusetts," *Proceedings of the American Antiquarian Society*,
   new series, 1936 (XLV); 29. Luther R. Marsh, ed.,
   Writings and Speeches of Alvan Stewart on Slavery (New
   York, 1860), 219–20.

9. Siebert, *Underground Railroad*, 95. Allan Peskin, ed., *North into Freedom: The Autobiography of John Malvin, Free Negro, 1795–1880* (Cleveland, 1966), 6, 10.

10. Larry Gara, *The Liberty Line: The Legend of the Underground Railroad* (Lexington, Ky., 1961), 27–28; hereafter cited as *Liberty Line*. *Genius*, Oct. 1831.

11. William Craft, *Running a Thousand Miles for Freedom* (London, 1860), 85. *Reminiscences of Levi Coffin* (Cincinnati, 1876), 107; hereafter cited as *Reminiscences*. Thornbrough, *Negro in Indiana*, 41.

12. Coffin, *Reminiscences*, 297. Wendell P. Dabney, *Cincinnati's Colored Citizens* (Cincinnati, 1926), 130. For Mitchell, see William M. Mitchell, *The Underground Railroad* (London, 1860). Siebert, *Underground Railroad*, 70. Jones to F. Douglass, Nov. 11, 1853, in *Douglass' Paper*, Nov. 18, 1853.

13. R. C. Smedley, *History of the Underground Railroad in Chester and the Neighboring Counties of Pennsylvania* (Lancaster, 1883), 355; hereafter cited as *Underground Railroad in Chester*. Still, *Underground Railroad*, 736. Whipper to White, Apr. 26, 1839, Leon Gardiner Collection. Smedley, *Underground Railroad in Chester*, 338.

14. Monroe N. Work, "Life of Charles B. Ray," *Journal of Negro History*, Oct. 1919 (IV), 371. *Weekly Anglo-African*, Sept. 17, 1859.

15. *Narrative of William W. Brown, A Fugitive Slave. Written by Himself* (Boston, 1847), 107–8.

16. Archibald H. Grimké, "Anti-Slavery Boston," *New England Magazine*, Dec. 1890 (new series, III), 458. Austin Bearse, *Reminiscences of Fugitive-Slave Days in Boston* (Boston, 1880), 8.

17. These abolitionist outfits are not to be confused with the horse-thief societies so common to the rural America of that day.

18. *Douglass' Paper*, Apr. 6, 1855.

19. *Emancipator*, Jan. 26, 1837. Ibid.

20. Wilson's arrest in *Colored American*, July 21, 1838. *Emancipator*, June 1, 1837.

21. *Herald of Freedom*, Mar. 8, 1839.

22. For the Charity Walker affair, see *Mirror of Liberty* (New York), July 1838.

23. In its August 20, 1840, issue, *The Standard* devotes six columns to an airing of the quarrel between Ruggles and the committee.

24. *First Annual Report of the New York Committee of Vigilance* (New York, 1837), 84. *Emancipator*, June 1, 1837. Ibid. Aug. 13, 1840. Ibid. June 17, 1841.

25. *Liberator*, Dec. 12, 1845. DeBaptiste to Douglass, Nov. 5, 1854, in *Douglass' Paper*, Nov. 17, 1854. *Provincial Freeman*, May 31, 1856. *Douglass' Paper*, Jan. 26, 1855.

26. Emerson to "Dr. S. G. Howe, and Associates of the Committee of Citizens," Sept. 23, 1846, in *Address of the Committee Appointed by a Public Meeting Held in Faneuil Hall, September 24, 1846, for the Purpose of Considering the Recent Case of Kidnaping from our Soil and of Taking Measures to Prevent the Recurrence of Similar Outrages* (Boston, 1846), 31.

27. See below, chapter 9.

28. *North Star*, May 19, 1848. *Bugle*, May 25, 1849. *Report of the New York State Vigilance Committee made at the Annual Meeting Held in New York, March 19, 1853* (New York, 1853), 4.

29. For the constitution of the Fugitive Aid Society, see *Douglass' Weekly*, Apr. 6, 1855. *Weekly Anglo-African*, May 5, 1860.

30. Minutes of the Philadelphia Female Anti-Slavery Society, Sept. 8, 1842, Historical Society of Pennsylvania.

31. See letter of White to Ruggles, Dec. 6, 1838, in Leon Gardiner Collection. On the makeup and operations of this organization see Joseph A. Boromé, "The Vigilant Committee of Philadelphia," *Pennsylvania Magazine of History and Biography*, July 1968 (XCII), 320–51.

32. Woodson, *Mind of the Negro*, 586.

33. Still, *Underground Railroad*, 83.

34. *Colored American*, June 8, 1838. *First Annual Report of the New York Committee of Vigilance*, 84. *Emancipator*, Sept. 19, 1839. Figures of donations to Vigilance Committee of Philadelphia compiled from the Minute Book of the

Vigilant Committee of Philadelphia, June 4, 1839, to March 20, 1844, which also includes other fund-raising activities of the committee.

35. *Liberator*, Mar. 5, 1852. *Douglass' Monthly*, Mar. 1859. Funds raised at Sunday collections compiled from *Liberator*, Aug. 28, 1846.

36. *Emancipator*, Mar. 19, 1840. *Northern Star and Freeman's Advocate*, Dec. 8, 1842. *North Star*, May 18, 1849. *Liberator*, July 8, 1858.

37. The woman's auxiliary reference is found in the Minute Book of the Vigilant Committee of Philadelphia, June 4, 1839, to March 20, 1844. All other citations may be found in the Minutes of the Philadelphia Female Anti-Slavery Society, 1839–1870 (8 vols., handwritten).

38. *Douglass' Paper*, Mar. 11, 1842. *Report of Edinburgh Ladies New Anti-Slavery Association for 1856 and 1857* (Edinburgh, 1858), 3. For Richardson's letters to Still (Vigilance Committee of Philadelphia), see Still's *Underground Railroad*, 604–8. *Report of the Edinburgh Ladies New Anti-Slavery Association for 1858*, 5.

39. Loguen to "Dear Friend," Feb. 7, 1859, in A.M.A. Papers.

40. Minutes of the Philadelphia Female Anti-Slavery Society, 1839–1870, Nov. 11, 1841.

41. Minute Book of the Vigilant Committee of Philadelphia, Dec. 4, 1839. *Liberator*, Aug. 7, 1845. *Standard*, Feb. 21, 1850. *Douglass' Paper*, Dec. 7, 1855.

42. *Standard*, Jan. 2, 1858. Harwood, Great Britain and American Antislavery, 712.

43. E. B. Chace, *Anti-Slavery Reminiscences* (Central Falls, R. I., 1891), 89.

44. Coffin, *Reminiscences*, 298.

45. W. Montague Cobb, "Martin Robinson Delany, 1812–1855," *Journal of the National Medical Association*, May 1952 (XLIV), 234.

46. Haviland, *Woman's Life Work*, 135. *Liberator*, Sept. 11, 1858. Thornbrough, *Negro in Indiana*, 42.

47. *Standard*, Sept. 21, 1848. Still, *Underground Railroad*, 746–47. Thornbrough, *Negro in Indiana*, 42. Still, *Underground Railroad*, 246–50.

48. *Liberator*, Dec. 21, 1849. *Weekly Advocate*, Jan. 14, 1837. Still, *Underground Railroad*, 739.

49. *Emancipator*, Dec. 8, 1836. Ibid. Dec. 15, 1836. *Pennsylvania Freeman*, Jan. 6, 1853. Beman to Douglass, Sept. 10, 1855, in *Douglass' Paper*, Sept. 14, 1855.

50. *Standard*, Sept. 13, 1849. Calvin Fairbank, *How the Way Was Prepared* (Chicago, 1890), 63.

51. J. C. Lovejoy, *Memoir of Charles T. Torrey* (Boston, 1847), 89. *Emancipator*, Aug. 14, 1844.

52. *Liberator*, July 10, 1846. Ibid. July 10, 1846. Ibid. Aug. 7, 1846.

53. Ibid. Daniel A. Payne, *Recollections of Seventy Years* (Nashville, 1888), 98.

54. For a good contemporary account of the Williamson episode, see William Still's lengthy article in *Provincial Freeman*, Aug. 22, 1855.

55. *Proceedings of Colored National Convention of 1855*, 25. *Case of Passmore Williamson. Report of the Proceedings* . . . (Phila., 1856), 165.

56. *Colored American*, Feb. 20, 1841. Albert Bushnell Hart, *Salmon Portland Chase* (Boston, 1899), 82, 84. *Liberator*, July 11, 1851. Robert Morris to Dana, Jan. 1, 1852; Morris to Hale, Jan. 1, 1852; Hale to Morris, Jan. 18, 1852, and Dana to Morris, Jan. 1, 1852, all in *Liberator*, Mar. 19, 1852.

CHAPTER VIII

1. *Standard*, May 23, 1857. Ibid. May 30, 1857. Ibid. June 7, 1849.

2. *Douglass' Paper*, June 15, 1855.

3. For Negro disfranchisement see Charles H. Wesley, *Neglected History* (Wilberforce, Ohio, 1965), 41–77; Litwack, *North of Slavery*, and the pioneer study, still useful, Emil Olbrich, *The Development of Sentiment on Negro Suffrage to 1860* (Madison, Wis., 1912); hereafter cited as *Negro Suffrage*.

4. *Douglass' Paper*, May 4, 1855.

5. Loguen to Douglass, Apr. 9, 1855, *Douglass' Paper*, Apr. 20, 1855.

6. *Colored American*, Mar. 11, 1837, and *Philanthropist*, Mar. 31, 1837.

7. *Colored American*, Sept. 2, 1837, and *Emancipator*, Sept. 7, 1837.

8. *Colored American*, July 4, 1838. Ibid. Oct. 6, 1838. Ibid. Aug. 17, 1839.

9. *Emancipator*, Dec. 31, 1840.

10. *Douglass' Paper*, Sept. 14, 1855. Ibid. Feb. 22, 1856.

11. *The Suffrage Question in Relation to Colored Voters in the State of New York* (no place or date, but undoubtedly New York, 1860), 2.

12. Olbrich, *Negro Suffrage*, 53.

13. *Appeal of Forty Thousand Citizens Threatened with Disfranchisement, to the People of Pennsylvania* (Phila., 1838), 18.

14. Joseph B. Braithwaite, ed., *Memoirs of Joseph John Guerney* (Phila., 1854), 131.

15. *Minutes of the State Convention of Colored Citizens of Pennsylvania, Convened at Harrisburg, December 13 and 14, 1848* (Phila., 1849), 10. Edward R. Turner, *The Negro in Pennsylvania, 1619–1861* (Washington, D. C., 1911), 191, n. 81.

16. *Memorial of Thirty Thousand Disfranchised Citizens of Philadelphia to the Honorable Senate and House of Representatives* (Phila., 1855). W. Still to *Provincial Freeman*, Mar. 15, 1857, in *Provincial Freeman*, Mar. 28, 1857.

17. Marion T. Wright, "Negro Suffrage in New Jersey, 1776–1875," *Journal of Negro History*, Apr. 1948 (XXXIII), 191.

18. *Proceedings of the State Convention of Colored Citizens of the State of Illinois, Held in the City of Alton, November 13, 14, 15, 1856* (Chicago, 1856), 3. *Bugle*, Jan. 19, 1850.

19. *Bugle*, Feb. 22, 1851. The Langston memorial is carried in *Douglass' Paper*, June 16, 1854. Ibid. July 25, 1856.

20. *Proceedings of the First State Convention of the Colored Citizens of the State of California* (Sacramento, 1855), 27.

21. *Douglass' Paper*, Dec. 7, 1855. Eugene H. Berwanger, "The 'Black Law' Question in Ante-Bellum California," *Journal of the West*, Apr. 1967 (VI), 218.

22. Still to Mary Ann Shadd, May 30, 1855, in *Provincial Freeman*, June 9, 1855.

23. *Bugle*, Oct. 6, 1849.

24. *North Star*, July 28, 1848. *Douglass' Paper*, Nov. 25, 1853. Ibid. Dec. 16, 1853.

25. *Minutes and Addresses of the State Convention of the Colored Citizens of Ohio, Convened at Columbus, January 10, 11, 12, and 13, 1849* (Oberlin, 1849), 15.

26. *Proceedings of State Convention of Colored Men*, 6.

27. Lillie Buffum Chace Wyman, *American Chivalry* (Boston, 1913), 107.

28. *Douglass' Paper*, Mar. 14, 1856. *Twenty-First Annual Report Presented to the Pennsylvania Anti-Slavery Society by its Executive Committee, October 6, 1858* (Phila., 1858), 15. Still to Shadd, Feb. 21, 1857, in *Provincial Freeman*, Mar. 7, 1857. *Norristown Reporter*, in *Standard*, July 4, 1857.

29. *Proceedings of a Convention of the Colored Men of Ohio, Held in Cincinnati, November 23, 24, 25, 26, 1858* (Cincinnati, 1858), 11.

30. Phillips to Charlotte, Jan. 18, 1857, in Anna J. Cooper, *Personal Recollections of the Grimké Family* (Washington, D. C., 1951), 17.

31. *Standard*, Nov. 27, 1858. Journal (handwritten) of Charlotte Forten, Nov. 19, 1858, Howard University Library. Ibid. Dec. 1, 1856. Ibid. Feb. 27, 1858.

32. *Liberator*, Mar. 30, 1838. Ibid. Feb. 25, 1842. Ibid. Feb. 10, 1843.

33. Ibid. Nov. 1, 1839.

34. *Standard*, Dec. 23, 1841.

35. *Rights of All*, Oct. 16, 1829. *Human Rights*, in *Herald of Freedom*, Dec. 22, 1838.

36. *Herald of Freedom*, Dec. 22, 1838. Olbrich, *Negro Suffrage*, 72. *An Address to the Three Thousand Colored Citizens of New York Who are the Owners of One Hundred and Twenty Thousand Acres of Land in the State of New York, Given Them by Gerrit Smith, Esquire, September 1, 1846* (New York, 1846). *Standard*, Nov. 8, 1849. *Douglass' Monthly*, Oct. 1860.

37. *Colored American*, Nov. 3, 1838. *Standard*, Jan. 26, 1843.

38. *Emancipator*, May 15, 1840. *Colored American*, May 23, 1840.

39. *Emancipator and Free American*, Mar. 4, 1842.

40. Wright to Joshua Leavitt, Oct. 19, 1844, in *Emancipator*, Oct. 30, 1844.

41. *North Star*, Nov. 24, 1848.

42. *Liberator*, Dec. 10, 1852.

43. Loguen to Douglass, Mar. 7, 1854, in *Douglass' Paper*, Apr. 14, 1854. Ibid. Apr. 7, 1854.

44. *Pennsylvania Freeman*, Oct. 13, 1853.

45. *Pro. of State Con. of Colored Men . . . 1856*, 2. *Douglass' Paper*, Oct. 3, 1856.

46. *Standard*, Oct. 9, 1858. *Proceedings of a Convention of the Colored Men of Ohio, Held in Cincinnati, November 23, 24, 25, 26, 1858, passim.*

47. *Weekly Anglo-African*, Aug. 6, 1859.

48. *Douglass' Monthly*, Dec. 1860.

49. *Proceedings of the State Convention of Colored Citizens of the State of Illinois, Held in the City of Alton, November 13, 14, 15, 1856* (Chicago, 1856), 7. *Proceedings of a Convention of the Colored Men of Ohio, Held in Cincinnati, November 23, 24, 25, 26, 1858* (Cincinnati, 1858), 5.

50. *Annals of Sixth Congress*, 229–30, 241–45. *Human Rights*, Jan. 1837.

51. *Liberator*, Nov. 17, 1832. Ibid. Apr. 27, 1833.

52. *Emancipator*, July 27, 1833.

53. Ibid. Aug. 5, 1837. *Minutes and Proceedings of the First Annual Meeting of the American Moral Reform Society . . . 1837*, 23.

54. Nina Moore Tiffany, *Samuel E. Sewall: A Memoir* (Boston, 1898), 70.

55. For the wording of these petitions, see *Emancipator and Free American*, Dec. 8, 1842.

56. Ibid. June 23, 1842. *Liberator*, Dec. 23, 1842. J. W. C. Pennington, *Covenants Involving Moral Wrong Not Obligatory Upon Man* (Hartford, 1842), 5.

57. *Journal of House of Representatives*, Twenty-fourth Congress, second session (Washington, D. C., 1837), 350. Charles Francis Adams, ed., *Memoirs of John Quincy Adams* (12 vols., Phila., 1874–77), X, 9. *Emancipator*, Dec. 1, 1842. *Liberator*, Aug. 25, 1843.

58. *North Star*, Apr. 21, 1848. *Bugle*, Apr. 7, 1848. *North Star*, Mar. 10, 1848. *Pennsylvania Freeman*, Mar. 9, 1848.

CHAPTER IX

1. *Standard*, Oct. 10, 1850, and *The Fugitive Slave Bill: Its History and Unconstitutionality: with an Account of the Seizure and Enslavement of James Hamlet, and His Subsequent Restoration to Liberty* (New York, 1850), *passim*.

2. *Bugle*, Nov. 16, 1850.

3. *Standard*, Oct. 10, 1850.

4. New York *Evening Post*, in *American Missionary*, Mar. 1851.

5. Irene Williams, "The Operation of the Fugitive Slave Law in Western Pennsylvania from 1850 to 1860," *Western Pennsylvania Historical Magazine*, July 1921 (IV), 152. *Weekly Anglo-African*, Mar. 10, 1860. Whipper to Still, Dec. 4, 1871, in Still, *Underground Railroad*, 737–38.

6. *Standard*, Oct. 10, 1850. *North Star*, Oct. 24, 1850.

7. Rollin, *Martin R. Delany*, 76. Pillsbury to Oliver Johnson, Oct. 18, 1850, in *Bugle*, Nov. 3, 1850.

8. *Chicago Daily Journal*, Oct. 3, 1850, in Mark Miles Fisher, "Negro Churches in Illinois," *Journal of Illinois History*, Autumn 1963 (LVI), 555. *North Star*, Dec. 5, 1850. *State Convention of Colored Citizens of Ohio, Convened at Columbus, January 1851*, 16.

9. *Nineteenth Annual Report of the Massachusetts Anti-Slavery Society* (Boston, 1851), 43.

10. *Boston Herald*, Oct. 15, 1850, in *Liberator*, Oct. 18, 1850.

11. *North Star*, Oct. 24, 1850.

12. Ibid.

13. *Pennsylvania Freeman*, Apr. 22, 1852.

14. V. Y. Bowditch, *Henry Ingersoll Bowditch*, I, 207–8.

15. *Liberator*, July 6, 1833. *Niles' Register*, Apr. 19, 1834, May 10, 1834.

16. Nina Moore Tiffany, *Samuel E. Sewall: A Memoir* (Boston, 1898), 63. For this whole episode, see Leonard W. Levy, "The 'Abolition Riot': Boston's First Slave Rescue," *New England Quarterly*, Mar. 1952 (XXV), 85–92.

17. Bessie L. Pierce, *A History of Chicago, 1673–1848* (1937), 252. Gara, *Liberty Line*, 110.

18. *Twentieth Annual Report of the Massachusetts Anti-Slavery Society, January 28, 1852*, 23.

19. For the names of these 49 Negroes, see Wilbur H. Siebert, "The Underground Railroad in Massachusetts," *Proceedings of the American Antiquarian Society*, 1936 (new series, XLV), 75–76.

20. Whittier to Bowditch, May 29, 1854, in V. Y. Bowditch, *Henry Ingersoll Bowditch*, I, 270. *Liberator*, July 7, 1854.

21. Journal of Charlotte Forten.

22. Laura E. Richards, ed., *Letters and Journals of Samuel Gridley Howe* (2 vols., Boston, 1909), II, 270.

23. Watkins to Douglass, Dec. 23, 1853, in *Douglass' Paper*, Jan. 6, 1854.

24. *Liberator*, Aug. 13, 1858.

25. For the Jerry Rescue, see May, *Some Recollections*, 374–84, and W. Freeman Galpin, "The Jerry Rescue," *New York History*, Jan. 1945 (XXVI), 19–34.

26. Ward to Whipple, Oct. 13, 1851, A.M.A. Papers.

27. Jermain W. Loguen, *The Rev. J. W. Loguen As a Slave and As a Freeman* (Syracuse, 1859), 442.

28. Allen to the *Pennsylvania Freeman*, Oct. 6, 1852, in *Douglass' Paper*, Oct. 29, 1852.

29. In its September 27, 1851, issue, the short-lived *Impartial Citizen* ran nine editorials from other journals on the Christiana affair. For scholarly versions, see W. U. Hensel, *The Christiana Riot and the Treason Trials of 1851* (Lancaster, Pa., 1911), and Roderick W. Nash, "William Parker and the Christiana Riot," *Journal of Negro History*, Jan. 1961 (XLVI), 24–31.

30. For the contribution of the San Francisco Negroes, see *Pennsylvania Freeman*, Feb. 12, 1852. For the meetings in New York, Columbus, and Chicago, see *Douglass' Paper*, Oct. 16, 1851, Nov. 13, 1851, and Jan. 8, 1852.

31. *Liberator*, Aug. 20, 1859.

32. For this case, see *Should Colored Men Be Subject to the Pains and Penalties of the Fugitive Slave Law? Speech of C. H. Langston, before the U. S. District Court for the Northern Dis. of Ohio, May 12, 1859* (Cleveland, 1859). Also John Mercer Langston, "The Oberlin-Wellington Rescue," *Weekly Anglo-African*, July 23, 1859, and Jacob R. Shipherd, *History of the Oberlin-Wellington Rescue* (Boston, 1859).

33. *Proceedings of a Convention of the Colored Men of Ohio, Held in Cincinnati, November 23, 24, 25, 26, 1858* (Cincinnati, 1858), 15.

34. *Weekly Anglo-African*, June 23, 1860.

35. Ibid. July 14, 1860.

36. For letter, see *Douglass' Paper*, Apr. 8, 1852.

37. *Speech of H. Ford Douglas in Reply to Mr. J. M. Langston Before the Emigration Convention at Cleveland, Ohio, Delivered on August 27, 1854* (Chicago, 1854), 16.

38. James Theodore Holly, *A Vindication of the Capacity of the Negro Race for Self-Government and Civilized Progress as Illustrated by Historical Events of the Haytien Revolution* (New Haven, Conn., 1857), 46.

39. Garnet to Douglass, Jan. 21, 1848, in *North Star*, Jan. 26, 1848. Ibid. Mar. 2, 1849.

40. Ibid. Mar. 2, 1849.

41. For the flight northward, see Fred Landon, "The Negro Migration to Canada after the Passing of the Fugitive Slave Act," *Journal of Negro History*, Jan. 1920 (V), 22–30.

Whipper to Gerrit Smith, Apr. 22, 1856, in Smith Papers.

42. *Provincial Freeman*, Dec. 1, 1855. For an analysis of this weekly see Alexander L. Murray, "The Provincial Freeman: A New Source for the History of the Negro in Canada and the United States," *Journal of Negro History*, April 1959 (XLIV), 123–35.

43. For a contemporary account of the Negro in Canada, see Benjamin Drew, *The Refugee: Or the Narratives of Fugitive Slaves in Canada, Related by Themselves* (Boston, 1856). An analysis of the lot of the Negro in Canada may be found in Pease and Pease, *Black Utopia*, 8–12, 161.

44. *The Standard* for May 3, 1849, devoted fourteen columns to this meeting. *The Colonization Herald* (Phila.), June 1848.

45. *Impartial Citizen*, Sept. 27, 1851. *Fifteenth Annual Report of the Pennsylvania Anti-Slavery Society, October 25, 1852* (Phila., 1852), 56. *Liberator*, Apr. 4, 1851.

46. *Standard*, Jan. 22, 1852.

47. *Provincial Freeman*, May 6, 1854.

48. *Thirteenth Annual Report of the American and Foreign Anti-Slavery Society at New York, May 1853* (New York, 1853), 193. Downing to Douglass, Dec. 6, 1854, in *Douglass' Paper*, Dec. 22, 1854. *Provincial Freeman*, July 22, 1854.

49. *Thirteenth Annual Report of the American and Foreign Anti-Slavery Society at New York, May 1853*, 193.

50. Allen to Douglass, May 6, 1852, in *Douglass' Paper*, May 20, 1852.

51. *Proceedings of Colored National Convention at Philadelphia, 1855*, 28. See also *Douglass' Paper*, Nov. 9, 1855.

52. *Weekly Anglo-African*, Sept. 10, 1859.

CHAPTER X

1. *Correspondence Between the Hon. F. H. Elmore . . . and James G. Birney*, 21.

2. Martineau, *Martyr Age*, 6.

3. *House Committee Reports, Twenty-Seventh Congress, third session, Report No. 283, Report on the Memorial of the Friends of African Colonization, Feb. 28, 1843,* 1026. *Standard,* Oct. 15, 1840. *Liberator,* Nov. 19, 1841.

4. *People's Press,* Mar. 17, 1842, in *Emancipator and Free American,* Mar. 31, 1842.

5. Ibid. Apr. 14, 1842.

6. For this address, see Herbert Aptheker, *A Documentary History of the Negro People in the United States* (New York, 1951), 226–33.

7. *Buffalo Commercial Advertiser,* in *Emancipator and Free American,* Oct. 12, 1843.

8. *Liberator,* Sept. 22, 1843.

9. *Emancipator and Free American,* Nov. 30, 1843.

10. *North Star,* Dec. 3, 1847. Henry Highland Garnet, *Walker's Appeal, with a Brief Sketch of His Life; and, also, Garnet's Address to the Slaves of the United States of America* (New York, 1848). *Minutes and Addresses of the State Convention of the Colored Citizens of Ohio, Convened at Columbus, January 10, 11, 12, and 13, 1849,* 18.

11. *Liberator,* June 8, 1849.

12. Loguen to Douglass, Aug. 5, 1853, in *Douglass' Paper,* Aug. 12, 1853. *Speech of H. Ford Douglas . . . before the Emigration Convention at Cleveland* (Chicago, 1854), 11. *Douglass' Paper,* July 18, 1856.

13. *National Convention of Colored People . . . Held in Troy . . . 1847,* 17. *Liberator,* Apr. 4, 1851. *Douglass' Paper,* Aug. 10, 1855. Ibid. Nov. 28, 1856.

14. *State Convention of Colored Men of Ohio, Held in Columbus, 1857,* 6. William Jay, *Miscellaneous Writings on Slavery* (Boston, 1853), 381.

15. *Douglass' Paper,* May 13, 1852. *Liberator,* Mar. 11, 1853.

16. *Liberator,* Sept. 14, 1855. *Douglass' Paper,* Sept. 7, 1855.

17. *Provincial Freeman,* Apr. 18, 1857. Ibid. Apr. 25, 1857.

18. Ibid. Mar. 28, 1857.

19. *Standard,* Apr. 18, 1857. *Two Speeches by Frederick Douglass; one on West India Emancipation . . . and the other on the Dred Scott Decision . . .* (Rochester, 1857), 31.

20. *Standard*, Aug. 7, 1858. See also *Liberator*, Aug. 13, 1858.

21. *Weekly Anglo-African*, Aug. 6, 1859.

22. Wendell Phillips, *Speeches, Lectures and Letters* (second series, Boston, 1891), 75–76.

23. *Liberator*, Mar. 12, 1858.

24. *Acts and Resolves passed by the General Court of Massachusetts in the year 1932* (Boston, 1932), 315.

25. *Proceedings of a Convention of the Colored Men of Ohio, Held in Cincinnati, November 23, 24, 25, 26, 1858*, 17.

26. Carter G. Woodson, *Negro Orators*, 246. *Weekly Anglo-African*, Nov. 12, 1859.

27. Oswald Garrison Villard, *John Brown, 1800–1859: A Biography Fifty Years After* (New York, 1943), 74; hereafter cited as *John Brown*.

28. F. B. Sanborn, ed., *The Life and Letters of John Brown* (Boston, 1891), 129. For the original, see "John Brown's Letter Book, Taken by C. W. Tayleure from John Brown's residence at the Kennedy Farm, Washington County, Maryland, on the evening of the day of the capture of Brown at Harper's Ferry, Oct. 18, 1859," at Maryland Historical Society, Baltimore, Md.

29. James Redpath, *Public Life of John Brown* (Boston, 1860), 50. John W. Wayland, *John Kagi and John Brown* (Strasburg, Va., 1961), 70.

30. See Brown's letter of instructions to the Gileadites in Sanborn, *Life and Letters of John Brown*, 125.

31. J. W. Loguen, *The Rev. J. W. Loguen As a Slave and As a Freeman*, 451.

32. For Delany's role in the Chatham meeting, see Rollin, *Martin R. Delany*, 89–90.

33. Copeland to Addison W. Halbert, Dec. 10, 1859, in "The John Brown Letters Found in the Virginia State Library," *Virginia Magazine of History*, July 1902 (X), 170.

34. Langston to the *Cleveland Plaindealer*, Nov. 18, 1859, in *Weekly Anglo-African*, Dec. 3, 1859.

35. Ibid. Nov. 19, 1859. James Redpath, *Echoes of Harper's Ferry* (Boston, 1860), 391.

36. *Weekly Anglo-African*, Dec. 3, 1859. Redpath, *Echoes of Harper's Ferry*, 419. Ibid. 418. *Weekly Anglo-African*, Dec. 3, 1859.

37. Villard, *John Brown*, 554. James M. Ashley to his family, *Toledo Blade*, Dec. 9, 1859, in Robert L. Stevens, ed., "John Brown's Execution: An Eyewitness Account," *Northwestern Ohio Quarterly*, Autumn 1949 (XXI), 146. David H. Strother, in Boyd B. Stutler, "The Hanging of John Brown," *American Heritage*, Feb. 1955 (VI), 9.

38. *Letters of Lydia Maria Child* (Boston, 1882), 137.

39. *Weekly Anglo-African*, Dec. 10, 1859.

40. Ibid. Dec. 17, 1859.

41. *Weekly Anglo-African*, Mar. 10, 1860. Ibid. Jan. 7, 1860. Ibid. Feb. 11, 1860. For a typical letter from Mrs. Brown, see *Weekly Anglo-African*, Mar. 10, 1860.

42. Ibid. Apr. 14, 1860. Ibid. June 23, 1860.

43. *Liberator*, Dec. 16, 1859. Douglass to Redpath, Jan. 29, 1860, in *Douglass' Monthly*, Sept. 1860. Ibid. Oct. 1860. *Weekly Anglo-African*, Dec. 24, 1859. Ibid. Dec. 31, 1859.

44. "Brown Letters in Virginia State Library," 383.

45. For these expressions, see *Works of Charles Sumner* (Boston, 1880), V, 170–72.

46. *Douglass' Monthly*, July 1860.

47. *Standard*, July 7, 1860.

48. *Providence Daily Post*, Feb. 2, 1861, in Howard C. Perkins, *Northern Editorials on Secession* (New York, 1942), 441.

49. *Douglass' Monthly*, Feb. 1861.

50. "Anti-Slavery Album of Contributions from Friends of Freedom, 1834–1858," Manuscripts Division, Library of Congress.

Index

Amalgamation, *see* Intermarriage
AME, *see* Bethel Methodists
American Anti-Slavery Society,
14, 21–22, 26, 28, 33, 45,
48, 51, 65, 71, 113, 131,
139, 231
  formation, 23–25
  split in, 54
American Baptist Free Mission
Society, 80, 114, 148
American Baptist Missionary Society, 82
*American Prejudice against Color,
The* (William G. Allen),
138
American Colonization Society, 4,
6, 19–20, 41, 78, 130, 131,
215, 216, 218, 219
  and Liberia, 12
American Convention for Promoting the Abolition of Slavery
and Improving the Condition
of the African Race, The
(federation of state societies), 9, 11–12
AMEZ, *see* Zion Methodists
American and Foreign Anti-Slavery Society, 45, 46
  clergymen, 68–69
  1853 annual meeting of, 220
American Missionary Association,
76, 79–80, 210
American Moral Reform Society,
55, 94, 102, 193
American Peace Society, 63
American Seaman's Friends Society, 100
American Society for Colonizing
the Free People of Color in
the United States, 4
  see also American Colonization
Society
American Union for the Relief
and Improvement of the Col-
ored Race, 51
American Wesleyan Anti-Slavery
Society, 80
Amistad (Spanish schooner), 76,
78, 226
Amistad Committee, 76–78
Anderson, Elijah, 148, 162

Anderson, Osborn Perry, 239, 240
Andrews, Charles C., 12
Anglo-African Weekly (newspaper), 122, 128, 240
Anti-Slavery Convention of American Women, 91
Anti-Slavery Harp, The (W. W.
Brown), 62
Antislavery sentiment, 9, 17, 48,
54, 62, 71, 81, 83, 117–18,
141, 143, 151, 152, 153,
159, 160, 169, 177, 182,
183, 187, 222, 232
  influence of press, 84–86
  see also Abolitionists; Slavery
Anti-Slavery Standard, The
(newspaper), 33, 34, 37,
47, 55, 225
*Appeal to the American Women
on Prejudice Against Color,
An*, 28
"Appeal to the Colored Citizens
of the World" (Garnet),
227
"Appeal of Forty Thousand Citizens Threatened with Dis-
franchisement to the People
of Pennsylvania," 173–74
*Appeal to the Women of the
Nominally Free States* (Angelina E. Grimké), 27
Artist Fund Society, 77
Ashman, Cecil, 12
Association for the Political Im-
provement of the People of
Color, 171, 172
Attucks, Crispus, 207
August First emancipation cele-
brations, 124–29, 165
  the first, 123–24
  see also Antislavery sentiment;
Slavery
"Auspicious Dawn of Negro Rule,
The," (Holly), 235
Avery, Charles, 110

Bacon, Leonard W., 220
  quoted, 221
Badger, George E., 60
Bailey, Gamaliel, 36, 62
Ballard, John, 165